FRANCE WITHOUT TEARS

Everything you always wanted to know about holidays in France but were afraid to ask

FRANCE
Without Tears

Everything you always
wanted to know about holidays in France
but were afraid to ask

Frank Barrett
Susie Boulton
and
Chris Gill

Published by
Telegraph Publications
in association with
Brittany Ferries

Published by Telegraph Publications
135 Fleet Street, London EC4P 4BL

First published 1987

© *Sunday Telegraph* 1987 / Good City Guides Ltd 1987

Produced by Good City Guides Ltd, Bath
Designed by Fox + Partners, Bath
Cover illustration by Sarah McDonald, London
Other illustrations are individually credited
Maps by David Perrott, Machynlleth
Typeset by Fox + Partners and PCS Typesetting, Frome
Printed in Great Britain by Richard Clay Ltd, Bungay

ISBN 0 86367 106 3

Contents

A childhood romance

I first went on holiday to France in 1962, when I was eight years old. In response to a newspaper small-ad we went – my parents, my brother and I – to a campsite near Dinard in Brittany. It was a curious and fascinating experience. Holidays abroad were not the everyday event that they are now, and France was still a distant country for the British.

Looking back, it is difficult to credit the strangeness of it all. There was the excitement of driving on to the car ferry at Dover; ferries were emphatically nautical in those days – cars were terrifyingly swung around by hand on a wooden turntable before driving off, and the passenger decks resembled nothing so much as an overcrowded submarine. Over the previous weeks there had been the anxiety of obtaining insurance certificates, International Driving Permits, French petrol coupons, and AA route plans to get us from home to Dover and from Dunkerque to Brittany. The whole family had pored for hours over the leaflet explaining French road signs, wondering if we would ever work out what to do at roundabouts where you not only went anti-clockwise but also had to give way to traffic coming from the right (and wondering how theory would be translated into practice, given my father's imperfect driving skills and uncertain mastery of our Commer Cob van.)

But from the moment we drove off the ferry on to the first of those cobbled French roads, our worries assumed their proper proportions. We were all captivated. Even after all these years, I can recall the first smell of the bread at the boulangerie, the first taste of a croissant, the first visit to a French village market, seeing the stalls piled high with varieties of fruit, vegetables and cheese never seen in Britain. And the thrill of trying to speak a foreign language. At the tender age of eight, I was in love.

My childhood romance with France changed my life. I went back the next year, and every year since. French inevitably became my best subject at school, I studied the language as part of my degree and, when I took up journalism, the early passion for travel engendered by that first expedition steered me with equal certainty towards travel writing. And last summer I went once again to a pre-erected campsite in France – this time in the Dordogne. Again, we went as a family – but now with my own two children, aged four and two, who between them have already clocked up more than a dozen trips across the Channel.

After 25 years, France still seems the supreme all-round holiday destination, with a powerful combination of scenery, sights and sandy beaches, and a way of life which I cannot resist calling simply seductive. But the process of getting to your destination is now entirely painless and largely pleasurable.

We crossed the Channel from Portsmouth to Caen on Brittany Ferries' elegant new *Duc de Normandie*, with its handsome cafés, croissant shop, bars and lounges – more like a mobile hotel than the Channel ferries of old – and comfortable, well-turned-out cabins. The drive down to the Dordogne was smoothly accomplished on fast, clearly signposted roads. Our tent was clean and impressively furnished, the campsite spotless and well appointed. The Dordogne countryside was as ravishingly beautiful as ever, and most days we ate out at good-value restaurants where Dan and Jessica were as welcome as my wife and I.

We discovered that several of the families sharing our campsite were making their first visit to France. Nearly all of them had previously taken package holidays to the Mediterranean but now, with young children, felt they had to try something different. What seemed to have surprised nearly all of them was how simple it was to get to France and to drive down to the Dordogne – and how much fun it was, compared with taking a charter flight to a tower-block Mediterranean resort.

'If we'd known it was this easy, and this much fun, we'd have come to France years ago,' said one man from Sheffield, who was already making plans to venture further south to Provence the following summer. 'You won't catch me on a charter flight package again,' he said, pouring out another glass of Muscadet and cutting himself another chunk of ripe Brie to spread on his French loaf.

But not everyone was so enthusiastic. Some couples were confused by the shops and the French way of doing things. They would have liked to eat out, but were sticking to self-catering because they were unsure how to order in restaurants or what to choose. One family had wanted to stay at a beach resort but had booked on impulse and wound up coming to the Dordogne. For the lack of the right information, they were seeing all the drawbacks of a holiday in France, and not appreciating its pleasures.

It was then that the idea of *France Without Tears* was born: a book which explains in simple terms how to get the best out of a holiday in France; which reveals French shops, restaurants and hotels as the delights they are, by removing from them the air of mystery that can be so off-putting to a relative newcomer; that equips you to handle the preparation and the driving without fuss; that spells out the merits of the popular holiday areas of France, and within them picks out the best places to head for, so that you are sure of getting the sort of holiday you want.

Susie Boulton, Chris Gill and I have pooled our experience to produce a book that does all that, and more. We don't guarantee that it will change your life in quite the way that my childhood trip to France did. But if we succeed in turning you on to the pleasures of this remarkable country, the risk of addiction is high. You have been warned.

Frank Barrett
Bath, January 1987

Using this guide

France Without Tears is divided into three parts.

The first part is mainly about the differences between France and Britain – the things that make trips across the Channel so fascinating but at the same time frustrating if you don't know the ropes.

At many points in part one there are references to the different regions of France; these are described in part two, starting with Paris. We cover the main holiday areas (shown on the map over the page) in detail, describing the most interesting sights and recommending hotels and restaurants; then we summarise briefly the less popular areas.

The final third of the book is largely about the practical business of getting to your chosen destination. But day-trippers and weekend-breakers should certainly consult *Channel ports* before deciding where to go; and the *Factfile* has detailed information of all sorts which you'll want to use at the decision-making stage.

At the end of most of the chapters in part one (and *Driving in France*, in part three) we highlight some particularly useful bits of information to smooth your path – sometimes emphasising key points from the main text, sometimes supplementing it. We also give a selection of useful French phrases and vocabulary relevant to that chapter.

Hotels and restaurants

In each of the chapters on major holiday areas (and in *Channel ports* and *Getting to the south*) we recommend reliable restaurants and attractive, comfortable hotels. Most of the hotels are good value, but we have not left out places which we know to be excellent just because they charge for their excellence; instead, we have given the hotels price ratings, so that you can judge for yourself whether you can afford the expense. These are explained in the box at the foot of the page.

At the end of each description we say when the hotel or restaurant is closed. This is an important consideration in France, where most establishments revolve around one or two key people and close when those people take a break. In holiday areas, we have not mentioned winter closing times; if you are going to these areas out of season, do check first that there are hotels open. But in *Channel ports*, which are popular out of season, we have included winter closing times. We abbreviate the days of the week and months of the year, and use D for dinner and L for lunch.

In 1987 our hotel price ratings translate *roughly* into the following prices **for a typical double room for one night:**

£	up to £15
££	£15 to £25
£££	£25 to £15
££££	£45 to £70
£££££	£70 to £100
£££££!	more

France at a glance

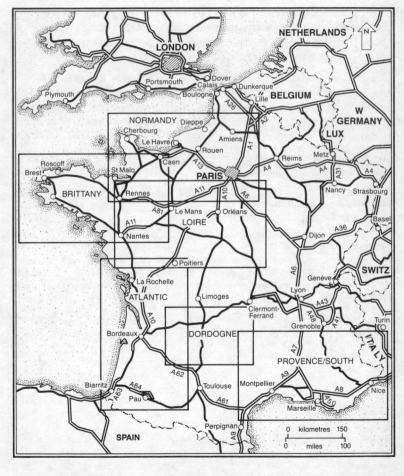

The boxes show the areas covered by the more detailed maps in part two, starting on page 73.

Part I

The pleasures of France

This part of *France Without Tears* has two aims: first, to give you a clear idea of what France has to offer the visitor; secondly, to explain how things work on the other side of the Channel, so that you get the most out of a visit.

At the end of each chapter you will find tips about what to expect and what not to expect, and translations into French of key phrases and words relevant to that chapter.

If you're preoccupied by the problems of driving in France, turn first to part three of the book.

What sort of holiday?

Ask a hundred different families on a car ferry to France what sort of holiday they are embarking on, and you'll get a hundred different answers. Certainly a lot of people go self-catering in rural cottages, or stay on campsites by the sea, or motor from hotel to hotel – but the variations on those themes are countless.

The range of holidays on offer in France also reflects the extraordinary variety of its landscape – mountains and lakes, rivers and forests, rich rolling vineyards, dramatic canyons, towering cliffs and miles of golden sands. Add blue seas and skies, a rich cultural heritage, the world's best food and wine, and you have all the holiday ingredients from which to concoct your own ideal recipe. You can hike in the Alps, bike in the vineyards of Beaujolais, ride horses in the Camargue, cruise on canals, shoot the rapids in a canoe on the river Ardèche, visit the châteaux of the Loire or merely laze on a Mediterranean beach. More specialist holidays range from pot-holing and gold-digging to courses in Gregorian Chant or mussel-breeding.

But most visitors to France don't find the need to give their holiday such a specific theme. You can happily devote days on end to the simple business of savouring the French way of life and the pleasures it brings. Things that would be a chore at home – assembling the ingredients of a picnic, for example – become a source of fun and satisfaction. Even doing absolutely nothing can be gently rewarding, if you're doing it outside a café in a leafy square, sipping wine while life goes on around you.

The idea of this chapter is to make a quick tour of the ways you can enjoy France. Practically everything we touch on here is covered in more detail later in the book, so we have not cluttered up the pages with references to other sections.

Day-trips

The fact that France lies just 21 miles from Dover means that it is possible to sample at least a few of its delights in a day. The quickest crossing to Calais or Boulogne is on the hovercraft, which takes little more than half an hour; but the fastest ferries take only 75 minutes. Either way, given an early start you can be there for lunch and have the time to spend the afternoon drooling over the delights of the food shops or hypermarkets.

The cross-Channel day-trip is not a modern invention. Before World War II it was a very smart thing to undertake – a quick flight to Le Touquet, a promenade along the front, then an indulgent and leisurely lunch in a grand hotel and a quick flutter in the casino. Though some people still cross the Channel mainly for the pleasure of a civilised French meal (and *The Good Food Guide* devotes generous space to eating places in the Channel ports as a result), many more take a day-trip for other reasons. Chief among these is shopping; some ferry operators even lay on coaches to take passengers to and from the hypermarkets, so great is the demand.

French shops in themselves make an interesting change – both the town-centre speciality shops and the huge, cheap-and-cheerful hypermarkets are different from anything you find at home. You can buy things in France that are difficult or impossible to get in Britain – particularly French foodstuffs (both fresh and preserved). And providing the pound is not in one of its weedy phases you can expect to pick up some bargains. One of the surest savings is on French bottled beer, which is ridiculously cheap by British standards – and tastes good too. Bringing back the 50 litres you're allowed to import without paying duty or tax is not easy without a car.

The other certain bargain, if you're a consumer of alcohol or tobacco, is the duty-free goods you can buy on-board the Channel ferries. Although the ferry companies make handsome profits on their duty-free sales, the savings on UK shop prices are still substantial, and often enough to recoup the cost of your crossing.

For families with younger children, a day-trip is an excellent introduction to France and the French way of life – a sort of test-drive, to see whether they would like to return again for a longer stay. For families with children studying French at school, a day-trip offers the chance to see that across the Channel people really do speak another language, and that learning French actually has some purpose – although in the main Channel ports, questions asked in faltering French are frequently responded to in English!

For the French, British Channel-hoppers mean big business. The shops prove so tempting that there are few tourists who leave empty-handed. Some shops are open on Sunday, hypermarkets are open late, and British money is sometimes accepted (though you shouldn't expect a generous exchange rate). There are large and colourful markets, quayside stalls with glistening fresh fish, *charcuteries* stacked with sausages, snails, pâtés and *foie gras*, and *pâtisseries* whose cakes, pastries and chocolates are a feast for English eyes.

Short breaks

If you have more time to spare, and you are keen to do more than shop and eat, it's worth considering travelling a little further (though for not very much more money) to Caen, Cherbourg or Dieppe in Normandy, or even to St-Malo or Roscoff in Brittany. All have more French character than Calais, and most have more than Boulogne.

They generally have more to offer the visitor, too – either sights within the town, or scenery outside it which is a great advance on the unremarkable hinterland of Calais and Boulogne. The western crossings are longer (the shortest, Newhaven to Dieppe, takes 4hr 15min, and Portsmouth to St-Malo takes 9hr), and too long for leisurely day trips, so they tend to be free of the rowdy trippers who prefer the proximity of Boulogne and Calais. Caen, a modern thriving town with two beautiful abbeys, is the latest addition to the Channel ports; the service from Portsmouth was inaugurated by Brittany Ferries in June 1986, and quickly established itself.

Taking a car with you adds substantially to the cost of the crossing, but a car is invaluable for lugging back huge packs of beer and heavy cases of wine – particularly as the big hypermarkets are often some way out of the port centres – and of course it makes forays deeper into France possible. The ferry companies have a number of tempting short-break offers for people taking their car. The particular deals vary slightly from company to company but a common pattern is to offer half-price tickets for those spending no more than 60 hours (effectively three nights) abroad, and smaller but still worthwhile reductions if you stay no more than 120 hours (five nights).

Paris is ideal for a short break: as well as being among the most captivating cities of Europe, it is easy to get to, with or without a car.

Accommodation

French **hotels** at their best offer value for money that few other European countries can match. The countryside is liberally endowed with small, charming hotels; there are hundreds of welcoming *auberges* (country inns), but you can also stay in mountain refuges, monasteries, converted mills or sumptuous mansions. Hotels in towns have less charm, except in Paris.

One of France's greatest attractions is its enormous variety of **self-catering** accommodation – cottages, flats, farmhouses, and châteaux in the countryside, and seaside villas, apartments and studios. *Gîtes* – rural houses or apartments – have become more and more popular with the British. They offer an excellent way of getting involved with local life and polishing up your French. The most popular areas for *gîtes* are Brittany, Normandy, areas inland from the Atlantic coast, the Dordogne and Languedoc-Roussillon. You need to book well in advance, especially if you want a *gîte* by the sea.

When going **camping** you can opt for anything from quiet, simple rural sites, where the only facilities might be a couple of cold showers, to the 4-star luxury of sites along the Côte d'Azur, where your pre-erected tent comes complete with electric lighting, a fridge, a double bed and other mod cons. There are sites all over France, many of them in beautiful settings, by rivers, lakes or in pine woods by the sea.

There are well equipped **holiday villages**, located mainly on the Mediterranean and Atlantic coast – often set back from the sea, perhaps in a pine grove a few minutes from the beach. Accommodation ranges from very simple bungalows to luxury chalets and facilities generally include a club-house, pool, tennis court and some form of evening entertainment.

Sightseeing and touring

France is probably the most civilised region in Europe for touring. Good-value hotels and good food make overnight stops something very much to look forward to. And the large number of sights and variety of landscape make for rewarding days on the road. With fast motorways and good minor roads you can cover a lot of ground in a short time if you need to, though it can be more rewarding if you try get to know one part of the country well.

Favourite touring areas are Normandy (sights and beautiful countryside), the Loire valley (châteaux, wine and riverside villages), the Dordogne (fine river valley, good food and prehistoric caves) and Provence

(Roman remains and sleepy hilltop villages), inland from the south coast. The Alps, which lie along the borders with Switzerland and Italy, offer spectacular scenery for adventurous motorist, hiker and mountaineer alike – though mainly without the picture-postcard charm of Austria and Switzerland. The Pyrénées, which form the border between France and Spain, are good walking and climbing country and are much less developed than the Alps as far as tourism is concerned. But the huge and remote mountainous region of the Massif Central is probably the best place to escape civilisation.

Package holidays

For many people, a package holiday has unpleasant overtones of charter flights, noisy overcrowded hotels and pushy reps selling unwanted excursions. There may be holidays to some south-coast resorts which are like this, but the great majority of packages to France are quite different. Tours are designed to give you as much flexibility and freedom as you want.

Short-break packages, with or without your car, are offered to places in Normandy, Brittany and the valley of the Loire by several tour operators including the ferry companies. Brittany Ferries, for example, offer all sorts of accommodation from a simple *auberge* to a Renaissance manor overlooking the Loire. There are longer stay-put packages to places such as Paris and Provence (including any sort of accommodation you can think of – hotels, simple country houses, apartments, tents). And there are a great many motoring holidays to choose from. Some tours provide a planned itinerary with all the hotels booked ahead for you, others book the first night's stay and give you vouchers for the rest of your holiday, leaving you to make reservations as you go along; others might just provide the bare essentials – ferry tickets and pre-paid bed and breakfast vouchers.

Most people underestimate the choice of packages to France, mainly because the brochures of small specialist companies are not widely available from local travel agents. It's a vicious circle: travel agents sell mainly sun-and-sand packages, so they fill their shelves with sun-and-sand brochures, so they sell very few specialist holidays, so specialist operators concentrate on selling direct to the public, so travel agents sell mainly sun-and-sand; and so on.

The obvious advantage of going independently is the complete flexibility and freedom to make up your own holiday. And the obvious disadvantage is the hassle of booking the travel and hotels (and sending deposits) or of fixing your accommodation as you go. It's not a complicated process but for a really successful holiday you need to do a lot of planning in advance.

Comparing the cost of packages with independent travel is tricky. Going on a package to Paris usually works out at about the same price as going independently, but often you have to book without knowing which hotel or

which area you'll be staying in – the brochure just gives a choice of hotel
category and you take pot luck (though there are some companies which
will tailor-make a holiday if you tell them where you want to stay). Most of
the Paris hotels used by tour operators don't fall into the 'small and
charming' category (see *Paris* for our recommendations).
For the south of France, package prices vary enormously for the same
hotels, and it's worth making a detailed comparison of brochures and
working out if it would be cheaper to do it yourself. If you plan to stay in a
simple hotel rather than a large resort hotel, it will probably be cheaper to
go independently.

Travel within France

If you have a car, the arguments for taking it with you, so that you can
explore France fully and easily, are compelling. But it is not essential.
Thanks to heavy government investment, the French have one of the best
railway networks in the world: fast, clean and frequent trains, with lines
extending to the rural areas as well as main cities – the main exception is
the mountains. Many lines use the comfortable, air-conditioned, sound-
proofed Corail trains or Turbotrains. The TGV (*Train à Grande Vitesse* –
high-speed train) will get you from Paris to Lyon, centre to centre, in just
two hours – which means it is faster by train than by plane. Some major
lines have the lst-class-only TEE (Trans Europ Express) trains – very
comfortable, with air conditioning, restaurant car etc. For overnight long-
distance journeys there are sleeper trains like those in Britain with single,
two-berth or three-berth compartments, but also cheaper *couchettes* –
compartments for four or six with drop-down bunks.

   With such an efficient rail network, **buses** play a minor role in France,
complementing trains rather than competing with them. There are bus
services in rural areas, some timed to link with trains, others timed to get
to the local market; and there are buses for getting around within cities.
But there are very few long-distance routes.

Family holidays

With thousands of kilometres of coastline and wonderful sandy beaches,
France is increasingly the number-one choice for an overseas family
holiday. Children are made welcome here: the French seem genuinely to
like children, and the hotels, campsites and restaurants are well prepared
for them. There are plenty of places with children's menus, small helpings
(or an extra plate so you can feed them from your own) and sometimes
high-chairs. Unhappily, children accustomed to baked beans on toast or
cottage pie will not necessarily appreciate gourmet meals or the three hours
it takes to eat them – so if you're taking the children out for a meal, it's
probably best to stick to the less formal eating places.

Brittany is particularly good for family holidays, and a great British favourite. There are big sandy beaches and jolly family resorts, with clubs for children where trained personnel organise games and activities, leaving you free to laze on the beach. It's also good value, with plenty of modest hotels and good campsites. The main drawbacks are big tides and some strong currents. Neighbouring Normandy also has a long coastline and a number of stylish resorts, but it is also good for touring and sightseeing.

In the south of France the Côte d'Azur (at the eastern end of the Mediterranean coast) offers rather more exotic beach holidays: glamorous resorts, glorious Mediterranean coastal scenery and beautiful countryside inland from the coast. The drawbacks are crowds, traffic jams and high prices. Special facilities for children in hotels, such as playgrounds and baby-sitting, are rarely available on this coast. But campsites are well equipped, with organised games and sporting events. Beach clubs with activities for children come to life in July and August, and there are plenty of places like pizzerias and hamburger bars among the more expensive restaurants.

The Languedoc-Roussillon coast, to the west, is less appealing scenically; but its vast, modern holiday complexes provide a tremendous variety of sports and activities. The long, sweeping Atlantic coast to the south of the Brittany peninsula provides some of the warmth of the south coast but its resorts are much better suited to families – much simpler and cheaper.

An important point to remember is that you don't have to be near the sea to sit on a beach. France has countless beautiful lakes, both natural and artificial, which are often fringed by sandy beaches; here you will find hotels, villas, campsites, bathing areas and facilities for watersports. Many rivers such as the Dordogne have their 'beaches', with beach-side campsites and other facilities.

Most travel and package operators offer worthwhile discounts for children. On Brittany Ferries services, for example, children under ten can cross the Channel free. Some companies offer free self-catering accommodation, others substantial discounts on hotel accommodation – children sharing a room with two adults sometimes stay free or for a minimal price, and in many hotels cots can be put in rooms at no extra charge. On trains and buses within France travel is free for children up to 4 years old, and half-fare from 4 to 12.

Specialist holidays

The range of **special-interest** holidays is huge. You can learn how to make *pâté de foie gras* and *confit de canard*, you can trek with dogs in the snowy wilds of the Jura, you can river-run in the Dordogne or hire a horse-drawn caravan (bag of oats and lessons on tangle-free harnessing provided). There are garden tours, bird-watching holidays, painting holidays, tours of steam locomotives, rambling tours, cave tours – and even battlefield tours. Programmes focusing on food and wine are among the most popular specialist holidays – though also among the most expensive. A cookery course might include visits to local food markets, vineyards, a croissant baker or a farmer who makes goat's cheese. Wine tours cover visits to châteaux, vineyards and cellars, with tasting all the way. Popular areas are the Loire valley, Cognac, Bordeaux, Rhône valley, Burgundy and Champagne.

Holidays on the French **waterways** are becoming more and more popular, providing a quiet contrast to crowded coasts. With over 8,000km of canals and navigable rivers, France is an ideal place for this sort of holiday. It's a very slow way of seeing the country – a barge goes at not much more than walking pace – but it does give you the chance to get to know a particular region well. One of the best areas is Burgundy, with a dense network of waterways and particularly beautiful scenery and sights to see *en route*. The longest waterway in the country is the Canal du Midi, an amazing feat of 17th-century engineering, connecting the Atlantic with the Mediterranean and passing through some beautiful Languedoc countryside on the way.

The comfiest boats are the commercial barges or *péniches*, converted into floating hotels and accommodating anything up to 24 people, with up to 8 crew to look after you. Some cruises put the emphasis on food and wine, with excursions to cellars and vineyards; others have an historic emphasis. There are also smaller boats for 6 to 12 people, where you drive yourself and provide your own meals. They are easy to drive; all you have to do is get the shopping in and make the meals (or go out for them). It's a fun family holiday: children can help operate the sluices of the lock-gates with the lock-keepers (*les éclusiers*), who are a particularly friendly breed – always ready to sell you (or sometimes even give you) eggs, vegetables, cheese and wine.

For a real taste of rural France there is no better way of getting around than by **cycling**. Keep to the back-roads and you can picnic on fruit and cheese from local farms, make friends with the locals and stay in country inns where you can rely on a very warm welcome – the French approve of cyclists. The best touring regions are Normandy, Brittany, the Loire valley, Burgundy, the Rhône valley and Provence, and for the really energetic, the Massif Central and the Jura. The easiest regions are Normandy, the Loire and the Médoc wine region. But if you really want to guarantee a gentle ride consider taking a 'Cycling for Softies' package holiday: you can cycle from one hotel to another only an easy day's ride away; or stay at the same hotel for a week and use the bike for leisurely exploration of the countryside; or stay the first two nights at a pre-booked hotel, then pedal off and find your own hotels with the help of a guidebook; see *Factfile*.

Biking and train travel are easily combined. There's a set price to register a bike as baggage on French trains however far you go (except that on some trains you can check your bike into the baggage car free), and bikes can be rented at many railway stations. Rates are very low but you have to leave a deposit or use a credit card. You can return the bike to another station which rents out bikes.

France has 32,000km of **hiking** trails. The Fédération Française de Randonnée Pédestre (see *Factfile*) marks out trails and provides details (in French only) of the individual itineraries, including the basic mountain huts and hostels where you can stay and eat *en route*. You can also get information on itineraries and accommodation from the *Topo-guides*, available in French bookshops. The major hiking trails, known as *sentiers de grande randonnée*, are clearly marked with red-and-white symbols. These are amazingly varied: one encircles the whole of Paris, another goes all the way from the north to the south of France (Luxembourg to Nice), another follows the route of the medieval pilgrims' way to Santiago de Compostela in northern Spain. The hardest walking is to be found on the mountain trails in the Alps, Pyrénées and Massif Central. Less energetic walkers may prefer the *randonnée du pays* trails (red-and-yellow markers) or the *petite randonnée* ones (yellow markers) which typically consist of one-day round-trips. Most local tourist offices will have information about points of interest along the trails.

Winter holidays

Although most people go to France for summer holidays or for short breaks just outside the main season, the south of France first became popular with the British as a retreat from the bitter winter of the north. It can still play that same role today – the climate is still mild, and the hotels are open for most of the winter even if they take a month or two off (usually between mid-November and mid-January). But no one should go in the expectation of meteorological miracles: for a reliable winter sunbathing holiday you need to head further south than the northern Mediterranean, which at some times out of season gets more rain than London.

In the same way that the French have purpose-built resorts on the Atlantic and Mediterranean coasts for summer holidays, they have developed resorts in the mountains for skiing. What is more, they have designed them so carefully and run them so efficiently that French resorts can fairly claim to be the best in Europe for the keen skier – that is, someone who wants to spend as much of their holiday as possible skiing and as little as possible waiting in queues for lifts, or sitting in bars waiting for runs and lifts to be re-opened after heavy snowfalls.

Many French resorts are also excellent for beginners and children – traffic is often kept well away from both skiing areas and village streets, reducing the risk of accidents, and the special children's ski schools are good at turning the early stages of skiing lessons into amusing games.

What purpose-built French resorts lack is the traditional Alpine charm of longer-established resorts in Austria and Switzerland. There are exceptions – Méribel has worked hard to build even its biggest apartment blocks in the style of mountain chalets, for example, and nearby Valmorel is rather like a Disneyland replica of a mountain village. There are also some resorts which have grown up gradually and kept a bit of Alpine atmosphere in the process – mainly in the northern Alps close to Geneva. For example, Megève is a fashionable and expensive resort, La Clusaz a more friendly family village, Chamonix an old mountaineering centre right next to Mont Blanc, now grown into a bustling town.

Choosing where to go skiing is not something to be done lightly, whether you're a beginner or not; it requires careful thought and as much information as you can lay your hands on. Widely acknowledged as the definitive guide to ski resorts in Europe is *The Good Skiing Guide*, which happens to be edited by one of the authors of this book; see *Factfile*.

Sightseeing

Wayne Allen

France has an exceptional cultural heritage and a mass of interesting things to see, from prehistoric cave paintings and Roman theatres to Gothic cathedrals and the great châteaux of the Loire.

Wherever you are, there's nearly always a church, château, museum or gallery – or some weird or wonderful natural phenomenon – that's worth a detour. But the particular delight of France is that the 'serious' business of visiting great cathedrals or important museums can be pleasurably combined with other diversions – leisurely lunches, rummaging through interesting markets, or merely ambling in picturesque towns and villages, and savouring the local atmosphere.

Even if you've opted for a cultural tour of the Loire châteaux, your holiday is unlikely to be confined to intensive sightseeing; other delights, such as liberal tastings of Muscadet or visits to sleepy riverside villages, will probably play just as big a role. Paris and its incomparable collection of art treasures can provide weeks of solid sightseeing, but the distractions of the city's streets and squares, cafés and restaurants are sufficient to make sure that most visitors don't 'do' the city in such a concentrated way. After all, the Louvre can always be left until the next time.

Sightseeing in France is not without its frustrations. Opening times change with alarming frequency, and sights or parts of them close for restoration without much warning. There are 13 French national holidays when doors are firmly closed. Museums, galleries and châteaux are not very generous with their opening hours – normally two or three hours in the morning and three hours in the afternoon (9am or 10am to noon, and 2pm to 5pm), apart from a few very famous sights which are open all day. The doors of some sights are shut ruthlessly at 11.45am (or even earlier) – much to the dismay of the poor tourist who has breakfasted at leisure and driven for an hour or so, only to find he has to wait until 2pm for the doors to open again.

While it is dangerous to generalise on such matters, it has to be said that on the whole museums, castles and other principal tourist sights are not managed with the flair that nowadays characterises their British counterparts. How much you get out of a visit is likely to depend on how much you've gleaned from guidebooks. Any serious sightseer should go equipped with a specialist guidebook – which for all practical purposes means the Michelin Green Guide for the area you're in. There are 23 altogether, 7 of them (covering the popular places like the Loire, Dordogne, Paris) translated into English. Sights are graded by stars, from one to three, which makes for a quick and useful point of reference. The only trouble with this system is that any sight awarded three stars will be invariably crowded with tourists clutching Green Guides. The first few pages of each volume are devoted to résumés on art and architecture, history, food and wine, and touring programmes. There are also useful maps, both for the whole region and main towns, pin-pointing sights.

Visiting châteaux

The word *château* embraces more than castles. It can mean a handsome mansion, the ruins of a fortress or bastion, a Renaissance palace or any building that we would call a stately home. Visiting châteaux is a popular pastime for both French and foreigners. Gracious, decorative, extravagant, and more often than not heralded by handsome grounds, châteaux are rarely disappointing from the outside. But the insides can be something of an anti-climax – particularly those that have been empty for centuries. The châteaux of the Loire are good examples. While the massive Chambord is a

Renaissance sensation, profusely decorated with chimneys, windows, spires and pinnacles, the 440 rooms inside are virtually empty. Where there are furnishings inside a château, the collections tend to bear little relation to the history of the building.

More often than not, a visit to a château entails a long, detailed and regimented guided tour in French. This can be fearfully boring for anyone whose French is anything but fluent (it's normally no barrel of laughs even for French speakers). The emphasis will almost invariably be on French history, with a long list of dates and battles, kings and queens: usually with frequent put-downs of the English (the battles of Agincourt and Waterloo still rankle). It does of course help if you already know the outline of French medieval history and can put the particular château in context. You may have to wait up to an hour for a tour to start, and the last tour may start up to half an hour before the closing times stated. Some of the châteaux are far too small to cope with the crowds they attract, and in the big popular ones like Fontainebleau you are forced to share the masterpieces with hordes of fellow-tourists.

French châteaux are not organised on the lines of English stately homes. There is rarely any interest or entertainment beyond the château itself – no amusements or playgrounds for children, no cream teas in the garden and no shops selling home-made fudge or linen tea-cloths. There are of course exceptions. Vaux-le-Vicomte, a superb château (the model for Versailles) not far from Fontainebleau, is owned by a count who has been so impressed by English stately homes that he has borrowed their ideas. As a result, his house is beautifully furnished, giving a good idea of the sumptuous life style of the 17th century hedonist who once lived there. There are hand-outs in English, attractive catering facilities and a shop with the sort of things you expect to find at a National Trust property.

Individuality is the essence of French châteaux and to get some idea of the variety it's worth seeking out some of the smaller, less popular ones. There are hunting lodges, towers, giant dovecots and follies, many of them still inhabited and far less formal than the huge well-known châteaux. There are many fortresses too – in the Dordogne for example you'll find them perched on rocky spurs or hilltops, overlooking the river and dominating small villages below. Some are no more than ruins, but they look splendid from afar.

Visiting caves

France has a wider range of impressive caves open to the public than any other country in Europe. These range from small rock shelters (*abris*) with animal carvings to large caves (*grottes*) and fairy-tale chasms with rock formations in the shape of things like palm trees and tortoise-shells (or so the guide will tell you); others have forests of white, staggeringly thin stalactites. Caves can be cold, damp and slippery, with steep paths or steps, so it's wise to take a sweater and sensible shoes. While most caves are covered on foot there are some where you penetrate the depths by train or boat. Guided tours are usually obligatory. Crowds can be an even bigger problem when visiting caves than when visiting châteaux.

Visiting churches and cathedrals

France has a wealth of religious architectural masterpieces, from the famous Gothic cathedrals to tiny lesser-known churches, often tucked away in the heart of the countryside. Admission is free, apart from treasuries and crypts. The major churches are almost always open all day, but you may find the smaller ones closed. If so, you can be sure they will open for Mass on Sunday morning; otherwise you can usually get a key from the verger, who almost certainly lives nearby; ask at a local shop or bar. (If you disturb him from his lunch or siesta, he'll probably expect a decent tip.)

Visiting museums

France has a huge range of museums, from the great art galleries of Paris to tiny, specialist local museums. There are wine museums, ceramic museums, tapestry museums, hunting museums, history museums – even a tobacco museum and a mushroom museum. Some are small and pleasantly informal, others large and sedate. Often the most notable museum in a town is the Musée des Beaux-Arts, or fine arts museum, with paintings by local or other French artists – there are some particularly good collections in the larger towns. Displays in other museums may be less interesting than the buildings (often medieval palaces) which house them.

Paris is packed with good museums, but towering above the others is the Louvre, which has the richest collection of art in the world. The sheer size of the place is daunting – and so are the crowds that throng in front of the Mona Lisa and Venus di Milo. In complete contrast is the modern Centre Pompidou, where the crowds are a positive asset, lending a festive air. For the most popular museums in Paris (including the Louvre) you can expect to queue for an hour or so at certain times of the year. But there are less well-known museums both in Paris and the provinces where you may be the only visitor.

Styles of building

There's not enough space here to go into French architecture in any depth, and if you are interested in such things you will certainly want to get hold of more specialised guidebooks than this, so as to appreciate fully the wonderful buildings there are to see in France. But even the most casual sightseer stands to gain from knowing something about the main styles of architecture employed in building the country's churches, cathedrals and grand houses.

The earliest 'buildings' in France are the mysterious stone monuments – the menhirs (upright stones) and dolmens (stone tables) – which are to be found all over France but concentrated in large numbers in Brittany. But it was with the arrival of the Romans in the 2nd century AD that the foundations of modern French culture were laid down. Provence, in the south, is the region richest in Roman remains, with many impressive monuments surviving almost intact – in particular, the perfectly preserved temple (Maison Carrée) and amphitheatre at Nîmes, the splendid theatre and Arc de Triomphe at Orange, the amphitheatre at Arles and the great Pont du Gard aqueduct.

The **Romanesque** building style, derived from that of ancient Rome and distinguished by rounded arches and barrel vaulting, persisted in one form or another for over a thousand years. France has an amazing number of Romanesque churches, cathedrals and monasteries, many of them in beautiful settings, dating from the 10th to the 12th century. Styles vary from region to region (churches in the north are plain and unadorned, and it was this style which William the Conqueror brought to Britain from Normandy, which is why we know it as Norman). Sculpture often features on the outside, or on pillars, doorways, walls and entrances.

The **Gothic** style succeeded the Romanesque and dominated church building from the 12th to the early 16th century, producing the great cathedrals of northern France; Notre-Dame in Paris and Chartres are prominent examples. The buildings are taller and lighter than the Romanesque, distinguished by the pointed arch, the flying buttress and the rib vault. Other features are delicate filigree-like rose windows, tall lancet windows, and elaborate doorways and façades. The last phase of the Gothic style, known as flamboyant ('flaming'), is characterised by an abundance of curves and ornate sculpture – the best examples are in Normandy.

In the early 16th century, artistic and architectural styles were influenced by the Italian **Renaissance**. The church was in decline in this period, and most of the notable Renaissance buildings are grandiose châteaux, built for kings and nobles around Paris and in the valley of the Loire. Blois, Chambord, Chenonceau and Fontainebleau are all good examples of this extravagantly ornamental style.

Gradually the Renaissance style became more restrained. The more extravagant designs were rejected in favour of building in a simpler and more **classical** style, of which the Louvre museum in Paris is a prime example. During the 17th and 18th centuries, the greatest buildings tended to reflect the inclinations of the king as well as the architectural movements of the time. The grandiose **baroque** palace of Versailles, built by Louis XIV, became a symbol of royal extravagance and a model for others. Under Louis XV, there was a reaction against the sumptuous excesses of baroque buildings and the more elegant and playful **rococo** style came to the fore. There was a further retreat from ornamentation in the latter 18th century with the rise of **neo-classicism** – a return to strict classical principles which resulted in solid, severe buildings, sometimes entirely devoid of decoration.

Sightseeing tips

Watch out for...
- closing times which mean you have to plan your sightseeing with military precision
- rip-off restaurants close to major sights, charging high prices for mediocre food

Don't be surprised if...
- most of the 'stately homes' you visit are bare of furnishings
- there are massive queues for major sights in high summer
- tour guides make no attempt to communicate with foreigners

Remember that...
- caves are cold, and often have slippery floors

Useful phrases

Où se trouve le syndicat d'initiative? – Where is the tourist information office?
Est-ce qu'on peut aller en excursion de la ville? – Are there any excursions from the town?
A quelle heure ferme le musée? – What time does the museum close?
L'entrée est combien? – How much does entry cost?
Est-ce que la visite guidée est obligatoire pour voir le château? – Is a guided tour the only way to see the château?

Est-ce qu'il y a une visite guidée du château? – Is there a guided tour of the château?
Est-ce qu' il y a un guide qui parle anglais? – Is there an English-speaking guide?
A quelle heure commence la visite guidée? – What time does the tour start?
Combien de temps dure la visite? – How long does the tour last?

Eating and drinking

Tim Duke

You don't have to be a great gourmet to find, after a trip or two to France, that among your most vivid recollections are the meals – not necessarily extravagant dinners in opulent restaurants, but all sorts of occasions when you have enjoyed the produce of France in lovely French surroundings. It might be a long, lingering lunch on the terrace of an elegant château or a gastronomic feast in one of the temples of *haute cuisine*, but it could equally well be a picnic of fresh crusty bread, ripe cheese and spicy *vin ordinaire* under a tree beside a stream, or a fish soup served in a quayside café.

Few food experts question French supremacy when it comes to cooking. France still sets the world standard in good food and wine; and for many people that alone is reason enough to cross the Channel. Even at the ferry ports the sumptuous displays of the food shops and the mouth-watering menus of the restaurants are sufficient to persuade hundreds of thousands of people every year to make a day-trip crossing from Britain.

To the French, good food is a high priority; its preparation and enjoyment are serious matters, in which compromises are not made. Top chefs in France have always been praised and revered as creators and artists; nowadays the great chefs are household names, and sometimes seem to get as much coverage in the press as film stars or opera singers. Paul Bocuse, the renowned chef from Lyon and 'Ambassador of French cuisine', is a star who has been honoured by the state and has made headlines in practically every magazine from Newsweek to Paris Match.

Whereas we British treat a trip to a restaurant as something of a special outing, to be reserved only for birthdays, high-days and holidays, eating out for the French is a national pastime. On Sundays restaurants are packed with families from all social backgrounds, with grannies and toddlers in tow. Even small towns have at least one ambitious restaurant, and by British standards restaurant meals are excellent value. The emphasis is on fresh local produce and even the humblest, dowdiest looking place may produce food of surprisingly good quality.

But that doesn't mean to say that you always eat well in France. Gone are the days when you could guarantee good quality wherever you went. In many city and town centres, particularly those popular with tourists, you need to beware of rip-off restaurants; and there's an increasing infiltration of fast food – much to the despair of serious food lovers. 'Le fast food' is fashionable with teenagers and there has been a rapid growth in *croissanteries* (croissant stalls), pizzerias and hamburger bars – McDonalds is well established in Paris's Champs-Elysées and elsewhere in France (although in fairness to the French, it must be admitted that the fast-food places do seem to cater largely for Americans indulging their homesickness). And a great many restaurants offer cheap and not particularly cheerful set menus, which typically include *bifteck frites* – an all-too-often chewy piece of beef with chips.

One school of thought holds the recent years of socialist government to blame for the decline in standards. Restaurant owners have been having a hard time in recent years; a crippling 30% tax was imposed on business entertainment in 1982, and higher personal taxes have meant that the French haven't been going out to eat quite so regularly as they used to. Nevertheless there are still thousands of menus in France which offer good food at reasonable prices.

French dominance in the matter of wine is less complete than it once was, with increasingly hot competition from the vineyards of the New World as well as other European countries. But you can rest assured that the best wines of France are as good as you will find anywhere, and (more importantly) that the affordable everyday wines are excellent value.

Styles of cuisine

The variety of French cooking is vast – ranging from simple stews to dishes as rich as goose liver pâté stuffed with truffles (rare fungi, found underground). Whatever your tastes, French cooking will have something to stimulate and satisfy the appetite; even vegetarians, once considered to have some kind of extreme personality disorder, are now usually treated with patience (though very few smart restaurants have much idea of how to cater for them).

There is no such thing as a typical French meal or menu, and attempts to explain and classify the different styles of cooking can be confusing – particularly now that restaurants increasingly offer a mixture of styles. But it's helpful to have a bit of background knowledge when you come to confront a menu.

The stuff of gourmets' dreams has traditionally been *haute cuisine* or *grande cuisine* – characterised by truffles, mushrooms, *foie gras* (specially fattened goose liver), butter, brandy, cream, cognac and everything else that's rich and forbidden. Until a few years ago you found these elaborate and sophisticated dishes in all the highly regarded and expensive restaurants, but many of these have turned to the lighter dishes of *nouvelle cuisine* (see below) in response to popular demand.

Although few French would like to admit it, their *grande cuisine* was imported from Italy – or at least greatly influenced by the Italians. The true foundations of French gastronomy were established about 400 years ago during the Renaissance, when Italian-born Catherine de Médicis (whose husband was to become Henry II of France) arrived in France with an impressive retinue of sophisticated Florentine cooks. Extravagance and ostentation were the essence of *grande cuisine* – at least until the Revolution. Louis XIV was a notorious glutton, consuming copious quantities of food and wine at Versailles. According to his sister-in-law, at one meal he managed to consume 'four plates of different soups, an entire pheasant, a partridge, a large plateful of salad, mutton cut up in its juice with garlic, two good pieces of ham, a plateful of cakes, fruits and jams'. Three of the greatest *grande cuisine* chefs were Carême, who created opulent displays such as classical temples and bridges out of spun sugar, glue, wax and pastry dough; Montagné, who in 1938 wrote the bible of French gastronomy, the great *Larousse Gastronomique*; and Escoffier ('king of cooks and cook of kings') who invented scores of new dishes, some of them (like Tournedos Rossini) named after friends and celebrities.

Great controversy has surrounded *nouvelle cuisine*, which means literally 'new cooking' and was pioneered in the 1950s by the late Fernand Point, considered by many to be one of the greatest modern French chefs. Rejecting the rich cream sauces of *haute cuisine*, it concentrates on lighter, natural dishes and new combinations. The accent is on prime, fresh ingredients, meticulous preparation and artistic presentation – often with a

Japanese influence. (With many *nouvelle cuisine* dishes, the often-heard complaint is that you don't know whether to eat it or hang it on the wall like a painting.) At a time when people were becoming more conscious of the links between diet and health, *nouvelle cuisine* was enthusiastically taken up by both restaurateurs and restaurant-goers, not just health fetishists and weight-watchers.

But over the last few years there has been an inevitable reaction against the trend. Gourmets reared on robust traditional dishes like *cassoulet* or *boeuf bourguignon* felt under-nourished and over-charged by restaurants serving dainty and costly portions of courgette flowers and baby carrots, and far-fetched dishes like kiwi fruit served with steak or raw duck breast with raspberry sauce. Not all the top French chefs were converted to *nouvelle cuisine* and, of those who were, many now offer classic dishes as well because it's evident that the majority of French – and foreigners too – still prefer the good old traditional dishes. The famous Bocuse still believes that cream, butter and wine are 'the holy trinity of the kitchen', along with perfect quality of produce. He despises the import of foodstuffs from places like Kenya, Chile and Mexico when there are so many excellent ingredients available locally.

Nouvelle cuisine is often confused with *cuisine minceur*, which was invented by Michel Guérard. The emphasis here is on non-calorific food, strictly for slimmers – no butter, cream, fat, flour or sugar. With *nouvelle cuisine* there's no calorie counting, and fattening ingredients are not necessarily forbidden – just used in moderation.

The longest established form of cooking is *cuisine régionale*, which centres on the use of fresh local produce. It might be seafood in Brittany, *confit* (potted meat, often duck) in the Dordogne or *bouillabaisse* (fish stew) in the south. But good local produce is becoming increasingly scarce – the best of it, particularly in the north, goes to the market at Rungis near Paris rather than to local markets. And some of the old regional specialities are gradually disappearing: you can spend days searching for specialities listed in guidebooks only to find that they are non-existent or available only once or twice a year.

We've pointed out the most characteristic and accessible specialities of each region in the *Region-by-region* section. Some of them you'll come across all over the country – *boeuf bourguignon*, for example, or *bouillabaisse*. Of all French food, cheese is the great upholder of regional identity. Virtually everywhere you go in France there are shops, markets and restaurants with an extraordinary choice of cheeses, many of them regional and made by traditional local methods (see *Shopping*).

Cuisine bourgeoise may sound rather insulting to the British, but it simply refers to plain, traditional dishes, served throughout France in unpretentious restaurants which aim primarily to offer their customers good value. *Cassoulet* (stew of beans and various meats such as pork, duck or goose) and *daube* (beef stew) are typical examples.

Choosing a restaurant

The *Michelin Red Guide* is indispensable for anyone with more than a passing interest in eating out. It recommends over 10,000 hotels and restaurants, most of which are inspected anonymously every year. For the British, it is difficult to comprehend fully the seriousness with which the Michelin guide is taken in France (by restaurateurs and restaurant-goers alike). Without getting too pretentious, it's fair to say that Michelin is more than just a guide to hotels and restaurants: it is treated as a form of Gospel. It can make – and break – establishments almost overnight. No joy can compare to the awarding of an additional Michelin star; on the other hand, no misery or shame can equal the loss of one.

But it is only a guide. Chefs of course move on, and a good restaurant can turn into a mediocre one overnight. Restaurants where the chefs are also the owners (which is quite normal) are theoretically more reliable, but these can deteriorate too, particularly if success goes to the head of the chef. This means no guide can really be up to date – and some critics hold that the Michelin guide is too slow to respond to changes.

The guide does take a lot of getting used to. The short entries are crammed with details – price of a set meal, degree of comfort, specialities, location on map (if in a town), days closed and so on. To get the most out of the guide, it does pay to do some homework before you use it and to sort out some of the curious hieroglyphics. There are no well-turned phrases and evocative descriptions, only symbols; but once these are mastered you will need no more than a glance to sum up a restaurant (experience will also help you to read between the symbols, as it were). The main thing to remember is the difference between knife and fork symbols, which indicate how smart the restaurant is, and the stars which are awarded where the food is particularly good. A restaurant with three stars is exceptional – places with 'marvellous food, great wines, impeccable service, elegant surroundings … and prices to match'. The 1986 guide listed no more than 20 of these temples of gastronomy. A restaurant with two stars is excellent and merits a detour, and a restaurant with one star is very good in its category. Any place with a star is likely to be expensive and popular – booking in advance is essential.

If the finances won't run to star restaurants and you're happy with simpler fare, head for the places in Michelin marked with a red R – restaurants which are usually quite simple but provide excellent value for money. You can rarely go wrong in this category.

The other worthwhile guide for those competent in French is *Gault Millau*, named after its original authors, two leading gastronomic critics and writers. It contains over 4,000 witty and opinionated reviews of restaurants (and some hotels) in France. Marks are awarded from 0 to 20 (a scheme subsequently adopted by Britain's *Good Food Guide*), and are based solely on cooking, though the reviews normally give you some idea of the décor, atmosphere and service. Restaurants scoring 13 plus are distinguished with one to four *toques* (chefs' hats); *toques* in colour indicate *nouvelle cuisine*, laurel wreaths indicate authentic regional cuisine and prices in colour mean excellent value.

Without a guide or recommendation the best way to go about choosing a place is by looking at the menu and the clientele. A hand-written (frequently indecipherable) menu in French is invariably a more promising sign than a typed or printed one – particularly one that has also been translated. And if the place is full of French, preferably locals, it's obviously a good sign. Restaurants which clearly rely on tourists for their trade aren't nearly so reliable. Don't take the décor as a guide to culinary standards; good food is often found in basic or uninspired settings.

Menus

The French word *menu* has a rather more precise meaning in France than in Britain – it means a meal consisting of several courses with a narrow choice of dishes, at a fixed all-in price. A list of individually priced dishes from which you can choose at random is a *carte*. Our expression for this – an *à la carte menu* – makes no sense at all to the French. A fixed-price menu is nearly always the better bet.

In a simple restaurant you will usually find just one or two set menus; in other places you can come across as many as six or more different menus at different prices. The cost shown will nearly always include service and tax. To give some examples, the cheapest menus will perhaps start with a home-made *pâté*, an *hors d'oeuvre* or salad dish, followed by a plain meat or fish dish and ending with cheese or dessert (usually ice cream, fruit or caramel custard). At the other end of the scale the gastronomic menu might start with *foie gras* or snails, followed by a fish dish (lobster or salmon, say), a main course of perhaps *Châteaubriand* or *côte de boeuf*, a trolley with umpteen mouthwatering cheeses and some exotic sweet to end the meal. A *menu dégustation* is usually a seven- or eight-course affair – all of the dishes small, exquisite specialities of the house. Apart from the menus, you might see advertised a *plat du jour* (dish of the day) which is the chef's selection for that particular meal – usually very good value.

Vegetables are usually served separately from the meat, and the choice can be disappointing given the huge variety you see in the markets. Side-salads are nearly always entirely green, and in a lot of places you make the dressing yourself with the glass bottles of oil and vinegar on the table. (Special salads,served as a main dish, can be much more interesting).

A good cheeseboard is said to be the sign of a good restaurant. At worst you're likely to get a choice of five or six cheeses, at best a trolley crammed with a couple of dozen. There are always the familiar Camemberts, Bries and Roqueforts,and in addition a bewildering range of lesser-known varieties,often locally produced, in all sorts of shapes and sizes and in all manner of straw and grass wrappings. Desserts are often limited to sorbets and ice-creams (both of which are usually home-made and excellent), chocolate mousse, fruit or caramel custard, though in more elaborate places you find a variety of tarts, gâteaux and generally more sophisticated desserts.

What's available when

Proper restaurants and hotel dining rooms (other than in the major cities) stick to pretty rigid hours, and meals are generally served earlier than in Britain. Lunch (*le déjeuner*) is usually a leisurely two-hour affair and the main meal of the day, except in cities where workers are steering more and more to the one-hour lunch break. Popular restaurants start filling up soon after noon. Dinner (*le dîner*) is usually served from around 7pm or 7.30pm until 8.30pm or 9pm; in some areas it's difficult to get dinner after 8pm, and in any restaurant the set menus may be unavailable if you arrive late.

Cafés, by contrast, are usually open all day, starting by serving coffee and croissants for breakfast (*le petit déjeuner*). That apart, the range of food they offer may be pretty limited – perhaps only sandwiches (usually half *baguettes* with rather mean fillings of *pâté*, ham or cheese) and the ubiquitous *croque-monsieur* (toasted cheese and ham sandwich) and *croque-madame* (the same with an egg on top). Many of the Parisian cafés have a lot more to offer, including main meals. Snack bars are quite common these days in the large towns and cities, and pizzerias have cropped up all over the country. A **salon de thé** (tea room) usually opens mid mornings for cakes and snacks – usually quite pricey, and the domain of elderly ladies. By far the best way to fill a gap is go to the local *charcuterie* for ready-made meat dishes, salads, pies, vol-au-vents etc (see *Shopping*).

A **brasserie** – in terms of atmosphere a larger, smarter and less intimate version of a café – is usually open all day for snacks or more substantial meals. You frequently find them near railway stations, and they're useful if you haven't the time to linger over a three-course meal. The smart Parisian 1900s brasseries are a special breed, with their crisp white table-cloths, bibbed waiters, and fashionable clientele. Traditionally these offer sauerkraut, seafood, home-made pâté and *foie gras*. You may also find the dishes we British traditionally associate with the French – snails and frogs' legs. Snails (*escargots* – though sometimes given facetious names on menus, such as *les rapides*) are sold in sixes, nines or dozens. They should taste neither slimy nor fishy. The usual way of serving snails is with loads of garlic and butter, with plenty of bread to mop up the sauce. The shell is held firmly in a small clamp while the snail is extracted with a special fork. Frogs' legs are often served lightly fried, or with a sauce; the flavour is very delicate, much like that of the sweetest meat of a young chicken. The best way to eat them – indeed probably the only way to eat them with any satisfaction – is with your fingers.

Wine

The eminent French scientist Louis Pasteur asserted that wine was a healthier drink than either milk or water. This may be one reason why the French drink so much of it; but price has something to do with it too. Table wines are barely more expensive than bottled water, so it is hardly surprising that wine has become an indispensable part of everyday living.

France makes over a fifth of the world's total production of wine; and the French are the world's second greatest consumers of wine after the Italians. Large quantities are exported but even larger quantities have to be imported to keep the nation happy. The choice of wines is enormous: everything from rock-bottom *vin ordinaire* in plastic bottles to the cream of the crop from Bordeaux and Burgundy – the best wines in the world.

French wines are subject to very stringent controls, particularly top quality wines. It's worth knowing the basic rules behind the main categories. The top category is *Appellation d'Origine Contrôlée* (AOC or, usually, AC). This guarantees the area of origin, grape variety, method of production, and so on – so an AC wine which bears the name of a village, for example, has not been blended with wine from any other area.

Although not every AC wine is necessarily a great wine, all the top French wines have AC status. An *appellation* may be limited to wine from a particular vineyard, or it may cover a village or a region; as a general rule, the more geographically specific the limits, the higher the quality of wine. For example, an AC Chambertin (an individual vineyard) should be superior to an AC Gevrey-Chambertin (the village), which in turn should be superior to an AC Bourgogne (the Burgundy area).

In Bordeaux the lesser wines will be marked AC Bordeaux or one of the main areas within the region, for example AC Médoc or AC St-Emilion. All the best Bordeaux wines are 'château-bottled' – bottled at the estate where the wine was produced – though the word château is not in itself any indication of quality. Many of the better Bordeaux wines are classified or grouped into categories called *crus classés*.

The next category down is *Vin Délimité de Qualité Supérieure* (VDQS), covering medium-quality wines, many from the south of France and good value for everyday drinking. The area of origin is always on the label. Then comes *Vin de Pays* – plain and simple country wines but coming from a specific area; like VDQS this group includes many good-value robust reds, many of them made in the south of France. The largest category of wine is *Vin de Table*, made of blended wines from various areas and even other countries. These wines are totally unpredictable. At the very bottom of the pecking order come the wines sold simply as *vin rouge* or *vin blanc* under a trade name or brand.

Wine lists are always divided into wine regions and it's worth knowing the general characteristics of the major areas. (But don't be afraid of trying the many wines from less prestigious areas such as Bergerac and

Roussillon.)

Burgundy produces soft, warm and 'velvety' wines. The area is small but the names are big – particularly along the Côte d'Or ('golden slope'), whose densely cultivated hillsides stretch from near Dijon to Santenay, south-west of Beaune. The villages here read like a who's who of wine: Gevrey-Chambertin, Morey-St-Denis, Clos de Vougeot, Nuits-St-Georges and so on. There are fewer whites but the names are no less prestigious: Montrachet is considered by some to be the best dry white wine in the world. Such wines are prohibitively expensive, but there are more affordable reds and whites which will give you at least a taste of what Burgundy is all about. Look for the non-village or non-vineyard names such as AC Bourgogne or Bourgogne Rouge.

The light, fruity Beaujolais, which causes such a fuss in England each autumn when people race across the Channel with the first of the new season's young wines, comes from the south of Burgundy.

Bordeaux is the other great wine-growing area, known mainly for its dry, elegant and slightly austere wines. Large quantities of both red and white wine are produced here. The reds (known to the British but not the French as 'claret') range from comparatively straightforward and simple table wines to the finest château-bottled wines such as Château Lafite, Château Latour and Château Margaux. (Some of these are actually cheaper to buy in England). There are good-quality still white wines, ranging from the fairly dry (eg Entre-Deux-Mers) to the very sweet and fragrant Sauternes, of which the leading name is Château d'Yquem.

A wealth of good-value wines come from the valley of the Loire: dry whites, sweet whites, rosés, reds and sparkling wines. Most of the wines are white, and best-known is the pale, fresh, dry Muscadet which is an excellent accompaniment to fish. Higher quality whites are the pale, fruity Pouilly-Fumé and Sancerre. Other wines you are likely to come across are the sparkling (or sometimes still) Vouvrays, the popular Rosé d'Anjou and the light, tart Gros Plant.

AC red wines are produced in huge quantities in and around the Rhône valley (between Vienne, south of Lyon, and Avignon). The wines tend to be heavy, full-bodied and robust – best drunk with red meat and stews. The favourite here is Châteauneuf-du-Pape, which is the model for other wines in the south of the area. In the north, Hermitage is the classic red.

Alsace produces wines which are German in character, though slightly drier than their German counterparts and distinctly fragrant. Unlike the rest of France, Alsace identifies its wines with the grape varieties they are made from, as in Germany. The best known is Gewürztraminer.

Unless you are very familiar with French wines, choosing from the wine list (la carte des vins) can be an intimidating experience. Some restaurants produce off-putting lists with pages and pages of wines, and prices which are very high indeed. It's not uncommon to find restaurants marking up top-quality wines by as much as 300 per cent.

Most restaurants, however simple, have a choice of reasonably priced middle-of-the-road AC wines such as white Muscadet and red Côtes du Rhône. There are no hard-and-fast rules about what wine should be drunk with what food, but the general rule is to drink red with red meat and white with fish and white meat. Foods which are not enhanced by wine are vinegar- or citrus-fruit-based dishes, curries (which you're unlikely to come across in France anyway) and chocolate-based desserts. If you're in a wine-growing region it's a good idea to choose a local wine: the choice is greater and, in theory at least, the wine is likely to go well with the food.

If in any doubt, the safest rule is to ignore the wine list and opt for the house wine (*la réserve de la maison*). This will almost always be better value than the cheapest bottle on the wine list, and is likely to be satisfactory whether it is an AC or VDQS wine or a *Vin du Pays*. Some of the more expensive restaurants don't have a house wine. If you want to play safe, consult the Michelin Red Guide, which gives a symbol to restaurants which provide house wine at moderate prices. At the other extreme are the restaurants which serve wine by the half-litre in carafes or in jugs (*en pichet*); some even include wine in the price of the menu – look for 'bc' or *boisson comprise* at the bottom of the menu.

Drinking in cafés

Wine is not the only good thing about drinking in France. You can while away endless hours in cafés, sipping coffee or aperitifs under a coloured parasol or in the shade of a leafy plane tree, watching the world go by. There are no restrictions on opening hours in France, and knocking back the brandies can start as early as five o'clock in the morning. Whereas in England pub doors are firmly closed for most of the morning and most of the afternoon, you can enjoy a civilised drink in France at almost any time of day. Although the majority of cafés are purely there for leisurely drinking, some cater for other popular French pastimes such as watching television, playing table football (*le baby foot*) or listening to the jukebox. The big advantage of French cafés for families is that children are normally welcome (though those under 14 are not allowed alcohol).

Cafés have been an integral part of French society since time immemorial. Many have been immortalised by well-known writers and artists, and you can still sit at tables where the literati churned out their novels or drew inspiration from the scenes around them. Such cafés today are fashionable spots for tourists and affluent French people – the Bohemian circles go elsewhere.

If the priority is quenching your thirst, then sitting at café tables is best avoided – you pay substantially more for drinks here than you do standing at the bar. Prices in fashionable Parisian places – in the Champs-Elysées and the Boulevard St-Michel, say – are very high, even for just a cup of coffee; but at least you can linger for as long as you like for the price of one drink. The cheapest cafés are those in back streets, away from the more fashionable boulevards of towns – also cheaper will be the basic village bars which cater for locals. The prices in any café have to be displayed, though more often than not the list is half hidden behind the bar.

The café system revolves around the waiter. You sit at a table while he goes to and fro, taking orders and delivering the goods. With each round he normally leaves a ticket from the till saying what it cost, and you can accumulate these until you're ready to leave; but you can pay as you go if you prefer, and in some places it is now expected. On the other hand, in a quiet café off the beaten track the waiter may keep track of what you've had and work out the cost at the end.

The French normally like their coffee strong and black in a small cup, espresso-style: this is simply *un café*. A white coffee is *un café crème*, and a larger cup made with hot milk (consumed at breakfast time with croissants) is *café au lait*. Tea is not a national drink and the French certainly don't make it 'like mother does'. If they do drink it, it's normally with lemon (*thé au citron*), probably because French milk is usually the UHT variety, which tastes quite nasty with tea. A pot of tea is nearly always made with tea bags with bits of string attached, which come dangling from the pot. Tea is a common drink for the elderly who are at death's door – so tea bags bought in France are notable for a complete absence of taste. (Self-caterers who want something better than mildly flavoured hot water should take their own tea.) Hot chocolate can be particularly delicious in France, often topped with cream.

British real-ale enthusiasts may find French beer a disappointment – it's lager-style *bière blonde*. But it's tastier than British lager, and is served refreshingly cool. Although bottled beer is cheap in shops, it's not in cafés – for the best value, ask for a draught beer (*une pression*). Most cafés don't have a wide selection of wines but you can always have *un vin rouge* (glass of red wine) or *un vin blanc* (glass of white wine). In a wine-growing area you may find a choice of cheaply priced local wines. Champagne or other sparkling wines are available in most cafés. Cider is the local drink of Normandy and Brittany. It can be flat or fizzy, strong or weak, but the best comes in bottles which have wired corks, like champagne.

Soft drinks are pretty international these days. Coke is ubiquitous, as are orange and lemon fizzy or still drinks. One of the best-selling French fizzy drinks is called *Pschitt*; happily it tastes better than it sounds. There are bright green minty drinks which may keep the kids amused, such as *menthe à l'eau*, which tastes like toothpaste. By far the most refreshing soft drink is *citron pressé*, freshly squeezed lemon juice served with water and sugar.

The French aren't really into pre-prandial gin and tonic (you can get it, but at a price). If you want to act typically French, the things to drink as an aperitif are Dubonnet (a red, sweet type of vermouth), Noilly Prat (white dry vermouth) and the aniseed-flavoured *pastis* (especially in the south) which can be drunk neat but is usually served with water which makes the clear liquid go cloudy.

France has an amazing range of brandies and fruit-based liqueurs, some very fine, others sweet and syrupy. In addition to the well-known Cognac and Armagnac (grape brandies) you'll come across Calvados (apple brandy made in Normandy) and fruit spirits such as kirsch (from cherries), *quetsch* (from plums) and *poire* (from pears). *Marc* is a hard-hitting drink made from grape skins. *Cassis* is a blackcurrant liqueur often mixed with white wine to make *Kir*, or with sparkling wine to make the more expensive *Kir Royale*; both are very refreshing drinks at any time of day.

Eating and drinking tips

Watch out for...
● waiters who bring the *carte* and don't offer you the cheaper *menu*
● dishes which may upset the squeamish: avoid *tête de veau* (calf's head), *tripes* (tripe), *cervelles* (brains), *ris de veau* (calf's sweetbreads)
● expensive mineral water (if you want to slake your thirst, ask for a jug of tap water – see below)

Don't be surprised if...
● you have difficulty getting lunch on Sunday without a booking
● service seems slow – meals are not meant to be rushed in France
● on Sundays and public holidays the cheapest menus are unavailable
● vegetables are served separately from the meat
● a simple restaurant has paper table-cloths and the waiter scribbles on them to tot up the bill
● a simple restaurant expects you to use the same knife and fork throughout the meal
● waiters or waitresses seem brusque; it's fairly standard in France

Remember that...
● you needn't be shy about sharing a dish
● a French restaurant expects to serve two proper meals a day and won't be terribly appreciative if you order only a salad or starter from the *carte*
● meat is normally served very rare or *saignant*; if you want it practically raw, ask for it *bleu*; if you want it rare but not bloody ask for it *à point*, for medium *bien cuit* (which in fact means well cooked)
● the French don't drink coffee or tea during meals
● the more expensive menus in a cheaper restaurant are often better value than the cheapest in a more expensive place
● there are strict drinking-and-driving laws and random breathalyser tests
● waiters aren't called *garçon* – use *monsieur, madame* or *mademoiselle*
● although children are very welcome in practically all restaurants, they are expected to behave themselves

Cheeses of France

Part of the fun of eating cheese in France is that there are always new varieties to discover and try out. 'Try anything once' should be your motto. But a little guidance may be helpful at first, so we list here 20 or so of the most common cheeses.

Regional cheeses

Bleu de Bresse – Factory-made blue cheese from the Lyonnais in the shape of a small cylinder; creamy and smooth.
Brillat-Savarin – Mild, creamy cheese from Normandy, named after the gastronome, ambassador and philosopher (1755–1826).
Cantal – Hard, strong, yellow cheese, with a nutty flavour, made in the Auvergne.
Chabichou – Small, cone-shaped goat's milk cheese, with strong smell and flavour; from the Poitou area.
Chaource – White, soft and creamy cheese from Burgundy, made in cylinders.
Dauphin – Soft, herb-seasoned cheese from Champagne-Ardennes area, said to be named after Louis XIV's son.
Epoisses Soft, whole milk cheese with spicy smell and flavour, made all over Burgundy and central France.
Olivet Bleu – Small, rich, fruity cheese with bluish skin, sometimes wrapped in plane tree leaves; it comes from the Loire.
Rollot – Cheese in the form of a disc with yellow rind, spicy smell and flavour.
Saint-Marcellin – Small, round, mild cheese made of cow's milk from the town of the same name in Savoie.
Tomme – Name for a large number of cheeses, mainly from the Alps. Usually mild.
Ste-Mauré – Soft creamy goat's milk cheese from Touraine.
St-Nectaire – Flat, round cheese with mild but aromatic flavour, made in the Dordogne.

Principal cheeses

You're likely to come across these major varieties of cheese anywhere in France.
Brie – Soft cheese always made in round discs, varying in size. A good one should be yellow, creamy but not runny. It is made by factories in Brie and other parts of France and often called by the name of the area where it is made, for example Brie de Meaux or Brie de Melun.
Bleu d'Auvergne – Blue mould cheese created by a 19th-century peasant. It is usually made from a mixture of goat's, ewe's and cow's milk.
Camembert – Small circular soft cheese invented in about 1790 by a farmer's wife, Mme Harel, whose statue you can see in the little village of Camembert, near Vimoutiers in Normandy.
Livarot – Soft, strong cheese with orange rind, from a small market town in Normandy.
Munster – Large, round supple cheese with orange rind, matured for three to six weeks, with strong smell and spicy flavour. Made in the Munster valley in Alsace.
Pont-l'Evêque – Small, square pungent cheese, made from whole or skimmed milk. It is ripened in cellars, usually for three to four months.
Port-Salut – Creamy, yellow, whole-milk cheese, first made at the Trappist Monastery of Port du Salut in Brittany.
Reblochon – Soft, smooth cheese from Savoie, with mild, creamy flavour; made of cow's milk.
Roquefort – The true Roquefort, made in the litte town of the same name in the Massif Central, is manufactured exclusively from ewe's milk. The unique feature of this expensive, pungent cheese is that the curds are mixed with a special type of breadcrumb, causing a green mould to develop. The cheeses are stored in damp, cool caves for 30 or 40 days. Experts say it should then be left to ripen for a year.

Useful phrases

Pourriez-vous me recommander un bon restaurant? – Could you recommend a good restaurant?

Je voudrais réserver une table pour deux personnes – I'd like to reserve a table for two

Nous arriverons à huit heures – We'll arrive at 8 o'clock

Est-ce qu'on peut manger ici? – Can we have something to eat here?

Avez-vous une table pour quatre? – Have you a table for four?

J'ai réservé une table au nom de... – I have reserved a table in the name of...

La carte, s'il vous plaît – The menu, please

Avez-vous un menu? – Have you a set menu?

La carte des vins, s'il vous plaît – The wine list, please

N'avez-vous riens de moins cher? – Don't you have anything less expensive?

Pourriez-vous recommander/conseiller un bon vin du pays? – Can you recommend a good local wine?

Avez-vous du vin en carafe? – Do you have carafe wine?

Que me recommandez-vous? – What do you recommend?

Nous voudrions... – We would like

Je voudrais... – I would like...

Qu'est-ce que c'est que ça? – What's that?

Quelles sont les spécialités de la région/maison? – What are the specialities of the region/house?

C'est pour moi – That's for me

C'est immangeable – It's inedible

Ce ne me plaît pas – I don't like this

Une autre bouteille/demi-bouteille, s'il vous plaît – Another bottle/half-bottle, please

Encore du beurre/de l'eau/du pain, s'il vous plaît – More butter/water/bread, please

Qu'est-ce que vous avez comme dessert? – What do you have for dessert?

C'est tout, merci – Nothing else, thank you

Du café seulement – Just coffee

L'addition, s'il vous plaît – I'd like the bill please

Est-ce que le service est compris? – Is service included?

Acceptez-vous les règlements avec carte de crédit/Eurocheques? – Do you take credit cards/Eurocheques

C'était très bon, merci – It was very good, thank you

Où sont les toilettes? – Where are the toilets?

Wine

une bouteille de... – a bottle of...
une demi-bouteille – a half bottle
cuvée/réserve de la maison/du patron – house wine
rouge – red
blanc – white
rosé – rosé
sec – dry
léger – light
corsé – full bodied
méthode champenoise – champagne method (ie sparkling).
mousseux – sparkling
brut – very dry
doux – sweet

Other drinks

de l'eau minérale gazeuse – fizzy mineral water
de l'eau minérale non-gazeuse (or *non-pétillante*) – still mineral water
de l'eau du robinet – tap water
un café – small black coffee
un café crème – white coffee
un café au lait – large milky coffee
un décaf – decaffeinated coffee
un chocolat chaud – hot chocolate
un thé au citron – tea with lemon
un thé au lait – tea with milk
une tisane – herb tea
une bière – beer
une pression – draught beer
un gin-tonic – gin and tonic
un porto – port
un vermouth – vermouth
sec – neat (straight)
avec des glaçons – on the rocks
jus de fruits – fruit juice
jus d'orange – orange juice
jus d'abricot – apricot juice
citron pressé – fresh lemon juice
une limonade – gassy lemonade

Starters

andouillette – pork sausage of chitterlings and tripe
bisque – shellfish soup
bouillabaisse – Mediterranean fish soup or stew
charcuterie assortie – assorted hams, sausages etc
crudités – raw vegetable salad
fonds d'artichauts – artichoke hearts
hors-d'oeuvre variés – assorted appetizers
jambon – ham
potage – thick soup
rillettes – highly seasoned potted pork
saucisse/saucisson – French sausage
soupe à l'oignon – onion soup
terrine – coarse type of pâté, served in slices
velouté de volaille – cream of chicken soup

Fish, seafood, snails etc

anchois – anchovy
anguille – eel
brochet – pike
colin – hake
coquilles St-Jacques – scallops
crevettes – shrimps
écrevisses – freshwater crayfish
escargots – snails
grenouilles – frogs
homard – lobster
huîtres – oysters
langouste – spiny lobster or crayfish
langoustines – large prawns
lotte de mer – monkfish
lotte de rivière – burbot
loup de mer – sea-bass
morue – cod
moules – mussels
palourdes – clams
rouget – red mullet
saumon – salmon
sole – sole
thon – tunny fish
truite – trout

Meat

agneau – lamb
bifteck – steak
boeuf – beef
canard – duck
carré d'agneau – rack of lamb
cervelle – brains
charcuterie – assorted pork products
châteaubriand – thick fillet steak
caille – quail
côte de boeuf – side of beef
côtelettes – chops
dinde – turkey
entrecôte – entrecote, rib steak
escalope – cutlet
filet –
foie – liver
gigôt – leg of lamb or mutton
jambon – ham
lapin – rabbit
poulet – chicken
poussin – baby chicken
ris de veau – veal sweetbreads
rognons – kidneys
rosbif – roast beef
tournedos – fillet steak
tripes – tripe
veau – veal
volaille – poultry

Ways of cooking

à la meunière – sauce of butter, lemon juice and parsley
au four – baked
beurre blanc – sauce of butter, dry wine or vinegar and shallots
à la vapeur – steamed
en croûte – in pastry
farci – stuffed
frit – fried
fumé – smoked
garni – with vegetables
grillé – grilled
à la provençale – sauce of tomatoes, garlic and olive oil
rôti – roasted

Vegetables

ail – garlic
artichaut – artichoke
asperges – asparagus
aubergines – aubergines
champignons – mushrooms
choucroute – sauerkraut
chou-fleur – cauliflower
endive – chicory
épinards – spinach
flageolets – small kidney beans
haricots verts – French beans
oignons – onions
petits pois – peas
pommes de terre – potatoes

pommes frites – chips
pommes lyonnaise – potatoes sautéd with onions
riz – rice
salade niçoise – mixed salad, usually with tomatoes, hard boiled eggs, potatoes, black olives, anchovy, lettuce, and tuna
salade panachée – mixed salad
salade verte – green salad

Dessert

coupe – usually a sundae
crème caramel – caramel custard
crêpes suzette – thin pancakes in flaming orange liqueur
fromage blanc – a cross between cream cheese and yoghourt
gâteau au chocolat – chocoate cake

glace au café/au chocolat/aux fraises/à la vanille – coffee/chocolate/strawberry/vanilla ice cream
mousse au chocolat – chocolate mousse
sorbet de cassis – blackcurrant sorbet
tarte aux pommes – apple tart

Fruit

abricot – apricot
ananas – pineapple
banane – banana
cerises – cherries
fraises – strawberries
framboises – raspberries
melon – melon
orange – orange
pêche – peach
poire – pear
pomme – apple

Accommodation

Wayne Allen

Whatever style of holiday accommodation you choose, with some care and a bit of luck you can expect it to add greatly to the enjoyment of your holiday – and to give very good value.

Hotels

To anyone whose experience of hotels is limited to Britain, French hotels are likely to come as a very pleasant surprise. Britain has its charming and characterful hotels, of course – but they're few and far between, and often too expensive for the ordinary traveller to afford. They're greatly outnumbered by dreary small hotels with incompetent service and barely edible food, and by big chain hotels where all is uniformity and plastic. The picture in France is quite different: the French intolerance of shoddy service and poor food, aided by a strong tradition of family hotel-keeping, has ensured that there is a plentiful supply of charming small hotels.

The biggest adjustment you have to make when you cross the Channel is to get used to the fact that in most French hotels food takes pride of place. One result of this is that in some hotels there are no public rooms other than the restaurant: it's not uncommon to find no lounge and no bar, and to have your drinks and breakfast in your bedroom. Another is that bedroom decoration and plumbing in simpler hotels can seem a bit behind the times. A simple *auberge* (a country inn) where the hotelier is also the chef may produce the best meal you have had for months; but the hectically patterned floral wallpaper, the desperately dim lighting, and the basin and bidet lurking behind a screen in your bedroom may come as something of an anti-climax.

But these sort of rooms are very cheap, and it's often worth sacrificing luxury in order to have more to spend on meals. For those whose creature comforts take priority, there is no shortage of French hotels which offer a lounge, bar and breakfast room, and elegant bedrooms with immaculate modern bathrooms – at a price, of course. And somewhere between these two extremes come all the enormously charming hotels that you find throughout France – ancient farmhouses with huge log fires and beams, skilfully converted mills beside streams, and lovely mellow old village inns.

Of course, not all French hoteliers are master chefs, or want to employ someone who is. But instead of running a mediocre restaurant, as they might in Britain, such hoteliers don't run a restaurant at all – they simply do bed and breakfast. (Naturally, hotels without restaurants are to be found mainly in towns, where there are plenty of other places to eat.)

As a rule, French hotels offer better value than British ones, particularly at the cheaper end of the market. But there are pronounced variations from place to place. In particular, the fashionable south coast is much more expensive than inland areas or the family-resort coasts of the Atlantic and the Channel; if you want to stay in a charming and comfortable hotel in the south, you must consider it a privilege and pay accordingly. Individual resorts, too, may have higher prices than their neighbours if they have the style to attract an affluent clientele.

Double beds are the norm in French hotels (the French delight in making jokes about the common British preference for twin beds). Twin rooms are usually a bit more expensive and not easy to come by – at least in small hotels. One child can usually be accommodated on a folding bed in a double room. Two children are sometimes expected to sleep in a double bed in another room (you'd rarely find a room in an *auberge* large enough to accommodate four people). Comfortable hotels will probably provide pillows (often kept in the cupboards); but it's not unusual in simpler places to have to make do with hard tubular bolsters.

The French have not traditionally gone in for bed-and-breakfast accommodation in private homes, perhaps because they have had access to plenty of good-value hotels. But things are changing, and there are now several alternatives to conventional hotels.

Under the *Château Accueil* scheme you can stay as a paying guest with aristocratic French families in their châteaux. The wealth tax introduced by the Socialist government under President Mitterand in 1982 has proved to be a very good reason for château owners to open their doors to paying guests. The scheme was started by a *vicomtesse* who began taking guests into her husband's family château in the late 1970s, and when the wealth tax came into effect she set up a cooperative with ten other château owners; now there are 37 in the group, many of them in the Loire. The French Tourist Office has a leaflet spelling out facilities and identifying which proprietors speak English (most do).

Many home-owners offering b&b are now organised under the *Chambres d'Hôtes* banner – offering a 'very warm family welcome' in country homes ranging from half-timbered cottages in Normandy to small châteaux in the Loire. And there's *Café-Couette* ('Coffee-Quilt'), an organisation which you have to join if you want to stay in any of the 1,000-plus homes it offers all over France. Details in the *Factfile*.

If the budget is really tight for your trip across France it is worth considering the *Relais Routiers*, traditionally staging posts or coaching inns, today truck-drivers' cafés which offer cheap palatable food and often very cheap accommodation too. Rooms are very basic (ask to see one before you commit yourself) but the main drawback is the noise – most of them are on main roads. Buying the *Relais Routiers* guide (see *Factfile*) entitles you to a reduction on lorry-drivers' menus.

French hotels are controlled and supervised by the Ministry of Tourism and classified in five categories – from simple one-star accommodation to four-star *de luxe* (there are also unclassified hotels which are too basic to be recommended to tourists). The star-ratings, which are usually displayed outside the hotels, don't give you much of an indication of what a place is like, as they are based on facilities – such as whether there is a bidet or telephone in every room, or 24hr room-service.

Prices are controlled, and every hotel should display its rates at reception and in every bedroom (they're often hidden behind the wardrobe door). Rates are quoted for a room, not per person, and normally are the same regardless of whether one or two people occupy the room; a child can normally be accommodated on a folding bed at little extra cost. Rates include service and tax (*service et taxes compris*), except in some *de luxe* hotels where the service charge is quoted separately. Most hotels offer special rates for *pension complète* (accommodation and full meals) or *demi-pension* (accommodation, breakfast and either lunch or dinner), but to take advantage of these special rates a stay of three nights is normally required.

Finding a hotel

Twenty years ago, one of the great pleasures of French holidays was finding superb hotels unknown to other tourists. Today, France is so thoroughly documented by hotel guides – particularly English hotel guides – that the scope for fresh discoveries is very limited. In this book we've recommended a selection of hotels in popular holiday areas; some of them have been (up to now) relatively unknown in Britain. But you mustn't be surprised if you find another GB plate in the car park when you arrive.

The hotels we have selected are ones which are above average for charm and atmosphere, for quality of food or for value for money – or a combination of all three. It is not a uniform selection – on the contrary, our hotels range from simple, modestly priced family-run *auberges* to elegant converted châteaux. A few very expensive but irresistible places have crept in – the sort of hotels you might consider for a very special occasion; but the majority are certainly not over-priced for what they offer, and many of them are remarkably good value, particularly in comparison with their British counterparts. Most have a restaurant where you can expect to be well fed, and only in the very simplest places are you likely to have a language problem.

We have limited ourselves to hotels in locations which are either attractive in themselves or which make a good base for exploring the surrounding area. If there is a lack of hotels in large towns it is for two reasons: first, French country hotels are nearly always more charming and atmospheric than their town equivalents (Paris excepted), and secondly it's much more relaxing to stay in the countryside, well removed from noisy town centres, and make day-trips into any nearby towns which you find interesting.

If you are positively horrified by the idea of finding yourself surrounded by your compatriots at dinner, the only safe solution is to draw up a 'blacklist' of hotels recommended by all the popular English guides (including this one) and to steer well clear of those places. But a good half-measure is simply to ignore the English recommendations and to employ French ones – which for all practical purposes means using the Michelin Red Guide. This fat annual volume recommends over 10,000 hotels and restaurants, from the simple to the extremely grand, on the basis of regular inspections. The two- or three-line entries are a bit intimidating at first, but they're crammed with information and once you've mastered the symbols and used the guide a few times you'll soon begin to get some idea of what to expect.

The Michelin 'gable' symbols give you a very good indication of the degree of comfort; if you want somewhere particularly nice it's worth looking for these symbols in red and/or an additional red symbol showing the Michelin man in a rocking chair (or a bird on a branch, depending which way you interpret it); strictly speaking this means only that the hotel is very quiet, but in practice it often means also that it's a rather nice place. The Michelin entry also gives details of the price of a room, cost of dinner and breakfast, days closed, parking facilities, credit cards taken, sports facilities and so on. Using the Michelin in combination with the book of Logis (see below) you cannot go far wrong.

Do not make the mistake of assuming that Michelin (or any other guide) is infallible. If you spot what looks like a welcoming and comfortable *auberge*, but find it's not in the guides, don't be put off. Ask to see a room, have a look at the menu, and if the signs are still good, give it a whirl. If the gamble pays off, the satisfaction is enormous. (Of course, if it doesn't…)

Chains and groups

In the last few years there has also been a rapid growth in the chain hotel/ motel business, with chains such as Ibis, Mercure and Novotel expanding across France and offering high-quality, functional accommodation at low prices – not the way to see rural France, but quite useful if you have no time to detour from main roads, towns or motorways. Novotel, for example, have 85 three-star hotels, mainly on motorways, on the outskirts of cities or at airports; the accommodation is usually reliable and not too expensive, but the food cannot be compared to that served by a privately-owned hotel of the same class. You pays your money and takes your choice, or *à chacun son goût*, as they say locally.

What is of more interest to most touring motorists is the fact that many individually owned hotels in France have come together into marketing groups. The grandest is the *Relais et Châteaux* group, paragon of the French hotel industry (though also embracing hotels in other European countries). There are over 100 French hotels in the group, spread throughout the country. A typical Relais et Châteaux hotel will be a converted grand building with beautiful grounds (and probably German or Swiss BMWs littered outside). It could be a castle by the sea in Brittany, a Renaissance manor overlooking the Loire, an ancient farmhouse in Provence or the Ritz in Paris. The accent is on comfort, elegance and fine food. Meals are usually sophisticated and menus normally feature *nouvelle cuisine*. The atmosphere can be somewhat formal, though rarely forbidding – the forbidding part is probably the price, which you can expect to be high (though still less than you might pay for similar style in the UK).

But perhaps the most characteristic of French hotels, and the ones that offer the best value for money, are the rural *Logis et Auberges de France*. These are privately owned, family-run hotels, mostly one- or two-star establishments, located in peaceful countryside or perhaps on the edge of some small market town or in a village square. These are dotted all over France, and offer a warm welcome, a pleasantly relaxed atmosphere and simple regional cooking. The *auberges* tend to be smaller and simpler than the *logis*. The guide lists over 4,000 hotels and is available from the French

Tourist Office in London, free of charge apart from postage. Bookings have to be made direct with the individual hotels.

In the more expensive hotel groups the emphasis is still on character and individuality. Slightly cheaper than the Relais et Châteaux are the *Châteaux-hôtels Indépendants et Hôtelleries d'Atmosphère* (Independent Châteaux Hotels and Inns with Character), the *Châteaux et Demeures de Tradition* (traditional establishments) and the *Relais du Silence*, where the accent is on peace and quiet.

Making a reservation

If you are going independently to France you can either telephone or write direct to the hotel to reserve a room. There's a good chance that you'll be able to speak to someone who can understand sufficient English to make a booking, but the amount of French you need to do it is in any case not great. You will almost inevitably be expected to send a deposit (*des arrhes*) – usually for the first night's stay, though if you're booking for several days you might be asked for three nights' deposit. The best way to do this is to write a Eurocheque in francs; failing that you can send a banker's draft. If you are writing to make a reservation and want a quick answer it is worth enclosing an International Reply Coupon, available from post offices. Bilingual booking forms are available from the French Tourist Office.

The main holiday season in France is August, when the French depart *en masse* for their annual break. But for any time in summer it is wise to make bookings well in advance of travelling. If you want to book hotels as you tour around the country, the *Accueil de France* offices in main towns will make bookings for personal callers for up to a week ahead; they're open every day of the year (there's a small charge for the telephone call or telex). Many hotels (for example, Logis and other chain groups) will book ahead for you. It's worth remembering that a lot of the smaller hotels close for one day a week; the reception and restaurant will be closed and only long-term guests are allowed to stay. The Michelin Red Guide states which days hotels are closed (it's usually mid-week).

Checking in

If you haven't sent a deposit it is essential to turn up at your hotel by 6pm. French hoteliers are famous for giving away rooms if you're late in arriving – even at two minutes past six. When you arrive, ask to see the room, even if you've already made a definite reservation. This is quite normal practice in France and avoids the risk that you'll be lumbered with the pokiest, noisiest or most expensive room in the hotel. Also, ask about special rates for full or half board if you are staying three nights or more – but bear in mind that you will get set meals with very little choice.

Although most of the *logis* and *auberges* have a reputation for friendliness, staff in French hotels (like the French everywhere) can be prickly, glacially polite or just downright rude. It's worth trying to disarm them with smiles, but don't take it personally if Madame remains unmoved; she's almost certainly just the same with her French guests too – particularly Parisians.

Meals

French hoteliers, particularly in rural areas, are renowned for pressurising guests into taking dinner in the hotel (if it has a restaurant). Legally you are entitled to insist on having only bed and breakfast, but remember that in France (unlike Britain) hotel food is often among the best. If you want to eat out in the evening and want to avoid this pressure, you can normally find a hotel without a restaurant (this is easy in towns, not so easy in the country). If on the other hand your priority is food, it is worth looking out for restaurants with rooms. These are listed in Michelin as a restaurants but 'avec ch' (*avec chambres*) and the rooms they provide are often excellent value.

Remote hotels with little passing trade usually offer three- or four-course set menus. The food is home-made but unelaborate and there are no gastronomic or superior menus. Small hotels in villages or well populated rural regions tend to be the mainstay of the local community, catering for the local residents as much as for tourists staying a day or two. Here you are likely to have a choice of more than one menu, and in some hotels you are allowed to choose a dish from the more expensive menus if you tire of the basic *pension* menu – provided you pay the difference in price.

Small family-run hotels are not really suitable for young children. There are insufficient staff to provide early meals and special menus – and you are unlikely to get a babysitter if you want to go out.

Breakfast in a French hotel can be a bit of a disappointment if you are looking forward to buttery croissants and *brioches*, fresh-ground coffee, crusty *baguettes* and home-made apricot jam. Four-star hotels may produce such fare (for the price of a set lunch or dinner in a *relais routier*); elsewhere you're likely to get pre-packed factory butter and jam, mediocre coffee and bread that isn't always fresh. A much better bet (in a town at least) is to go to a local café, where for half the price you can get reliably good coffee and croissants.

Self-catering

One of the big holiday success stories of recent years has been the enormous popularity of self-catering holidays in France, and in particular of *gîtes* – simple country houses or apartments, usually available for a relatively low weekly rental. The *gîte* has done more than anything to make France accessible to many thousands of British families.

Freedom, privacy and 'getting away from it all' are the great pleasures of a do-it-yourself holiday. What's more, prices can be very reasonable, particularly if you opt for a place inland. And in France you have an unrivalled choice of styles of self-catering accommodation – farmhouses, cottages, converted barns, chalets, old mills, studio flats, bungalows, villas on the sea and modern high-rise apartments.

For tranquillity and a real taste of rural France there's no better choice than a *gîte*. Only a few years ago, few foreigners even knew what the word meant; now the word seems to be applied to every kind of self-catering property in inland France, and there are 30,000 of them altogether. The term has no real English equivalent but the official description is a privately owned, self-contained rural property, modernised with government help and supervised by the non-profit Gîtes de France organisation. *Gîtes* don't offer luxury – even a top-graded property can't match the comforts of a three-star hotel – but what most *gîtes* can offer is local character, charm and seclusion. A *gîte* could be a half-timbered house in Normandy, a rustic stone cottage in the Auvergne, a village house or even an apartment in a Loire château; it could also be a newly built property, squeezed into the category of 'modernised character cottages'. Some *gîtes* are very remote, others are in groups, either on a farm or in apartments.

A farm *gîte* has distinct advantages: milk from the churn on your doorstep, fresh eggs, vegetables and herbs from the garden and farm-made cider or brandy from the landlord – together with endless lectures on the evil of English lamb, Greek potatoes and the other evils of the EEC Common Agricultural Policy. It's an excellent way of improving your French, and great for children who can help the farmer milk his cows or tread the grapes. French farmers are quite unlike their British counterparts (many of them are communists, which gives you some idea of the extent of the difference – no Range Rovers and green wellies here). French farming families are usually quite friendly – more so than the staff in a lot of French hotels – and, providing it's not harvest time, they'll be happy to give you advice on what to see and where to eat and shop. Farms are probably the most peaceful places to stay – provided you don't mind the cocks crowing and the dawn chorus.

Sightseeing on a *gîte* holiday often takes second place to shopping in local markets and leisurely two-hour lunches; the slow pace of rural life is infectious. But you don't have to take the self-catering tag too literally – since it can be almost as cheap to eat out in France as it is to cook a meal at home, there's no compulsion to slave over the kitchen stove all day.

The *gîte* makes a near-ideal holiday for families, or at least for some sorts of family. Travelling out, you can load the car up with all the family essentials. Once you've arrived, you can relax, safe in the knowledge that your hyperactive children are not disturbing anybody else. But bear in mind that by its very nature a *gîte* tends to be rather remote from other human life. This is fine if your children are capable of amusing themselves, less attractive if you have to keep organising entertainment. If your children will be bored without companions of their own age, you may be better off camping.

Most companies quote different prices for different numbers of people staying in the same property. Going in a large party to a large property is usually the cheapest way of renting accommodation. By going off season, in May for example, you can save as much as 35 or 50 per cent on a holiday in August.

Choosing a gîte

The two biggest organisers of *gîte* holidays in the UK are the Gîtes de France organisation (attached to the French Tourist Office), which simply acts as a go-between to simplify the process of making a booking, and Brittany Ferries, who offer all-in package deals including the crossing to Caen, St-Malo or Roscoff. (They can book any hotels you're likely to need *en route*, too.)

The Brittany Ferries *gîte* brochure is available free from travel agents or direct from the company. It offers hundreds of properties, most of them officially approved in the same way as those offered by Gîtes de France. There's a colour picture and description of each one, and they are categorised in four price bands.

To get the Gîtes de France handbook, which has 1,600 properties available for rent, you need to be a member (an '*ami*') of Gîtes de France. Alternatively you can turn up at the Gîtes de France office in London and leaf through the handbook on the premises. There are photographs, descriptions and gradings by *épis* (ears of corn). One *épi* means a basic unit, perhaps a small and not very conveniently located annexe of a farmhouse, with no comfy chairs and a tiny kitchen and bathroom; a property with two *épis* would be more comfortable, perhaps with a couple of armchairs in the sitting room, and would probably be in a more desirable area; a *gîte* with three *épis* is the most comfortable and the most convenient, perhaps with recreational facilities such as a lake nearby or in an area with outstanding sights.

However simple the property, it's unlikely to be dirty or pokey, and it will conform to minimum standards of equipment: bathroom with shower, inside WC (and not the stand-up Turkish type), fridge etc. Furnishings and kitchen equipment are usually very French, which means you are unlikely to find a kettle or teapot. Linen is usually not provided – you either take your own or hire it out there.

Cooking is usually done on gas stored in huge refillable cylinders. This is a very common system in France and it may be assumed you'll know how to change the cylinders – if you don't, get the landlord to do it for you. Ask him too about the water-heater and the heating (usually an oil stove).

If you're considering renting a *gîte* or other property in mid-summer it's essential to book several months in advance – particularly if you're looking for something near the sea. The Gîtes de France handbook comes out in October and most of the properties within striking distance of the sea are fully booked for the July and August period by December or January. And if you leave it a lot longer you won't get a *gîte* at all. If the UK agents have no suitable vacancies you can always try to book directly by writing to the local *syndicat d'initiative* (tourist office) in your chosen area for a list of the other *gîtes* available. Tourist office addresses are given in the Michelin Red Guide.

Villas and apartments

While *gîtes* are typical of inland France, the coasts have different sorts of self-catering accommodation – apartments, studios, holiday complexes and villas. The Mediterranean coast has a huge choice, including luxurious and exclusive villas on the stretch between St-Tropez and Menton. (Don't expect these places to work out any cheaper than taking a hotel holiday.) There are also spanking new purpose-built apartment blocks, closely interlocked low-rise developments, and holiday villages which have communal facilities such as a pool, snack bar and mini-market. Few of them are actually on the beach and some are a fair distance from the sea. On the Atlantic coast there's also a good choice of individual villas and apartments but fewer complexes with elaborate facilities than the south of France.

There are lots of companies offering holiday homes in France, either simply acting as agents for the properties or selling complete packages with travel facilities of one sort or another – those using air travel sometimes include a hire-car at your destination, or offer to arrange one as an extra. Some of the smaller companies don't distribute brochures to travel agents and prefer to talk to clients direct about their various properties. The French Tourist Office in London can provide a useful list of tour operators, giving details of where they go.

Camping

Camping is a word that strikes fear into the heart of many thousands of Brits – ex-Boy Scouts and Girl Guides who still have nightmares about miserable weekends spent in chilly tents on the annual camp, waking up shivering in sleeping bags covered with morning dew.

Camping in France isn't like that. For one thing, the weather in France (particularly towards the south) is generally more suitable for outdoor life. Secondly, family camping has become a rather less spartan affair. No longer do you have to bed down on the hard ground – comfortably sprung double beds are available to campers; so are double-burner gas stoves, fridges and all other mod cons. This sort of luxury is probably frowned upon by the serious camping fraternity, who prefer to erect their ridge tents far from the madding crowd, but most people are happy to do without the hardship. Thus liberated from discomfort, you are free to enjoy to the full the pleasures of camping – the freedom and flexibility it offers, as well as the fresh air.

Campsites are good places for getting to know people. With communal washing and sports facilities, bars and restaurants, you're more than likely to strike up a few acquaintances. But the other side of the same coin is that privacy is limited. Any family rows you have tend to become part of the campsite entertainment (your rows may be an embarrassment, other peoples' rows of course are usually quite good value!). And camping still does require you to rough it just a little. Even the best maintained campsites find it difficult to keep toilet blocks and washrooms up to scratch all day every day. Unless you're terribly fussy this won't be too much of a problem.

The other major problems about camping – buying all the necessary equipment which you will probably use only once a year, and having to pack it all into your car – are also now easily resolved. A number of companies now offer fully furnished pre-erected tents at dozens of sites all over France – and at very attractive prices. The equipment is very well maintained and regularly replaced. Electric power and lighting is normal, and most of the tents can even have an indoor toilet added on if you choose!

The campsites themselves are usually well maintained, too. One of the favourite holiday horror stories recycled every August by the national press used to be the Great French Campsite Disaster. There would be photographs of disgracefully overcrowded sites on the Mediterranean coast, with close-ups of overflowing toilets and rotting rubbish. Things have improved enormously on the Mediterranean coast in recent years, but even so you would be well advised to choose another location during the peak season. The Atlantic coast around La Rochelle is a growing favourite. And there are quite a few inland sites: the Dordogne, for example, has a number of excellent locations.

There are other attractions of camping with a tour operator. The company will have a British French-speaking representative on the site to help sort out any problems you may have. There will also be other British people for you to talk to, and British children for your kids to play with – and normally there will be organised acitivities laid on by the holiday company rep to keep them amused for at least a part of the day. Most of the sites will also have restaurants or a take-away food service, so you don't even have to cook if you don't want to.

If you're happy to buy or hire your own tent and other equipment, and want to take to the open road and do your own thing, then France is still the place to go. The French regard themselves with some justice as the

most camping-conscious nation in Europe. There are over 7,000 sites in the
country, varying from small, thoroughly rural sites to massive complexes
(more akin to holiday camps) on the south coast. The big four-star sites
along the coast have the sort of luxury you might expect from a hotel: you
may well have a pool, tennis courts, shops, restaurant, bar and more. Such
is the self-sufficiency of some sites that campers can happily stay put for
several days, particularly if it's on or by a beach.

For the French, *le camping* usually means going laden with trailers,
radios, TVs, crates of wine and the dog. They are no less serious about
cooking while camping than they are when they're preparing the two-hour
lunch back home. (Even if they're stopping by the roadside for a picnic,
out come the tables, chairs and cooking paraphernalia.) This may mean
smells of garlic wafting over the campsite – which can of course be rather
nice. Meanwhile the British are more prone to big brunches, beans on
toast, camp take-aways or the local restaurant.

The big campsites are great places for keeping children and teenagers
amused without too much supervision. If however your idea is 'to get away
from it all', then opt for a quiet rural inland site where there's plenty of
space and privacy – ideally in the grounds of a farmhouse, or perhaps even
of a château.

Choosing a site

Every region of France has camping facilities, but the most popular areas
are Brittany (which has more campsites than anywhere else in the country),
Normandy, the Atlantic coast, the south coast and the Dordogne. If you're
thinking of going to the coast in high season it's essential to make a
reservation: either go with a tour operator (with or without your own tent)
or book independently by writing direct to the campsite enclosing an
International Reply Coupon (available from post offices).

Campsites are graded from one to four stars. One-star sites have minimal
facilities – perhaps just a couple of cold showers and loos. On a four-star site
you can expect hot water, telephone, shops, launderette and perhaps a pool
or lake nearby. Theoretically, more stars means more spacious pitches, but
this isn't always so in high season. Many small towns have municipal sites;
they are usually rated one-star or two-star (so they aren't luxurious) but
they often have attractive settings by a river or on the edge of town, and are
always good value. The management is usually very laid back – there may
even be no one on duty to take your money. Camping rough (or *sauvage*) is
not allowed on beaches or in nature parks or reserves. But you can nearly
always pitch in a field as long as you ask the owner's permission.

There are various sources for finding a campsite. The French Tourist
Office issues a useful leaflet. Michelin produces an excellent guide –
Camping Caravaning France; it's in French but has English translations
where relevant and most of the information is given in symbols. There is

also an official guide to campsites published by the Fédération Française de Camping-Caravaning – again in French. Both these guides have a wide range of sites and include small details like whether there are power points or a grocery shop on site. If you're looking for something rather special the *Castels et Camping Caravaning* group contains over 40 high quality four-star sites. There are more details of these sources in the *Factfile*.

Tips for self-catering and camping

Remember that...
● there are several excellent campsites within easy striking distance of central Paris
● if you're looking for a campsite in high season you can get information on current availability of sites throughout the country from tourist offices and from information centres on some motorways
● it's worth getting an International Camping Carnet – certain luxury sites won't admit you without it
● Camping Gaz International and Butagaz are available everywhere in France, but other brands of gas are not
● camping charges are worked out in different ways: on 1- or 2-star sites there are usually separate charges per person, per car, per caravan and per pitch; on 3- or 4-star sites there are often fixed charges per pitch regardless of how many of you there are and what equipment you have
● If you stay on a campsite until after mid-day you will normally be charged for an extra night

Don't be surprised if...
● French farmers (and their dogs) take a dim view of camping in fields without permission
● your *gîte* or apartment lacks the props of British life such as a kettle and teapot; when in France...
● the really attractive *gîtes* in the brochures are booked up for the summer months by the end of the previous year

Watch out for...
● campsites (particularly in the south) with little or no shade – tents can get unbearably hot in the Mediterranean sun
● campsites which squeeze too many tents and caravans in during high season; if possible, inspect your plot before committing yourself
● charges at smart château or seaside campsites which can mount up to more than you might expect
● extra costs on self-catering holidays – fuel, electricity and cleaning, for example

Tips for hotels

Watch out for...
- hoteliers who expect you to take dinner in their restaurant whether you want it or not
- extras at breakfast (fresh orange juice may seem less attractive when you realise it costs £2 a glass)
- room rates in posh hotels which don't include service and tax

Don't be surprised if...
- breakfast is served in your bedroom
- you have to ask for a pillow or a decent towel
- you're offered a room with wash basin, bidet (possibly on wheels!) and shower cabinet but no loo
- your bath is only three feet long and the hot water supply is erratic
- credit cards aren't accepted
- in a small hotel you are given a key to the front door to let yourself in after about 10.00pm
- hotels recommended in guidebooks such as this one attract other British visitors besides you

Remember that...
- breakfast will normally cost extra, and won't seem such good value as the room itself
- few hotels will keep a room for you if you are late in arriving and haven't sent a deposit
- it's normal to inspect the room you're being given, and to object if you don't like it
- smaller hotels may close one day a week, and most country hotels close for regular annual holidays
- in areas which are mainly popular for summer holidays, most hotels close down in winter

Booking by letter
If you want to make your own hotel reservation but don't trust your ability to do it over the phone, and if you are making your plans well ahead of departure, you can book by letter. A suitable letter with English translation is shown on the facing page. We haven't given full postal addresses of the hotels in this guide; the information we have given is normally sufficient for a letter to find its way to the hotel, but if in doubt check with the French Tourist Office or in the Michelin Red Guide.

```
                              Chez Nous
                              99 Basingstoke Road
                              Orpington
                              Kent

                              Le 25 Janvier 1987

    La Direction
    Hôtel de la Gare
    20 av République
    Colombey-sur-Orb
    50100
    Manche
    France


    Monsieur,

    J'aimerais réserver une chambre pour deux
    personnes avec salle de bain à partir du 15
    Juin jusqu'ua 19 Juin.

    Pouvez-vous confirmer la réservation dès que
    possible et me faire savoir le prix de la
    chambre?

    Je vous prie de croire, Monsieur, à
    l'expression de mes sentiments distingués.




    Henry Gibson
```

Dear Sir,

I would like to reserve a room for two with bath from 15 June to 19 June.

Could you confirm the reservation as soon as possible and let me know the price of the room?

Yours faithfully

Henry Gibson

Useful phrases

Hotels

Je m'appelle... – My name is...
Nous arriverons à sept heures – We will be arriving at 7 o'clock
J'ai réservé une chambre au nom de... – I've reserved a room in the name of...
Avez-vous une chambre... – Do you have a room...
pour deux personnes – a double
avec un grand lit – with a double bed
à deux lits – with twin beds
pour une personne (or *à un lit*) – single room
avec salle de bain – with bathroom
avec douche – with a shower
Quel est le prix d'une chambre pour deux? – How much is a room for two?
Est-ce qu'il y a des toilettes privées? – Is there a private toilet?
Quel est le prix... – How much does it cost...
avec petit déjeuner – with breakfast
sans les repas – without meals
avec demi-pension – for half board
avec pension complète – for full board
Est-ce qu'il y a une réduction pour les enfants? – Is there a reduction for children?
N'avez-vous rien de moins cher? – Haven't you anything cheaper?
Nous resterons quelques jours – We'll be staying a few days
Nous resterons jusqu'à dimanche – We'll be staying until Sunday
Nous resterons seulement une nuit – We'll stay just one night
Puis-je voir la chambre? – May I see the room?
La chambre est trop petite – The room is too small
Avez-vous quelque chose de plus grand/plus tranquille? – Have you anything bigger/quieter?
Ça va – That'll do fine
Non, je ne l'aime pas – No, I don't like it
A quelle heure devons-nous quitter la chambre? – By what time do we have to vacate the room?

A quelle heure servez-vous le petit déjeuner/le dîner? – What time do you serve breakfast/dinner?
Où est-ce que je peux garer la voiture? – Where can I park the car?
A quelle heure ferme l'hôtel? – What time does the hotel close?
Je vais rentrer tard; avez-vous une clef de la porte d'entrée? – I am going to be late getting back; have you got a key for the front door?
Est-ce que je peux avoir... – Can I have...
ma clef – my key
du savon – some soap
des oreillers – some pillows
des serviettes – some towels
Je voudrais la note s'il vous plaît – I'd like the bill please
Est-ce que je peux payer avec ma carte de crédit? – Can I pay by credit card?
Acceptez-vous les chèques de voyage? – Do you take travellers' cheques?

Self-catering and camping

Est-ce qu'il y a un bon restaurant près d'ici? – Is there a good restaurant near here?
Qu'est-ce qu'il y a à voir/à faire dans la région? – What is there to see/to do in the region?
Comment marche le chauffe-eau/la cuisinière? – How do you make the water heater/cooker work?
Peut-on avoir une autre bouteille de gaz? – Can we have another bottle of gas?
Comment la change-t-on? – How do you change it?
Que devons-nous faire avec les ordures? – What do we do with the refuse?
Nous avons passé un excellent séjour. – We have had a very enjoyable time.
le gaz – gas
les draps – sheets
les serviettes – towels
le propriétaire – owner, landlord
l'inventaire – inventory

Shopping

Eileen Knight

Nowhere is the culture gap between Britain and France clearer than in the matter of shopping. As usual, the French logic is immaculate. Certain sorts of goods, and particularly foodstuffs, require specialist attention if they're to be sold at their best – so every town has highly specialised little shops doing a roaring trade in their speciality. Supermarkets have their place, but to offer a really attractive range of goods and really low prices they need to be really big – so every sizeable town has one or two huge hypermarkets on the outskirts. Furniture needs space to be displayed, and easy access to the shop for delivery vans – so furniture shops are built on green-field sites out of town. Sunday lunch would be incomplete without a splendid *tarte* for dessert – so many *pâtisseries* are open on Sunday mornings, whatever the Church may say about a day of rest.

The novelty of French shops is attractive in itself, but it is the care and flair that the French put into the preparation and selling of food which most visitors find remarkable. Shopping for food is unquestionably one of the highlights of a holiday in France. Stalls and counters, even in small provincial towns, provide a feast for the eyes and a delight to the nose – wheels of oozing Brie, serried rows of sausages, strings of garlic, fresh herbs and spices, and piles of perfect fruit and fresh vegetables to make English markets pale in comparison.

Preparing and consuming a picnic or a meal in your *gîte* can be every bit as satisfying as eating out. You could do all the shopping under the one roof of a hypermarket but it's more fun and more French to go to tiny specialist shops in villages or towns – the *boulangerie* for crusty white loaves, the *charcuterie* for a bewildering variety of cold meats, pâtés, salads and ready-made *hors d'oeuvre*, the *pâtisserie* for mouth-watering fruit tarts and gâteaux.

The fact that there are *Appellation d'Origine Contrôlée* labels to certify the quality of chickens and cheese, as there are for classy wines, gives you some idea of how seriously the French take their food. AC Bresse chickens are fat, yellow and raised on maize, AC Brie is butter-gold, creamy soft and aged for a month. Locals claim that there is a cheese for every day of the year and no one doubts there are at least 300. The variety is enormous – from the salty *chèvre* (goat's milk) to the pungent, appropriately named *Vieux Puant* (old stinker).

Every town and sizeable village has regular markets, from early morning to mid-day once or twice a week, which are the best source for fresh fruit and vegetables and, depending where you are, often for things like cheese, meat and fish. Prices are always lower here than the shops. But the market is usually also an endlessly interesting spectacle, with plenty of local colour. The variety is huge – everything from live rabbits to wild strawberries and a lot of weird and interesting things in between like dandelions and nettles. You may find one stall entirely devoted to garlic, another to herbs, another to wild mushrooms or walnuts.

If you're based in a tiny hamlet without a market or proper shops, don't worry – you won't starve. There will be visits from mobile bakers, butchers and grocers about twice a week, and probably eggs, milk and poultry from the local farms.

The French-invented hypermarkets can be a boon to self-caterers. Of course they lack the intimacy of the traditional little village or town shops and offer few opportunities to practise your French (possibly a blessing), but to compensate there's a huge range of high-quality food (fresh as well as frozen and processed) plus endless household and DIY goods. And, as you would hope, hypermarkets are cheap. Day-trippers to French Channel ports know that by judicious hypermarket shopping they can easily recoup the cost of the ferry. Among the best bargains are table wine, bottled beer (you're allowed to take home 50 litres), coffee beans, olive oil and Le Creuset casseroles. What's more, they normally accept Eurocheques. The only occasional snag is long queues.

Hypermarkets usually lie on the outskirts of towns and are not always easy to find. Look for billboards pointing the way, bearing such names as Carrefour, Continent, Mammouth and Rallye, which are the biggest chains. Normally the main shop will be surrounded by lots of smaller satellite shops – garden centres, boutiques, banks, cafés and restaurants.

Clothes shops, particularly boutiques, are generally stylish and elegant but expensive. The *grands magasins* (department stores) are the best places to head for – they're particularly stylish in Paris (concentrated in and around the Boulevard Haussmann).

To the French, shopping is an important business – even buying a small piece of cheese can be something of an occasion. Local housewives have no qualms about keeping other customers waiting while they discuss at length the ripeness of a Brie or melon, or the merits of a home-made pâté. If your French isn't up to that sort of debate, it's essential at least to proffer a '*Bonjour messieurs-dames*' when you arrive and be profuse with your thanks when you leave. Knowing the word for everything you want is not necessary – pointing goes a very long way, particularly with a few stock phrases like *une tranche de celui-là s'il vous plaît* (a slice of that one please), *un comme ça* (one of those) and *c'est tout* (that's all). We've listed a few essential phrases later in this chapter, plus the weights you're likely to need.

Most small shops open early in the morning and stay open well into the evening but have a long mid–day break; many close all day on Monday. Hypermarket opening hours are long – usually 8am or 10am to 10pm, including Mondays. In the rest of this chapter, the main specialist food shops are described in turn – in alphabetical order, ending with a short section on buying wine. Then come shopping tips, and French vocabulary.

Boulangeries – bakers' shops

Bread is indispensable to every French meal, and because it doesn't keep its texture for long it has to be very fresh – which is why every village is required by law to have either a bakery or a *dépôt de pain* where fresh bread is delivered, and why it's not uncommon to see the local housewives, grannies or blue-clad workers with four or five sticks under their arm before breakfast. You might even see them coming back for more at midday – most *boulangeries* are expected to bake twice a day. The fresher the bread the better, and anything left over the next day is fit only for fattening the geese. If your experience of 'French' bread in Britain makes you wonder what all this fuss is about, that's because the stuff you've had at home isn't the same thing at all. It may *look* like French bread, but very rarely has the superbly brittle crust and light-as-air texture of the real thing (though purists say that even the real thing isn't what it was in the days before preservatives and electric ovens).

To buy a loaf all you really need do is say *un pain comme cela* and point to the relevant loaf. French loaves come in various shapes and sizes, but the traditional (some would say the only) bread is the long thin crusty white *baguette*. Although the French have been slow to latch on to the wholefood craze, more and more bakers are producing wholemeal as well as country and ryebread – all of which keep longer than the white loaves. For those who still believe there's nothing like sliced bread, the French equivalent – *pain de mie* – is sold in groceries and supermarkets.

Baking cakes and pastries is a specialised business – so for a good choice you go to a *pâtisserie*. But bakeries also sell a limited selection of pastries – in particular, croissants. These delicious flaky breakfast treats are now common in British supermarkets; the genuine French article is of course somewhat superior – though the croissant is not a French invention. (The story goes back to 1668, when the Turks besieged Budapest and dug tunnels to get under the city walls. Bakers working in the quiet hours between dusk and dawn heard the sound of the tunnelling, gave warning and saved the city. Their reward was permission to make pastry shaped in the form of a crescent – the Turkish emblem.)

Boucheries – butchers' shops

High quality and meticulous preparation are the trademarks of a French butcher, so prices might seem higher than you would have expected. A general butcher sells *volaille* (poultry), *agneau* (lamb), *bifteck* (cheap steak), *filet* (fillet steak) and all the other meats you would expect to find in a British butcher's, except that you sometimes have to go to a *charcuterie* for pork.

In addition you can usually buy things like rabbits and hares and there is a wider choice of poultry including *poussin* (baby chicken), *pintade* (guinea fowl) and *caille* (quail). Some of the best chickens come from Bresse, and like fine wines are subject to government quality control: a *poulet de Bresse* is a free-range chicken fattened on maize and buckwheat, killed and plucked by hand and bathed in milk to give a pearly effect. Butchers also sell hearts, sweetbreads and tripe – not guaranteed to excite the appetites of the average British customer. (Such things turn up in restaurants too – see *Tips*, page 40.

Speciality butchers are the *volailler* (devoted to poultry), the *triperie* (specialising in tripe and other British pet hates) and the *boucherie chevaline* which sells horse-meat (you may find the idea of horse-meat rather unpleasant, but it actually tastes remarkably like steak and is sometimes more expensive). You can often recognise a horse butcher by the gilded horse-head outside the shop.

Charcuteries – delicatessens

Shopping in a good French *charcuterie* is one of life's great pleasures. Even a distinguished English delicatessen can't rival its magnificent range of pâtés, terrines, sausages, ready-made *hors d'oeuvre*, quiches and pizzas, pastries, puddings and pies. Every small town in France is likely to have at least one *charcuterie*; if it has several there is bound to be one that is generally considered the best.

Originally, a *charcuterie* (literally a cooked-food shop) sold exclusively cooked pork; pork is still the prime speciality but *charcuteries* sell all sorts of cooked meats and other dishes. The choice can range from a few pâtés, sausages and *andouillettes* to a great kaleidoscope of food ready-made for a memorable picnic – vol-au-vents, salads, pastries stuffed with cheese and so on. Pâtés are an indispensable part of the French diet: from the expensive *pâté de foie gras* (goose liver) down to *pâté de veau* or *pâté de porc* for picnics. Hams include the mild *jambon de Paris* and *jambon de York* (not unlike English ham) and the smoked hams, many of them eaten raw, such as *jambon de Bayonne* (superb with melon). There is usually a veritable forest of sausages from salami to pure pork.

For the more adventurous palate there are *boudins noirs* (black puddings) which vary enormously but are generally lighter, spicier and more interesting than the English equivalent – often eaten with fried apples; *boudins blancs* (white puddings), which can again vary from region to region – they're made of pork, poultry or game, with fat, eggs and cream (but no blood) and in parts of France are regarded as great delicacies; and other French specialities such as *andouillette* (brawn) and *rillettes* (potted pork, best from Le Mans). In addition there are always the specialities of the individual *charcuteries*.

If you want something more substantial there are delicious spit-roast chickens, which are sold in bags that keep in the heat and juices – ideal for self-caterers. Some *charcuteries* also provide other ready-cooked dishes such as *boeuf bourgignon* or *coq au vin*.

Crémeries and fromageries – dairy and cheese shops

In regions such as Normandy which are rich in dairy products, specialist *crémeries* (dairies) are common; elsewhere you would probably buy milk, eggs, butter and cheese from the local *épicerie* or supermarket.

Milk lies at the heart of a fundamental cultural divide that separates the British from the French. For most French people, the only sort of milk worth buying is UHT – heat-treated milk which keeps for months. The French, of course, don't go in for breakfast cereals or milky tea, so they never have to confront the taste of the stuff, which bears no resemblance to that of real milk. One British government minister memorably remarked that not even his dog would drink UHT milk. You can buy non-UHT pasteurised milk in France, but you will have to hunt around for it.

Crémeries also sell *crème fraîche* (fresh cream) but it's not the type of cream you get in Britain – it's slightly sour, rather like yoghourt, and is often used in cooking, but it's also delicious on fresh strawberries, tarts and other sweets.

There are various sources for cheese. You can get it at the market, in an *épicerie* (see below), a supermarket or hypermarket; but a specialist cheese shop is known as a *fromagerie*. Nobody knows the exact number of cheeses that exist in France but you've only to look at a market cheese stall or the cheese trolley in a good restaurant to get some idea of the bewildering variety – the mild Brie, Reblochon and Mimolette; the sharp, tangy Livarot, Pont-l'Evêque, and Bleu de Bresse; the high-fat Chaource, Pierre-Robert and Fougéru; the Vignelait wrapped in vine leaves; the fluffy Fromage de Fontainebleau, the prized Roquefort, the garlicky Boursin – just to name a few.

There are basically three categories of cheese – fresh cream cheeses (*fromages frais*) such as *fromage blanc* and *petit suisse* which can be served with sugar or fruit, or with herbs and salt; pressed and hard cheeses such as Comté and Beaufort; and soft cheeses which include the familiar Camembert and Brie. Although most are made from cow's milk, there are dozens of local goat's-milk cheeses – from the mild and fresh to the mature and strong – and quite a few made from ewe's milk.

Authentic Bries and Camemberts are made from unpasteurised farm milk. Look for the label *fermier* or *au lait cru*. Given the range and complexity of French cheeses it's well worth asking the advice of the cheese merchant. These experts appreciate the interest and are usually delighted to give advice. Even if you can't hope to become a connoisseur of French cheeses, you can at least get to know some regional specialities.

Epiceries – grocers' shops

This is equivalent to the British grocery shop or small supermarket – the place where you get all the basics. Obviously you don't find the fresh quality of the specialist shops but you can always get commercial cheeses and other dairy products, pre-packed cakes, canned food, wine, beer, coffee, tea and frequently fresh fruit and vegetables. Don't spurn French tinned food. The quality is usually superior to the British equivalent, particularly when it comes to things like *petits pois* (peas), green or haricot beans, fish, and tinned soups.

More and more *épiceries* are turning to the self-service supermarket system. This of course lets you lightly off any language problems, but in case your local *épicerie* still gives personal service, we've listed the French words for basic foods and drinks.

Pâtisseries – cake/pastry shops

Most high-street cake shops in Britain these days offer a dull array of iced
slices, Chelsea buns, dense doughnuts and cardboard puffs stuffed with
syrupy jam and ersatz cream. But, happily, the cake-maker's art is alive
and exceedingly well – and living in France. Shop-window displays of the
pâtisseries are wonderful; among the forbidden delights they contain are
freshly made strawberry tarts, rich *brioches* and croissants, éclairs, choux
buns, *petits fours* and beautiful light home-made cakes. At Easter there are
chocolate rabbits and hens, at Christmas luxurious chocolate logs and
every weekend there is a special display for Sunday lunch (the French
rarely make their own desserts). It is all very difficult to resist; but prices
are high, and you soon realise that indulging in *pâtisseries* is something of a
luxury.

The epoch of great *pâtissiers* (pastry cooks) was the beginning of the 19th
century. The great chef Carême was famous for his lavish cake and pastry
displays; he designed massive, elaborate table decorations called *pièces
montées* (mounted pieces) as an outlet for his passionate interest in
architecture, and created some of the things (such as *mille-feuille*) which
you see in virtually every *pâtisserie* today.

Poissonneries – fish shops

You have only to glance along the quay at any Channel port to get an idea
of the vast variety of fresh seafood for sale in France – stalls piled high with
cockles and mussels, clams and crabs, squid and shrimps, oysters and
crayfish and of course whole, fresh fish. There are far more fish stalls in
France than proper fish shops.

The best and cheapest places to try are the local markets where
fishmongers have permanent stalls. Obviously, the nearer you are to the sea
the fresher the produce – but even inland there's a surprisingly good
choice. The selection will probably range from the tiniest winkles to tunny
fish of massive proportions. There are plenty of fish that you can take
home and simply grill – sole, trout, prawns for example – but there are also
many less familiar sights and some that are only fit for soups and stews;
naturally these are the very cheapest fish. At the other end of the scale
there are sea bass, lobster (rarely seen in markets – these go straight into
restaurant tanks) and crayfish. Fish stalls give prices per kilo and usually
the name of the fish – but the variety is such that it isn't always easy to
identify a fish even with the help of a good dictionary. Fishmongers will
willingly clean and gut (*vider*) the fish for you.

Oysters are excellent value in France, particularly if you're close to
oyster beds. There are two basic sorts – the *huître plate* or *Belon* and the
huître creuse or *Portugaise* – the first is a rounder, flatter oyster, much more
expensive than the second. The general rule for oysters is that you should

eat them only when there's an 'r' in the month (not in summer when
they're breeding) although the argument is somewhat controversial and
many ignore it. By combining oysters with mussels, prawns, clams and
other seafood you can make up your own *plateau de fruits de mer* – an
expensive dish in any restaurant but one which you can put together fairly
cheaply if you're not too far from the coast. Fresh sardines and anchovies
are also excellent value and easy to deal with.

Fish farms (*viviers*) are becoming increasingly popular in France, and if
you're self-catering it's worth finding out if there's one close to where
you're staying – prices are quite reasonable. A lot of the farm-bred trout are
taken to markets where they are sold live.

Buying wine

Wine can be extraordinarily cheap in France – about the same price as
mineral water if you don't mind basic *vin ordinaire* in a plastic screw-top
bottle. But in other respects, given the quality and variety of French wines,
wine shops in France are often something of a disappointment. While you
don't expect much more than plonk from the local grocer, and reasonably
priced everyday wines from the hypermarket, expectations are greater
from a specialist; but more often than not the choice is mediocre, the
atmosphere rather superior and the prices high. If you go for very fine
wines, you can easily pay more than you would in Britain.

Tasting and buying wine in the areas where it is produced is a different
matter. This is comparatively easy in France, and good value is much more
likely. You can either go to a *cave coopérative*, where wines from small local
vineyards are made and sold to a *maison du vin* (wine information centre)
where many locally made wines are available for comparison, or direct to
the vineyard. You can buy a bottle or a barrel at the *coopérative* but the
cheapest way is to buy *en vrac* – ie unbottled wine – from either the
vineyard or the *coopérative*. You have to supply your own containers but
some coopératives sell plastic containers holding about five litres.

A sign saying '*dégustation*' by the roadside means wine-tasting. This
could mean a free tipple or two although by the time you've knocked back
a few samples you may well feel under obligation to buy. Look out too for
signs saying *vente directe* – direct sales.

At a *maison du vin* you may be charged a few francs for tasting and
there's no compulsion to buy. In Beaune, for example, you can linger as
long as you please, imbibing the finest wines of Burgundy and paying less
than a fiver for the privilege – but if you want to buy here (and it's easy to
do so in a drunken stupour) you pay high prices. Alternatively you can
follow the *Route des Grands Crus*, and taste some of the greatest wines of
Burgundy at the vineyard where they are made; but you'll feel some
pressure to buy and you'll need to be affluent to do so.

If there are no local vineyards or caves to visit try the local hypermarket

– prices are very reasonable and there are frequently special offers. But try to experiment, and learn from experience before you start buying by the case. There will be good wine and bad, and no way of distinguishing the two except trial and error. You can find *vin ordinaire* in any *épicerie* or small food shop, often in a plastic bottle. Where the bottles are glass you pay a small deposit unless you're taking back an empty bottle.

Shopping tips

Remember that...
• you can import more booze without paying import tax and duty if you buy it from French shops rather than duty-free shops
• you can buy half a loaf of bread if a whole one seems too much for your immediate needs

Don't be surprised if...
• in small towns you have difficulty buying your picnic lunch after noon – everything stops for lunch, shopping included
• service is slow at the butcher's: the dicing, trimming, mincing, rolling and butchering is all done on the spot

Watch out for...
• elderly shopkeepers in rural areas who still talk in terms of 'old' francs – so they say *mille* when they mean ten

Useful phrases

Je voudrais... – I would like...
un morceau de – a piece of
une tranche de – a slice of
celui-là – that one
un/une de ceux-là – one of those
ça suffit – that's enough
encore un peu – a little more
plus grand que ça – bigger than that
plus petit que ça – smaller than that
Donnez m'en pour deux personnes – Give me enough for two helpings
C'est trop – That's too much
C'est tout – That's all
Quelles sont les fromages de la région? – Which are the regional cheeses?
Est-ce prêt pour manger aujourd'hui? – Is it ready to eat today?
Avez-vous quelque chose de moins fort? – Have you got something less strong?
Combien je vous dois? – What do I owe you?

Boulangeries – bakers' shops

baguette – standard long thin white loaf
bâtard – shorter, stockier type of baguette
biscottes – rusks
brioche – sweet yeast-bread roll
chausson aux pommes – apple turnover
couronne – round (crown shaped) loaf
croissant – crescent-shaped, light flaky pastry
demi-baguette – half a *baguette*
ficelle – thinner, smaller, crustier version of *baguette*
flûte – long, thin loaf (between a *baguette* and a *ficelle*)
gressins or *longuets* – bread sticks
gros pain – large crusty loaf
miche – large round loaf
pain d'avoine – oatmeal bread
pain bis – brown bread

pain brioché – slightly sweet cross between white bread and *brioche*
pain de campagne – large round white loaf
pain complet – wholemeal bread
pain doux – sultana bread
pain d'épi – bread shaped like a stalk of wheat
pain d'épice – spiced gingerbread
pain de froment – wheaten bread
pain de gruau – fine wheatened bread
pain d'orge – barley bread
pain aux raisins – raisin bread
pain de régime – diet bread
pain de seigle – rye bread
pain au son – bread with added bran
pain de sucre – sugar loaf
pain viennois – *brioche*-like loaf
petit pain au chocolat – flaky pastry in shape of a sausage roll with chocolate filling
petit pain – bread roll
Saint-Ouen – short, fat loaf

Boucheries – butchers' shops

agneau – lamb
agneau de pré-salé – lamb reared on salt meadows
bifteck haché – mince
châteaubriand – thick double fillet
cheval – horse
contrefilet or faux-filet – sirloin
côte de/côtelette – chop
dinde – turkey
entrecôte – rib steak
entrecôte minute – small *entrecôte*
épaule – shoulder
foie – liver
gigôt – leg of lamb or mutton
lapin – rabbit
lièvre – hare
mouton – lamb (not an old animal as in Britain)
noisettes – small round cuts from the fillet
porc – pork
poulet – chicken
poulet de Bresse – *Appellation Contrôlée* chicken (ie the best) – free-range fattened on maize and buckwheat and bathed in milk
rognons – kidneys
rosbif – beef for roasting
tournedos – thick cut from the fillet

Charcuteries – delicatessens

andouille/andouillette – pork sausage of chitterlings and tripe
boudin blanc – white sausage-like pudding made of white pork meat, poultry or game and fat, eggs and cream
boudin noir – black/blood pudding,
cervelle – brains
chorizo – red peppery sausage
crêpinettes – small flat cakes of sausage meat in white fat
échines – spare ribs
friandises – small sausages in puff pastry
fromage de tête – brawn
galantine de porc – pork cooked in jelly, quite like brawn
jambon – ham
jambon de Bayonne – smoked, raw ham
jambon cru – raw ham
jambonneau – mildy cured ham
lard – bacon
pâté de campagne – farmhouse (pork) pâté
pâté de gibier – game pâté
pâté de lapin – rabbit pâté
pâté de lièvre – hare pâté
pieds de porc – pig's trotters
poitrine – breast of lamb, veal etc
porc – pork
rillettes – potted pork seasoned with herbs or spices
saucisson à l'ail – garlic sausage
saucisson sec – dry sausage eg salami
tête de porc – pig's head

Crémeries and fromageries – dairy and cheese shops

Cheeses are dealt with at length in *Eating and drinking*
pas fait – unripe
fait – ripe
fromage de vache – cheese made from cow's milk
de brebis – from ewe's milk
de chèvre – from goat's milk

Epiceries – grocers' shops

beurre doux – butter, unsalted
beurre salé – butter, salted
bière – beer
bouteille – bottle

café – coffee
eau – water
huile – oil
lait – milk
oeufs – eggs
poivre – pepper
sel – salt
sucre – sugar
thé – tea
vin – wine
vinaigre – vinegar

Pâtisseries – cake/pastry shops

baba – cake made of leavened dough, mixed with raisins and steeped in kirsch or rum
brioche – bun made from light yeast dough, usually in the shape of a cottage loaf (a ball surmounted by another ball)
choux à la crème – cream pastry
croissant – crescent-shaped, light flaky pastry
flan – custard tart filled with fruit, custard or cream
macaron – macaroon, not necessarily made with almonds
madeleine – small sponge cake in the shape of a shell
mille-feuille – as the name ('thousand-leaf') suggests, this consists of thin layers of flaky pastry interleaved with cream or other filling
palmier – small sweet pastry puff, in the shape of a heart
Savarin – cake made with a yeast dough mixture, soaked in flavoured syrup with rum or kirsch added.
tarte aux pommes/fraises – apple/strawberry tart
truffes – truffles

Poissonneries – fish shops

anguilles – eel
bar – bass
bigorneaux – winkles
brochet – pike
colin – hake
coquilles St-Jacques – scallops
crevettes – shrimps
écrevisses – freshwater crayfish
encornets – cuttlefish
escargots – snails
espadon – swordfish
homard – lobster
huîtres – oysters
langouste – spiny lobster or crayfish
langoustines – large prawns
lotte de mer – monkfish
lotte de rivière – burbot
loup de mer – sea-bass
morue – cod (rarely fresh and usually salted)
moules – mussels
poulpe – octopus
praires and palourdes – small clams
rouget – red mullet
seiches – squid
sole – sole
thon – tunny or tuna fish
truite – trout
turbot – turbot

Weights and measures

un kilo is 2.2 lbs
cinq cent grammes or *un demi-kilo* (sometimes called *une livre*) is 1.1 lb
cent grammes is just over 3 oz

There are more metric conversions in the *Factfile* starting on page 171.

Part II
France region by region

This part of *France Without Tears* describes (as fully as space allows) the areas of France you're likely to think of first when planning a holiday. Each of the following is the subject of a separate chapter; near the beginning of each chapter is a map of the region.

But you shouldn't get the idea that the rest of France has nothing to be said for it; the parts of France which do not repay exploration are very few, and very small. So we end this part of the book with a quick summary of the other main regions:

Paris

'The last time I saw Paris, her heart was warm and gay, I heard the laughter of her heart in every street café,' wrote lyricist Oscar Hammerstein II, making his own well-known contribution to the bulging Parisian Romantic Song-book – to be put alongside 'April in Paris', 'I love Paris in the springtime', 'Under the bridges of Paris' and the rest. Everyone knows about the romance of the French capital. Ask a hundred couples which Continental city they would choose for a romantic weekend, and all but a handful (Venice has its attractions, too) will say Paris. And a weekend there is far from being an impossible dream – the city is now a package holiday resort which attracts more British travellers than summer-holiday favourites such as Torremolinos and Benidorm.

The city is packed with museums, galleries and monuments. There is an extraordinary range of sights, from the dazzling canvases of the impressionists, in the new gallery created in the 19th-century Gare d'Orsay, to the less aesthetic pleasures of the sewers and catacombs. If you haven't been to Paris before, you will want to go up the Eiffel Tower, have a look at the Mona Lisa in the Louvre, visit the cathedral of Notre-Dame, watch the artists at work in the Place du Tertre in Montmartre, walk up the Champs-Elysées to the Arc de Triomphe, explore the Rodin museum, look for bargains in the fascinating flea-market (Marché aux Puces) at Porte de Clignancourt and marvel at the controversial inside out plumbing of the extraordinary Pompidou Centre. And you'll be delighted to find that all these sights are every bit as good as you imagined them to be.

But people love Paris not just for art treasures or beautiful buildings but for everything else that makes the place so captivating: the style, the elegance, the infectious *joie de vivre*. However fast-paced and glamorous it is, Paris has at the same time a small-town feel. It is cosmopolitan, yet very French, and part of the pleasure is just strolling and absorbing the atmosphere. Each district or quarter of Paris has its own distinct character: the heart of the 'right bank' of the Seine for smart shops, galleries and grandiose vistas, the Marais for quiet unspoilt corners, the Latin Quarter (the essence of 'left bank' Paris) for lively markets, street stalls and bookshops, Clichy/Pigalle for lively nightlife, the Boulevard St-Germain for fashionable boutiques and cafés, Montmartre for touristy but picturesque 'Bohemian' life.

The nightlife of Paris is legendary, buzzing until the early hours of the morning: discos, jazz clubs, cabarets, rock and reggae as well as classical concerts, theatre and opera. There is a huge choice of films and evening cabarets (which are offered as excursions) featuring can-can girls and topless dancers in exotic costumes.

Embodying so much that is modern and vital in both culture and fashion, Paris is never dull. The only real drawback to the city is some of the rude and arrogant Parisians, who don't usually welcome visitors with open arms. But then Paris wouldn't be Paris without them – which is why it's not a good idea to visit the city in August, when many Parisians are on holiday and the city seems lifeless despite the many tourists. Spring, early summer and autumn are the best times to go.

If you are travelling to the south, you will inevitably be tempted to break your journey in Paris either on the way out or on the return journey. It makes good sense, as you can then almost enjoy two holidays for the price of one. If you have children learning French, a trip to Paris can add immeasurably to their understanding of France and its culture.

Eating out

Don't assume that every meal in Paris will be a memorable experience. There are plenty of good places to eat but a lot of tourist traps too. It's worth spending some time consulting one or two of the many restaurant guides which cover Paris, particularly the English-language guide to the city produced by Gault Millau (see *Food and drink*).

Prices vary dramatically: you can pay the same amount for a sandwich, salad and drink in a '*drugstore*' on the Champs-Elysées as you would for a three-course set menu in a back street on the Left Bank. Fixed-price menus are almost invariably the best value. There are no such things as Parisian specialities but a wide range of regional cooking from all over France and a host of ethnic restaurants. More and more snack places have opened over the last few years: sandwich bars, fast-food joints, *croissanteries*, cafés galore – and there is as always a superb choice of do-it-yourself meals from street markets and gourmet food shops.

Getting around

Being so compact, Paris is an ideal city for strolling; but for a faster way of getting around, there's nothing to beat the underground Metro. This is not only quick, efficient and cheap; it's attractive too, with green art nouveau signs heralding each station and interesting artwork decorating the tunnels. One of the best examples is the Louvre station, which is itself rather like a museum. Finding your way around is quite simple as long as you remember that the lines are called by the names of the station at each end (there are two names for each line) and that when you want to change trains you follow signs saying *Correspondances*.

There are very useful electronic maps – you just press the button beside the name of the station you want, and the lines and stations you have to follow light up. Within the city centre, one ticket covers one journey, however far you're travelling, but if you're making several journeys it's

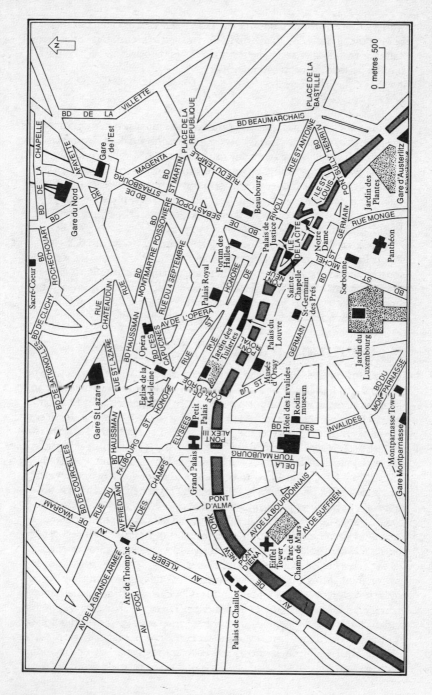

worth getting a *carnet* – a book of ten tickets which works out cheaper than buying them individually; alternatively you can get tourist 'rover' tickets valid for two, four or seven days. Metro tickets can also be used on buses, but the network is less comprehensive.

Sightseeing

Opening hours vary but the main thing to remember is that most museums close on Tuesday, some close on Monday and some on both. Entrance prices can be quite steep but many museums are free or half-price on Sunday (which is naturally the worst day for crowds) and/or Wednesday. The most enjoyable and least expensive town excursion is a trip along the Seine on a *Bateau Mouche* (a glass-topped river boat). It lasts about 75 minutes; alternatively there are coach tours of Paris, showing the highlights of the city both by day and by night.

The Ile-de-France which surrounds Paris provides a wealth of sights. Kings lived out here in preference to Paris, so there are grand palaces as well as museums and cathedrals. There are excursions from Paris to the huge, magnificent palace of Versailles, the smaller but no less interesting Fontainebleau (see *Getting to the south*), the glorious cathedral of Chartres and the romantic Renaissance château of Chantilly.

Accommodation

There are hundreds of hotels in Paris, from the de luxe Ritz down to basic one-star bed-and-breakfast places. In between there are a lot of small, charming hotels, which offer superb value in comparison with London hotels; most of them are on the left bank (*rive gauche* – south of the river). We have selected 20 or so central hotels, some on each bank. Most are two- or three-star places – it's not really worth paying for luxury in a city where there's so much to do and see both by day and by night, and where only your sleeping hours are likely to be spent in the hotel. They range widely in price; naturally, prices in Paris are generally higher than elsewhere, but none of our hotels is outrageously expensive.

Our recommendations are listed at the end of this chapter under *arrondissements* (rather like the postal districts of London). They cover six of the most central areas, and we have included some clues to the character of each area before the details of the hotels.

You might also think about self-catering. For example, Brittany Ferries offer three-, four- or seven-night holidays in Paris apartments including travel on their Portsmouth–Caen crossing. There are apartments available either in the 12th *arrondissement*, in the south-east of Paris near the Bois de Vincennes, or in the 17th *arrondissement* in the north-west. For two adults sharing, three nights in an apartment costs from £95 per person, including ferry crossing.

Main sights

Louvre A palace of massive proportions housing the world's richest collection of art. There are seven museums and countless masterpieces, including the Mona Lisa and the Venus de Milo. The size is overwhelming, and a guide to the rooms (available in the museum or in the Michelin Green Guide) is indispensable. Don't attempt to do more than one section at a time. The Musée des Arts Décoratifs (fine furniture, fabrics, ceramics, tapestries etc) is also housed in the Louvre but as a separate museum with a separate entrance charge.

Notre-Dame cathedral A perfect example of Gothic harmony, which has become one of the most familiar landmarks in Paris and is nearly always crowded with tourists. A strenuous climb up the tower gives good views of the gargoyles and a fine panorama of Paris – but no hunchback these days!

Musée d'Orsay 19th-century station recently converted into a splendid museum and gallery dedicated to 19th- and 20th-century art. It houses the world's finest collection of impressionist and post-impressionist paintings, many of which used to be in the crowded Jeu de Paume museum.

Pompidou Centre Controversial centre of modern art, resembling a multi-coloured oil refinery. The happenings outside in the piazza are as entertaining as those within the building: clowns, fire-eaters, jugglers, breakdancers and anyone else who feels like joining the fun.

Eiffel Tower The subject of bitter controversy when it was built in the 1880s, this is now recognised the world over as the symbol of Paris, and is visited by hundreds of thousands of tourists each summer. Lifts take you up to three levels, with cafeteria or restaurant on each floor. The staircase is cheaper but quite terrifying.

Hôtel des Invalides Built by Louis XIV as a home for wounded war veterans, now housing one of the finest military museums in the world; but the main focus is the fine Church of the Dôme, housing Napoleon's grandiose tomb.

Sainte-Chapelle Masterpiece of Gothic art, built by St-Louis to house the relic of Christ's Crown of Thorns. Beautiful stained glass windows.

Conciergerie A medieval palace turned Revolutionary prison, where Marie-Antionette and others were sent to await their execution. Visits cover the Prisoners' Gallery, Marie-Antionette's and Robespierre's cells and a small museum of the Revolution.

Grand Palais and Petit Palais Exuberant art nouveau buildings, created for the 1900 World Exhibition. The Grand Palais now houses the Science Museum and Planetarium, the Petis Palais the Museum of Fine Arts.

Sacré-Coeur Eye-catching white church in Montmartre whose lack of architectural charm is more than compensated for by the views of Paris from its steps, or better still from the dome.

Musée de Cluny Outstanding collection of medieval painting, sculpture, jewellery, relics, furniture and so on. Highlights are the tapestries and the Gallo-Roman baths. **Musée Rodin** Fine collection of Rodin sculptures, spanning his whole career.

Musée Carnavalet Intriguing museum which focuses on the history of Paris, in a beautiful mid-16th-century house.

Musée d'Art Moderne de la Ville de Paris Municipal modern art museum covering all the great French artistic movements of the early 20th century.

Hotels

1st arrondissement
The heart of the right bank – an expensive area to stay, with several four-star de luxe hotels including the Ritz. More reasonable alternatives are the family-run **Tuileries** 10 rue St-Hyacinthe ££££ ☎ (1) 42 61 04 17 – elegant rooms in a pretty 18th-century house; and the cheaper, traditional **Prince-Albert** down the road at 5 rue St-Hyacinthe £££ ☎ (1) 42 61 58 36. Super value, and as a result nearly always booked up, is the **Hôtel Family** 35 rue Cambon ££ ☎ (1) 42 61 54 84.

4th arrondissement
Right bank, slightly upstream of the centre – a quiet area to stay. The **Bretonnerie** 22 rue Ste-Croix-de-la-Bretonnerie £££ ☎ (1) 48 87 77 63 is full of old-world charm; **Célestins** at 1 rue Charles-V ££ ☎ (1) 48 87 87 04 is an attractive small hotel on a quiet corner with good-value rooms. There are three very charming hotels on the island of St-Louis-en-l'Ile, prettily converted from 17th-century houses: the two nicest are the **Deux-Iles** 59 rue St-Louis-en-l'Ile £££ ☎ (1) 43 26 13 35, and the **Lutèce**, 65 rue St-Louis-en-l'Ile £££ ☎ (1) 43 26 23 52.

5th arrondissement
Left bank, slightly upstream of the centre – the student or 'Latin' quarter. The **Colbert** 7 rue de l'Hôtel-Colbert ££££ ☎ (1) 43 25 85 65 is quiet and elegant. Much cheaper is the charmingly eccentric 17th-century **Esmeralda** near Notre-Dame, 4 rue St-Julien-le-Pauvre ££ ☎ (1) 43 54 19 20.

6th arrondissement
The fashionable heart of the left bank, with a lot of agreeable hotels. Expensive, but worth the cost, are the lovely **Abbaye St-Germain** 10 rue Cassette ££££ ☎ (1) 45 44 38 11, a peaceful and particularly elegant retreat off a noisy street; and the **Relais Christine** 3 rue Christine £££££ ☎ (1) 43 26 71 80, a beautifully converted 16th-century abbey with courtyard and garden. There are plenty of cheaper but still charming places to stay: the **Angleterre** 44 rue Jacob £££ ☎ (1) 42 60 34 72 is good value for a civilised central hotel; the **St-Germain-des-Prés** 36 rue Bonaparte ££££ ☎ (1) 43 26 00 19 has traditional charm; the **Deux Continents** 25 rue Jacob £££ ☎ (1) 43 26 72 46 is friendly and good value; the **Scandinavia** 27 rue de Tournon £££ ☎ (1) 43 29 67 20 has few facilities but is richly furnished with portraits, armour and antiques – and offers a warm welcome. A cheaper, simpler but satisfactory place is the **Récamier** 3 bis pl St-Sulpice ££ ☎ (1) 43 26 04 89, which is by the Church of St-Sulpice.

7th arrondissement
Left bank, downstream of the centre – not a very exciting area to stay, though it does have the Eiffel Tower and Invalides, and some of the hotels border the livelier 6th *arrondissement*. The **Lenox** 9 rue de l'Université £££ ☎ (1) 42 96 10 95 (in the Faubourg St-Germain) is traditional, civilised and good value; the **Suède** 31 rue Vaneau £££ ☎ (1) 47 05 OO 08 is peaceful and elegant but in a rather dull quarter near Les Invalides; and the **Pavillon** 54 rue St-Dominique £££ ☎ (1) 45 51 42 87 is a tiny enchanting hotel converted from an 18th-century convent, in a small street near the Eiffel Tower. The **Verneuil-St-Germain** 8 rue de Verneuil £££ ☎ (1) 42 60 24 16 is simple but adequate.

8th arrondissement
Right bank, downstream of centre around the Champs-Elysées, with a number of luxurious hotels. One of the smaller, more personal (but not inexpensive) places is the **Résidence Lord Byron** 5 rue Châteaubriand ££££ ☎ (1) 43 59 89 98 with quiet and very comfortable rooms, some built around a courtyard. The **Bradford** 10 rue St-Philippe-du-Roule £££ ☎ (1) 43 59 24 20 (near the Champs-Elysées) is one of the less expensive hotels in the area: comfortable and elegant.

Normandy

Normandy is one of the most under-rated regions of France, with great attractions for lovers of the countryside. Picture it in springtime: orchards bursting with apple blossom, the morning air fresh and clear, cows grazing in lush, high-hedged fields, black-and-white half-timbered cottages nestling beside bright, glistening streams. Irresistible – and equally delightful in summer, or in autumn when the trees are heavy with apples and the evening air is thick with the smell of log fires.

There is lots to see, too – a surprising variety of scenery, and many important historical sights. Yet Normandy is a place that few British people have so far properly explored; its very closeness to Britain seems to make it less interesting for many travellers. Most visitors tend to go for a short weekend break, or pause for a meal or an overnight stop at the beginning or end of a holiday taken further south in France. At first glance, it's easy to conclude that the Norman scenery isn't all that spectacular, and that its D-Day landing beaches are poor affairs compared with those of Brittany or other regions further south. But there's a lot more to Normandy than first meets the eye, and with Brittany Ferries' successful introduction of a ferry service from Portsmouth to the Norman heartland of Caen (strictly speaking, to the nearby port of Ouistreham), there are signs that the British are now taking Normandy more seriously.

Given its geographical proximity and strong historical links with Britain, it is hardly surprising that Normandy makes you feel closer to home than almost any other area of France. The land is familiarly green and rolling, there are apple trees, stud farms and the risk of rain (there's always a small price to be paid for green-ness!). But the region varies widely in character.

The heart of Normandy is a lush, pastoral landscape of rolling plateaux. Unlike Brittany, this is a prosperous land; there are beautiful old farmhouses, handsome châteaux, stone manors, sleek stallions and rich pastures; the dairy produce – butter, cheese and cream – is the pride of the region and the envy of the world. In a couple of inland areas, river valleys provide scenery that verges on the dramatic. The optimistically named Suisse Normande is no match for the Matterhorn – indeed there are no actual mountains – but it nevertheless is a charming area of woods and valleys, cliffs and crags. The Pays d'Auge, stretching inland from the popular seaside resorts of the Côte Fleurie, is the lush country of famous cheeses – Camembert, Livarot and Pont-l'Evêque. To the east, at the Seine valley, the scenery changes: beyond the port of Le Havre and the city of Rouen is the less welcoming, more exposed area of Seine-Maritime.

The coastline – over 600km of it – ranges from the sheer white cliffs and shingle beaches north-east of Le Havre to the long, shelving sandy beaches of the west coast, where the sea can retreat for miles. The most popular stretch is the Côte Fleurie, between Cabourg and the charming little port of Honfleur, where Deauville still holds sway as the most elegant and fashionable resort. In the 19th century the English came here in large numbers to pursue their new-found pleasure of sea-bathing; and once the railway was established from Paris to Rouen, the French aristocracy followed suit.

The great granite Cotentin peninsula juts out at the north-west corner of Normandy. Its west coast is flanked by cliffs and high headlands, with the occasional small, beautifully located seaside resort. Inland the main cultural diversions are the fine Romanesque abbey at Lessay and the magnificent cathedral of Coutances which escaped wartime devastation. The beaches on the east coast of the peninsula, and north of Bayeux, are broad and desolate, inextricably linked with the Allied landings of 1944. The code names of these beaches – Omaha, Utah, Juno, Gold and Sword – still carry a powerful meaning even to those born long after the June 1944 *débarquement*. War museums, tanks, cemeteries and military debris are constant reminders of the biggest armada ever launched.

Rouen is the only big city of Normandy, its industrial tentacles spreading for miles. It lies on the bank of the river Seine, which meanders through a varied landscape of eastern Normandy, flanked by factories, forests and occasionally by a beautiful and evocative abbey or château ruin. Massive sea-going tankers glide up the Seine looking quite out of place – and coming as something of a surprise if you happen to be picnicking on a quiet bend of the river.

What sort of holiday?

Normandy is the perfect destination for a weekend break. There are dozens of short-break packages on the market, which allow you to take your car either on a pre-arranged itinerary or on a tour of your own choosing. A number of operators allow you to take a *gîte* for a weekend. From the south coast there are regular crossings to Caen, Cherbourg, Le Havre, Dieppe and St-Malo (only just outside Normandy). For a longer stay, Normandy makes good touring territory, with straight and empty roads, an abundance of good restaurants and some delightful small hotels.

There are the usual sports of sailing and windsurfing along the coast, and riding and golf close to the main seaside resorts. Inland there are walks in wooded hills, and rock-climbing and canoeing in the Suisse Normande. Other diversions, more specific to Normandy, include watching sleek stallions exercise at stud-farms (Haras du Pin is one of the finest), touring the D-Day beaches and visiting Monet's glorious garden at Giverny.

The battle which raged through Normandy in 1944 reduced many towns and villages to ruins. But, mercifully, many of the architectural treasures were left intact, or at least have been restored to their former splendour.

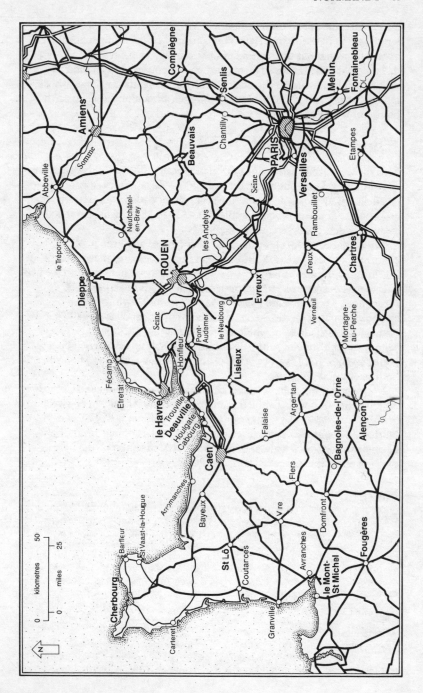

There are calm Romanesque churches, soaring Gothic cathedrals, handsome Renaissance châteaux and the majestic ruins of beautiful abbeys. Throughout the region, and particularly in the centre and east, there are old, half-timbered farms and manor houses, surrounded by orchards. The town with the greatest number of sights is Rouen, whose medieval heart and glorious Gothic churches miraculously survived the bombs of World War II.

Food and drink

Rich dishes, with lavish use of butter and cream, are part of the pleasures of Normandy. Look out for *poulet à la vallée d'Auge* – chicken in an apple, cream and Calvados sauce – and the many other dishes cooked with cream and apples. *Tarte aux pommes* (apple tart) is found everywhere and is absolutely delicious.

Camembert cheese is now made all over France and even in other countries such as Denmark, but the real thing originates in Normandy and was invented by a Norman farmer's wife (you can see her statue in the little village of Camembert near Vimoutiers). The Camemberts you get throughout Normandy are usually a far cry from the white chalky examples you find on the shelves of British supermarkets. A really good Camembert is made from whole unskimmed milk and should be pale yellow, smooth and not runny. Look for *lait cru* or unpasteurised cheese. Pont-l'Evêque and Livarot are the other well-known cheeses of Normandy, both strong and pungent.

Normandy is not wine country; the local drinks are cider and Calvados (apple brandy), both consumed in huge quantities. Cider can be sweet (*doux*) or dry (*brut*), flat or fizzy but the best comes in heavy corked bottles. To counteract all the cream and butter of a copious meal, the Normans knock back a glass of Calvados between courses – the hole-blowing effect it has is called a *trou normand*.

Gazetteer

Bayeux

For most people the name Bayeux means just one thing: its tapestry. But there is a lot more to this pleasant little town than its famous length of medieval needlework. Largely unscathed in 1944, it still has well-preserved old houses, cobbled streets and a beautiful cathedral.

What to see

Bayeux tapestry Very long and totally fascinating tapestry depicting William's conquest of England in 58 cartoon-like scenes, recently rehoused in a new building which also offers a wealth of information on its creation and background. The tapestry is amazingly vivid, lively and graphic, and provides a remarkable insight into the customs and costumes of the time. Cassette guides help you pin-point the details. Allow two hours at least, and be prepared for queues at peak times.

Hotels

The old British favourite is the **Lion d'Or** 71 rue St-Jean £££ ☎ 31 92 06 90, an old coaching inn, set in a cobbled courtyard near the centre. The décor is not exactly refined or co-ordinated, but it's a comfortable base with easily the best restaurant in town. Slightly cheaper is the **Argouges** 21 rue St-Patrice ££ ☎ 31 92 88 86, a charming, small family-run hotel, set in a courtyard in the centre of town. (No restaurant.)

Cabourg

The casino and the Grand Hotel, built for rich aristocratic Parisians during the last century, are still Cabourg's focal points. The long straight promenade and the formal, fan-shaped pattern of tree-lined roads radiating from the casino give the place a formal, rather sedate air. One of its principal claims to fame is that author Marcel Proust stayed at the Grand Hotel and made Cabourg and surroundings the inspiration of the imaginary resort of Balbec in *A la Recherche du Temps Perdu*. Nearby is Houlgate, a prosperous family resort set between wooded hills.

Hotel

About 7km out of Cabourg, off the road to Caen, the **Hostellerie Moulin du Pré** route de Gonneville ££ ☎ 31 78 83 68 is one of the most popular places to stay in the whole of Normandy – booking in advance is essential, particularly as there are only ten rooms. A modern reproduction of a traditional farmhouse, the Moulin is quiet and isolated. Food is all home-made and first-class. (Closed Sun D and Mon exc high season.)

Caen

A mostly modern city lying in the rich region of the Pays d'Auge, Caen was once the favourite city of William the Conqueror. Not as pretty as other Norman towns perhaps, but it's certainly worth visiting for its two splendid abbeys, stylish shops and particularly good restaurants. See *Channel ports* for details.

Hotels

If you don't want to stay in Caen itself, there are quieter alternatives further south. At Thury-Harcourt, 26km south-west, the **Relais de la Poste** ££ ☎ 31 79 72 12 is a creeper-clad stone building in the centre of town with ten elegant, delightfully furnished rooms. Cheaper and more rural is the **Auberge du Pont de Brie** at Goupillières, 8.5km north £ ☎ 31 79 37 84 – a restaurant with rooms in a wooded valley close to the river Orne. (Closed Wed exc high season.)

Caudebec-en-Caux

On the right bank of the Seine, under the shadow of the Brotonne bridge, Caudebec is a charming little town – particularly so during its Saturday morning market. Almost completely destroyed in World War II, Caudebec itself has one notable surviving building – the fine, flamboyant Gothic church. There are three great abbey churches in the vicinity: the old abbey church of St-Wandrille, whose Benedictine monks will give you a guided tour; the lofty, evocative ruins of Jumièges; and the well-renovated former abbey church of St-Georges at St-Martin-de-Boscherville.

Hotels

Probably the best-value hotel is the simple, modern **Normandie** 19 quai Guilbaud ££ ☎ 35 96 25 11 on the banks of the Seine. There are 13 adequately comfortable rooms and a reliable restaurant. (Restaurant closed Sun D exc public hols.) The smartest hotel is the next-door **Marine** 18 quai Guilbaud ££ ☎ 35 96 20 11 which has recently been redecorated. (Restaurant closed Sun D.)

Cherbourg

A big bustling ferry port on the north coast of the Cotentin peninsula, Cherbourg is not a place likely to detain the sightseer for long. But it has a hypermarket handily placed for the ferry port. See *Channel ports* for details.

£	up to £15
££	£15 to £25
£££	£25 to £45
££££	£45 to £70
£££££	£70 to £100
£££££!	more

Deauville

An elegant 19th-century resort, Deauville is still fashionable and affluent, although a little faded. The rich and famous are still drawn here by the glamour of the smart hotels, horse races, polo, regattas, nightlife and annual film festival. The sands are wide and golden, backed by bars, restaurants and pools. But the place to be seen is (and always has been) Les Planches, a wooden walkway which runs along the back of the beach. The season is short-lived; outside July and August Deauville loses a lot of its gloss.

Hotel

There is no such thing as a cheap or really good-value hotel or restaurant in Deauville; but one of the less expensive places to stay is **La Résidence** 55 av République ££ ☎ 31 88 07 50, which has 16 attractively furnished rooms.

Dieppe

Dieppe is the most northerly port and resort of Normandy – and the closest to Paris. It's one of the liveliest towns of the region, combining a big beach, worthwhile sightseeing and excellent shops and restaurants. See *Channel ports* for details.

Etretat

The wind and waves have been battering away for years at the cliffs between Dieppe and Le Havre, and nowhere is this more evident than at the small resort of Etretat where the houses are crammed between dramatically carved cliffs. A rather elegant resort in its 19th-century heyday, frequented by artists and literati, Etretat is now slightly faded, and the best things about it are the cliff walks and boat trips. Out of season it can be pretty bleak.

> Don't assume that a sight you want to see will be open: many museums and historic buildings close for a couple of hours over lunch, and often one or two days a week as well. Check with a *Syndicat d'Initiative*.

Hotel

The **Welcome** av Verdun ££ ☎ 35 27 00 89 is a cheerful, family place with a medley of furnishings and a reasonably priced restaurant. It lies a few minutes from the beach, set back from the main road going through town. (Closed Tue D and Wed.)

Fécamp

One of the main attractions of this rather drab fishing port is the free glass of Benedictine you get after a guided tour of the famous distillery. It is claimed that the liqueur was invented in 1610 by a local monk who had the idea of distilling the aromatic plants on the cliffs of Fécamp. The tour is a great tourist attraction – but the distillery itself is a neo-Gothic-cum-Renaissance atrocity. More impressive is the huge, imposing Gothic church of La Trinité.

Le Havre

The principal Atlantic port of France, spaciously but impersonally rebuilt after World War II. See *Channel ports* for details.

Honfleur

Honfleur is the most appealing coastal resort of Normandy – provided beaches are not your priority. It is touristy but the town succeeds in retaining its charm and manages to look pretty no matter how great the number of visitors. Its picturesque beauty and the quality of its light attracted an important colony of landscape painters in the latter half of the 19th century, including Sisley, Boudin, Cézanne and Pissarro. The artistic associations are still strong, and there are lots of studios you can visit.

Honfleur is a busy working harbour, which is part of its charm. The waterfront, with its cobbled quays, remains relatively unspoilt and the inner harbour, packed with boats and flanked by tall, narrow slate-roofed houses, is a delightful scene. The main drawback is the lack of reasonably priced places to stay.

What to see

Eugène Boudin museum Well displayed paintings, mainly of artists who worked locally. The emphasis is on Boudin, whose luminous seascapes and harbour scenes had a profound influence on Monet.

Ste-Catherine Unique church made of wood by the port's master shipwrights at the end of the Hundred Years' War.

Hotels

The **Ferme St-Siméon** route Adolphe Marais £££££! ☎ 31 89 23 61 can't be overlooked despite its extremely high prices. Once the meeting place of Monet, Sisley, Cézanne, Pissarro and Courbet, it's now a luxury hotel and anything but Bohemian. An 18th-century farmhouse, it is quiet and secluded, set in lovely gardens which overlook the estuary. Inside are antiques, old beams and some lovely big bedrooms. Despite the price it is very popular, so booking is essential. (Restaurant closed Wed L exc public hols and high season.)

There is not a lot of choice for those of modest means. The **Cheval Blanc** quai Passagers £££ ☎ 31 89 13 49 is the next-best place to stay, though perhaps over-priced these days. (Restaurant closed Mon.) The **Tour** 3 quai Tour ££ ☎ 31 89 21 22 is cheaper and reliable, but modern and not very inspiring.

Lisieux

Visitors mostly come to this industrial town on a pilgrimage to the modern basilica, dedicated to Ste-Thérèse who lived and died here. A much finer building is the old cathedral in the centre, and most holidaymakers will find more to interest them in the countryside around – the Pays d'Auge, a land of orchards, valleys and grazing cows. It's also the land of cheeses, with the towns of Pont-l'Evêque to the north, Livarot and Camembert to the south.

Nearby

St-Germain-de-Livet (6km S) A delightful little moated château whose towers and ramparts rise in a checker-board of grey stone and glazed brick.

Le Mont-St-Michel

You may have seen countless pictures of Mont-St-Michel – the fortress-like island of churches and spires which rises out of a silted bay like a mirage – but there's nothing to rival the first glimpse of the real thing. No other site in France outside Paris attracts more tourists than this amazing granite pyramid, crowned by the spire of its abbey. Inside the city walls, it's disappointing to discover the intense commercialism. The Grande Rue is a frenetic scene of tourists, souvenirs, cafés and crêperies. But this commercialism is nothing new – pilgrims were accosted by hucksters back in the Middle Ages. Less than half of today's visitors go up to the abbey, thereby giving some breathing space to those who go to see the impressive Romanesque and Gothic churches (guided tours only).

At low tide the sea is about 15km from the shore-line; when the tide comes in, it covers an enormous expanse of sand at astonishing speed – leaving a single causeway connecting the island to the mainland.

Hotels

Staying overnight has the great advantage that you see the place when one day's crowds have left and have the chance to visit the abbey before the next day's arrive. There are hotels on the mainland and a few in the village itself. The hotel with the most character on the island is **La Mère Poulard** ££ ☎ 33 60 14 01. Bedrooms are not exactly luxurious, but you eat well: good Norman and Breton dishes as well as Mme Poulard's famous fluffy omelettes cooked over an open fire. (Closed out of season.) A cheaper alternative is the **Auberge de la Sélune** 2 rue St-Germain ££ ☎ 33 48 53 62 at the village of Ducey, 15km west – a small, well-cared-for hotel whose main features are the gardens, river and excellent-value restaurant. (Closed Mon out of season.)

£	up to £15
££	£15 to £25
£££	£25 to £45
££££	£45 to £70
£££££	£70 to £100
£££££!	more

Pont-Audemer

Despite substantial damage in the war, Pont-Audemer is still a charming town, with timbered houses lining the streams which cut through it.

Hotel

The **Auberge du Vieux Puits** £££ ☎ 32 41 01 48 is one of the loveliest buildings (though not in one of the loveliest areas); its quaint rustic rooms and pretty garden have made it a great hit with British and American visitors. (Restaurant closed Mon D and Tue.)

Rouen

Don't be put off by Rouen's industrial sprawl: the core of the city is beautifully restored and easily explored on foot. There are splendid Gothic churches, beautiful squares, narrow alleyways and quaint half-timbered houses – and excellent shops and restaurants.

What to see

Cathedral A masterpiece of Gothic architecture, spanning three centuries. The western façade became the subject of several Manet paintings, each one a study in the changing patterns of shadow and light. There are two distinctive towers – one simple Romanesque/Gothic, the other (the Butter Tower) in fine, flamboyant style – and a central, soaring iron spire, added in the 19th century.

Gros Horloge A familiar landmark of the old town is this ornate gilt 14th-century clock, mounted in an archway over a lively pedestrian street.

St-Ouen Beautiful flamboyant Gothic church, less elaborate than the cathedral.

St-Maclou Another very fine Gothic church, standing in a picturesque square of half-timbered houses. Don't miss the church's former charnel house (Aître St-Maclou) beyond the church, with spooky frieze carved on the beams.

Palais de Justice Early 16th-century law courts, restored to their Gothic beauty after World War II.

Museums There are several museums in Rouen, of which the finest is the Musée des Beaux-Arts, with ceramics and a very extensive collection of paintings (16th- to 20th-century, mainly Flemish and French).

Hotels and restaurants

The **Cathédrale** 12 rue St-Romain ££ ☎ 35 71 57 95 is a quiet, pleasantly old-fashioned hotel in the heart of Rouen, with rooms overlooking a flower-filled courtyard. Further north, the **Morand** 1 rue Morand ££ ☎ 35 71 46 07 is another quiet hotel, with some rooms overlooking a courtyard. Neither hotel has a restaurant but there are plenty nearby. There are no less than three Michelin-starred restaurants in Rouen, of which the best is the **Beffroy** 15 rue Beffroy ☎ 35 71 55 27 – intimate and elegantly rustic. (Closed Sun and Mon.)

Trouville

Trouville became the most fashionable resort of the 1860s, frequented by the aristocracy for its casino and beach, and popular with artists. Now it's far less chic and rather more homely than neighbouring Deauville. Streets, shops and hotels are down-to-earth and unsophisticated, but it still has a casino and a beach with *planches*, just like Deauville.

Vironvay

This quiet village, high above the Seine, close to Louviers and 30km from Rouen, is listed simply for its hotel.

Hotel

Les Saisons £££ ☎ 32 40 02 56 has 15 peaceful rooms in delightful cottages around a garden. The food is classical and competently produced. (Restaurant closed Sun D and Mon.)

Brittany

Jutting out like a jagged claw at the north-western corner of France, Brittany is geographically out of the mainstream of French life; but it's culturally distinct, too. In some ways, the Bretons are more strongly linked with Britain than with the rest of France: like the people of Cornwall, Wales, Scotland and Ireland, they have their roots in Celtic culture. Their spirit of independence is more pronounced than in almost any other part of France. Traditions and the deep local patriotism die hard. Medieval *pardons* (religious processions) are kept alive, a few people still speak the Breton language – close to Welsh – and there is a typically Celtic belief in things supernatural. There are legends of lost cities, magicians and monsters, spirits and saints; while the mighty megaliths that dot the landscape are constant reminders of a mysterious race that existed long before the Celts. The landscape, too, has clear echoes of the western extremities of Britain, and not much in common with other parts of France.

In the past few years, Brittany has consistently been one of the most popular parts of France with British holidaymakers. One of its attractions, particularly for families with young children, is that it is an easy drive from the ferry ports of St-Malo and Roscoff. There are modestly priced hotels and a plentiful supply of *gîtes* and campsites. But the main appeal of Brittany is its beaches and resorts – the most popular in France after those of the Mediterranean. Less sophisticated than those of the Côte d'Azur, they're also less crowded. Even in the height of summer you're rarely crammed together cheek-by-jowl.

Brittany has a long and extraordinarily varied coast. There are red, rose and mauve cliffs, mounds of boulders, offshore islands, reefs, estuaries and inlets. The Atlantic waves have battered away at the stubborn rocky shore, moulding rocks into weird shapes and forming towering escarpments, headlands and grand peninsulas. There are hundreds of excellent beaches, from tiny coves to huge sweeping sands.

Arguably the prettiest and certainly the most popular stretch is from Quiberon to Bénodet, in the south-west, where small pretty resorts nestle in wooded inlets and estuaries. The rugged western peninsulas are windswept beauty spots, some too exposed for tourist resorts. In contrast the north coast has long, flat sandy beaches, huge rocks and well established family resorts. The loveliest stretch here is the Pink Granite Coast, from Perros-Guirec to Trébeurden, characterised by piles of pink boulders.

The only real drawback of the beaches (along with the risk of clouds and rain) are the huge tides which can mean long walks to the sea and great expanses of mud, rocks and seaweed. But this is good news for seafood enthusiasts: there are crabs, clams, shrimps, mussels, cockles, sand eels and sea urchins, all of which are enthusiastically eaten by the locals.

Inland Brittany is generally reckoned to have less to offer the tourist. But away from the coast you can find lush pastures, rolling farmland, peaceful forests and wild, melancholy moorland, which some will prefer to the busy beach resorts. The most scenic area of inland Brittany is the Armorique Regional Nature Park, covering the Montagnes d'Arrée, the highest peaks in Brittany. Not spectacularly high (the tallest peak is under 400m), their desolate summits provide good views of heather moors, woodland and the valleys of rivers and streams.

Small towns and villages of inland Brittany are sober, their houses hewn from hard grey granite; and the few inland large towns are generally less rewarding than the coastal resorts and seaports. It's worth bearing in mind however, that *gîte* and hotel prices are much less expensive away from the coast – so if you feel you can manage without a beach immediately on hand, staying in inland Brittany may be a good way of saving money.

What sort of holiday?

Brittany is a place for summer holidays rather than off-season breaks; from October to May a lot of hotels, restaurants and even whole resorts shut down. It is good value, with plenty of reasonably priced small hotels and restaurants, and excellent opportunities for self-catering and camping. It's a poor place for anyone seeking exciting nightlife but good for a family seaside holiday.

The big Breton beaches are a paradise for bucket-and-spade enthusiasts and in the bigger resorts there are clubs which organise all sorts of games and activities for children on the beach. The indented coastline provides sheltered bays which are ideal for sailing – there are plenty of sailing clubs – as well as windsurfing and some waterskiing. Boat trips are popular – around inlets, to islands or along some inland waterways. One of the most popular excursions is to Le Mont-St-Michel, which lies just inside neighbouring Normandy.

The area is not one for the keen sightseer. But all over Brittany there are traces of pre-historic people – huge and powerful menhirs (standing stones) and dolmens (stone tables, generally thought to have been burial chambers). The greatest concentration of menhirs is at Carnac, where they stand in long parallel lines running from east and west and ending in a semi-circle or cromlech. They appear to be astronomically set, which would suggest that sun worship had something to do with the arrangement.

These megaliths probably influenced the stone Calvaries that you find in Brittany – small granite religious monuments representing the Crucifixion,

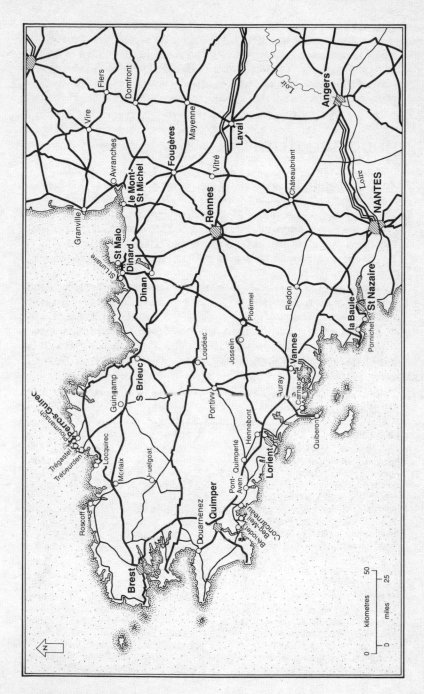

many of which were built to ward off a plague epidemic in 1598, or as an act of thanks after it had ended. Look out for the ornate Breton parish close: a church, small square, Calvary and charnel house. A few of the old town centres are worth visiting (notably Dinard, Quimper, Vannes) and there are countless churches and chapels which testify to the Breton religious fervour. A handful of châteaux are open to the public, including some forbidding fortresses close to Normandy.

Food and drink

Prime fresh ingredients are the essence of Breton cuisine, particularly superb seafood. Dishes aren't full of rich cream and butter as they are in nearby Normandy. A *plateau de fruits de mer* is probably the most common dish in Brittany: a huge platter of prawns, oysters, mussels, clams, scallops and other seafood, sometimes served on a bed of seaweed. In comparison with the quality of the fish, meat is sometimes rather disappointing – though *agneau de pré-salé*, lamb grazed on salt meadows near the sea, is a prized regional dish.

Pancakes are the main local speciality, and are served at stalls, cafés and specialised restaurants (*crêperies*). To anyone used to thick, heavy British pancakes, lace-thin Breton ones come as something of a revelation. There are the buckwheat *galettes*, stuffed with cheese, bacon or other savoury filling, usually washed down with local cider, and the wheat *crêpes* with sweet fillings. One pancake makes an ideal snack, two or three a more-than-modest meal.

Gazetteer

La Baule

Affluent, lively and sophisticated, La Baule is not a typical Breton resort. Its beach, a gathering place for the young and beautiful, is one of the most attractive in France. But not much is left of the resort of the 1880s – La Baule is mostly modern, with big apartment blocks and huge hotels. Activities and entertainment are endless: all varieties of sports, smart shops, cocktail bars, discos and nightclubs.

Bénodet

A very popular beach resort lying on the Odet estuary, south of Quimper. The site is rather more picturesque than the resort itself, which is modern and straggling, but there's plenty to do, with sports, nightlife and boat trips.

Carnac

Mysterious giant megaliths and a spacious, sheltered beach have made Carnac one of the most popular seaside resorts on the south coast of Brittany.

What to see

Menhirs There are nearly 3,000 of these standing stones, some of them over ten feet high. Local legend has it that the menhirs are Roman soldiers turned to stone by the Pope, St Cornelius, after they had pursued him from Rome to Brittany.

St-Michel tumulus Big mound with burial chambers; you can go inside and there are good views of the menhirs from the top. Most things found inside are now in the remarkable museum (see below).

Prehistoric museum Crammed with ancient finds, including beautiful examples of pottery and jewellery, and plaster casts of menhir carvings.

Hotel

The **Lann-Roz** av de la Poste ££ ☎ 97 52 10 48 is a delightful rustic restaurant with rooms and gardens, a few minutes from the beach. (Closed Wed out of season.)

Concarneau

One of the largest fishing ports in France, specialising in tunny and sardines. But apart from the appeal of its seafaring life (which includes a fish auction and a fishing museum with an Azores whaleboat, harpoon gun and giant Japanese crab), tourists come to see the walled city of Concarneau, which stands in the middle of the harbour, surrounded by granite ramparts. Despite crowds and commercialism, the town still manages to preserve something of its authentic atmosphere and there are good views of the port from the ramparts.

Nearby

The coastal drive south takes you to the conventionally pretty town of **Pont-Aven**, home of Gauguin and followers in the late 1880s; further south there is a fine beach at **Raguenès-Plage**, the delightful fishing village of **Port-Manech** and the busy resort of **Le Pouldu**, where Gauguin lived when he had grown weary of the crowds at Pont-Aven.

Hotels and restaurants

The Hotel-Restaurant **du Port** at Port-Manech ££ ☎ 98 06 82 17 is a small simple inn, with splendid views over the estuary and deliciously fresh seafood. (Closed winter, restaurant closed Mon.) **Chez Pierre** at Raguenès-Plage ££ ☎ 98 06 81 06 is an old stone house with light, modern rooms and a well-deserved reputation for home-made cooking. (Closed winter, restaurant closed Wed.)

Dinan

Perched high above the port, overlooking the deep-green Rance estuary, Dinan is one of Brittany's most beautifully preserved cities. It is also lively, and makes a good base for coast and inland excursions. Within the ramparts is a labyrinth of leafy streets, paved with cobbles and lined by pale grey granite houses. Specific sights, which include the château of Dinan, are not especially interesting – this is more a place for ambling.

Hotel and restaurant

The **d'Avaugour** 1 pl du Champ-Clos £££ ☎ 96 39 07 49, an old building backing on to the ramparts, is the most comfortable and appealing of Dinan's hotels. The best restaurant is the **Caravelle** 14 pl Duclos ☎ 96 39 00 11, whose inventive dishes have earned it a Michelin star. There are 11 basic cheap rooms in the annex. (Restaurant closed Wed out of season.)

Dinard

It was largely due to affluent English aristocrats that in the mid 19th century Dinard turned from a fishing village into one of the most fashionable resorts in France. Luxury hotels, Victorian villas and gardens with fig trees and palms are all evidence of that illustrious era; now it is slightly sedate, but still retains a certain old-fashioned charm.

Nearby

It is worth exploring the coast to the west, with its craggy headlands and sweeping beaches. Favourite resorts are **St-Cast-le-Guildo** – a good family resort with an excellent beach; **Sables-d'Or-les-Pins** – a fine beach but little else; and **Erquy** – a busy fishing port with good beaches nearby.

In 1987 our hotel price ratings translate *roughly* into the following prices for a typical double room for one night:

£	up to £15
££	£15 to £25
£££	£25 to £45
££££	£45 to £70
£££££	£70 to £100
£££££!	more

Locronan

A cobbled square of quaint, granite houses, an ancient well, church and chapel combine to make an extraordinarily picturesque ensemble – so picturesque that Roman Polanski chose it as a location when shooting his film version of Hardy's novel *Tess of the d'Urbevilles*. Inevitably it has become a focus of tourism, with more than enough craft and antique shops and cafés.

Hotels

The **Manoir de Moëllien £££** ☎ 98 92 50 40, 3km to the north-west of the village, is full of old-world charm. (Closed winter.) Cheaper and not quite so charming is the **Hôtel au Fer à Cheval ££** ☎ 98 91 76 67, lkm south.

Morgat

Chief resort of the rugged Crozon peninsula, at the western end of Brittany, Morgat has a lovely setting, with a fine beach framed by cliffs and caves.

Nantes

Largest town in Brittany, Nantes became the seat of the ducal court in the 16th century and the leading port in the trade of sugar and slaves – the 'ebony trade' as it was known. Today Nantes is a big industrial city, but behind the suburban sprawl is a historic centre with some beautiful streets and buildings.

What to see

Ducal castle This striking though much remodelled 16th-century structure was the residence of nearly all the kings of France from Charles VIII to Louis XIV. The rooms house museums devoted to the history of Nantes and Breton art and folklore.
Cathedral Flamboyant in style despite the austere façade which was added in 1930.

> Except in *Channel ports*, we have not mentioned winter closing times of hotels and restaurants: if you are going out of season, do check first that hotels are open.

Museums Of the small specialist museums, the Musée des Beaux-Arts is the finest: large impressive galleries mainly devoted to French, Italian and Dutch schools from the 15th to the 20th century.

Paimpol

Fishing and oyster breeding are still the main local activities of Paimpol; tourism is incidental, and the old cobbled streets and market square have remained unspoilt.

Hotel

Le Repaire de Kerroc'h 29 quai Morand **££** ☎ 96 20 50 13 is a late 18th-century harbour house, converted to a stylish hotel with seven luxury rooms and a particularly good fish restaurant. (Closed Mon and Tue out of season.)

Perros-Guirec

This is one of the most popular family resorts, on a beautiful stretch of the northern coastline. The town, on a rocky promontory, rises above the fishing harbour and the two fine, gently sloping beaches. There are boat trips to the sea-bird reserve of Sept Iles and exhilarating cliff walks to Ploumanac'h, a smaller resort with a pretty beach and working port. Further along the coast Trégastel-Plage is characterised by pink granite boulders and secluded beaches, and to the south Trébeurden is a family resort whose broad sandy beaches are sheltered by green, wooded promontories.

Hotel

The **Manoir de Lan-Kerellec ££££** ☎ 96 23 50 09 at Trébeurden is a beautiful, elegant manor-house with sea view, garden and terrace. Excellent food too, with lobster as a speciality. High prices, but a good choice if you want to spoil yourself a little. (Hotel closed winter, restaurant closed Mon out of season.)

Quiberon

Lying at the tip of a long peninsula, Quiberon is modern, lively but slightly lacking in charm. The main attractions are the beach, the spectacular island of

Belle-Ile, reached by ferry, and the Côte Sauvage – a wild, rugged stretch of the peninsula where stormy seas pound dramatically against the cliffs.

Quimper

Capital of the ancient kingdom of Cornouaille, this is the oldest city in Brittany and one of the liveliest. It lies in a pretty, wooded valley at the junction of the Steir and Odet rivers, and the medieval quarter is beautifully preserved, still retaining its tall, timbered houses and narrow cobbled streets. Pottery and lace are the local crafts – both sold in the shops.

What to see
Cathedral Splendid Gothic edifice, with two soaring 19th-century towers.
Museums The Bishop's Palace with its cloisters and fine spiral staircase is rather more interesting than the Breton Museum it houses. The Musée des Beaux-Arts in the Hôtel de Ville has a mixed collection, from 17th-century Dutch and Flemish paintings to the rather more interesting 19th-century Breton scenes.

Hotel and restaurant
There are no very special hotels in Quimper, but the simple Sapinière, route Bénodet £ ☎ 98 90 39 63, 4km out of town, makes a cheap and reasonably quiet base. No restaurant here, but the best-value place to eat in town is **La Rotonde** 36 av France Libre ☎ 98 95 09 26. (Closed Sat L and Sun, and late Jun to mid-Jul.)

Rennes

In 1720 a drunken carpenter set fire to a heap of shavings with his lamp. His house burned down and so did most of the old city of Rennes, leaving only a handful of old houses standing. As a result, modern Rennes doesn't have much to interest the sightseer. But it's a prosperous place with some smart shops and well-stocked hypermarkets which will interest the self-catering holidaymaker.

What to see
Museum of Brittany One of the better museums of its kind: history, costumes, tools and furnishings – though surprisingly very little about the region's Celtic history.
Musée des Beaux-Arts Major collection of paintings from the 16th century onwards.
Palais de Justice Impressive courts, in the former Houses of Parliament of Brittany.

Roscoff

A friendly little town which is now well established as a car ferry port – see *Channel ports* for details.

St-Malo

Ferry port, beach resort and much-restored historic town – see *Channel ports* for details.

Ste-Anne-la-Palud

A tiny isolated hamlet 7km to the north-west of Locronan, with windswept walks and a splendid beach hammered by big Atlantic rollers. On the last Sunday of August it becomes the focus for thousands of Bretons, flocking here for one of the greatest *pardons* (religious processions) of the province. For the rest of the year, it is relatively quiet.

Hotel
The **Plage** ££££ ☎ 98 92 50 12 stands on the edge of the beach, with beautiful views, quiet rooms, garden, pool and consistently good food – one of the most appealing places to stay in the whole area. (Closed winter.)

Tréguier

No beaches here, but the historic centre – old streets, timbered houses and magnificent cathedral – and the beautiful setting at the confluence of two rivers make the town well worth visiting.

£	up to £15
££	£15 to £25
£££	£25 to £45
££££	£45 to £70
£££££	£70 to £100
£££££!	more

Vannes

Seat of the Breton kings until the 16th century, Vannes is one of the most handsome towns of the region. Ignore the suburban sprawl and head for the old quarter, enclosed within the city walls. There are narrow cobbled streets, quaint timbered houses and the ruins of its great château.

Nearby

Gulf of Morbihan Tours by boat are available from Vannes. There used to be hundreds of islands in the gulf, but now there are only about 50, most of which are owned by the rich and famous. The Ile-aux-Moines is the largest, with pine groves, heather moors, beaches and dolmens. The pretty little resort of Locmariaquer, on the western side of the gulf, is another site of prehistoric monuments. Avoid the gulf at low tide, when it's no more than than a huge expanse of mud.

Hotel and restaurant

No very special hotels or restaurants in Vannes itself but **Le Roof** ££ ☎ 97 63 47 47, 4.5km south-west at Conleau, is a restaurant with 12 modest, pleasant rooms and good, down-to-earth seafood. A lovely spot, overlooking the Gulf of Morbihan. (Closed Mon out of season.)

The Loire

For many people, the valley of the Loire means the valley of châteaux: fairy-tale Chenonceau, spanning the river Cher; mighty Chambord, crowned by a forest of spires; Azay-le-Rideau, set like a jewel in the waters of the Indre; Amboise, perched high on a promontory over the Loire – and a hundred others which are less well-known. The splendour and variety of the châteaux concentrated in and around the Loire valley are unmatched in France, or anywhere else in the world for that matter – helping to make the Loire one of the favourite regions in France for British visitors. Its attraction is enhanced by accessibility: it's an easy day's drive from the Channel ports of Normandy and Brittany.

But there's more to the Loire than châteaux. The landscape is smiling and civilised and the climate is mild all year round. There are peaceful orchards, gently rolling farmland, green pastures, neatly tended vineyards, wine-tasting cellars, gastronomic restaurants, ancient towns and quiet, flower-decked villages nestling in the shadow of churches.

Visiting the châteaux of the Loire is a journey through French (and English) history. Despite its modern serenity, the Loire has seen plots, devastation and massacre. Not all its châteaux were built purely as palaces of pleasure for kings, queens and mistresses. Feudal lords, powerful barons and some of the counts of Blois and Anjou built châteaux primarily for defence. They warred against each other and against the English who persistently fought for the French crown here until Joan of Arc stormed the English strongholds and freed the city of Orléans in 1429.

In the 15th and 16th centuries, the region was the favourite abode of the royalty and nobility. It was a period of decadent court life, with intrigues, scandals, and scheming hostility between queens and mistresses. It was also a period of flourishing culture, which saw the patronage of great Italian masters who embellished the châteaux in opulent Renaissance style.

The Loire itself is the longest river in France but not always the most attractive (it lacks the simple charm of the Dordogne, for example). Broad, shallow and sometimes muddy, it meanders placidly through low-lying fertile farmland, in summer exposing broad expanses of sandbank. Châteaux rise up intermittently along its banks, as do towns, villages, industry and nuclear power stations. But once you get away from the flat, wide valley of the Loire and follow its tributaries, the countryside becomes rather more seductive. The Cher flows through rich pastures, the deep Indre is hidden among willows and poplars and the Vienne skirts the moors of plateaux. These narrower rivers conceal châteaux just as remarkable as those along the Loire.

What sort of holiday?

Sightseeing is the great attraction. The temptation is to try to do too much:
don't attempt to cram in visits to all of the famous châteaux at the expense
of visits to the other delights of the Loire. It's also easy to get very bored
with the regimented, crowded guided tours of the châteaux, many of
which are the only way to see the building (see *Sightseeing*). Roaming freely
round a château in the Loire is a privilege; if you have the opportunity,
take it; if not, find out first from a guidebook if there's anything worth
seeing inside. It may well be more-or-less empty and the façade may be the
finest thing about it. Don't neglect the small, charming unknown
châteaux, which can be just as rewarding and a lot less crowded than the the
the big ones.

Most of the châteaux are open at least from Easter to the end of
September. Some are closed on Tuesday, or occasionally Monday, and they
are nearly all closed for lunch. This may mean having to get there by
11.30am, or even earlier, for the last morning visit. (Make sure you arrive
well before the time of closing stated in guidebooks.) Many of the châteaux
have *son et lumière* performances – melodramatic presentations of voice,
music and lighting, centred round a historic theme relating to the
particular château or area. These are fairly informal events and rarely last
more than half an hour or so; when done well, on a fine summer evening,
they can be delightful.

The châteaux are the obvious highlights of the Loire but don't neglect
some of the other great attractions – for example, the gardens at Villandry
(outside Tours), the Romanesque abbey at St-Benoît-sur-Loire and cities
such as Le Mans, Bourges and Tours.

This is not really an area for sport, although one or two of the lakes have
been developed for watersports and there are special swimming areas along
the rivers, sometimes with pedaloes and rowing boats for hire. Pollution
and currents put most people off swimming in the Loire. Riding, fishing
and walking are popular pursuits; temporary fishing permits can be
bought locally and there are national footpaths and smaller circuits.

Hotels are plentiful, most of them small and quite simple, often in rustic
style. Self-catering covers all sorts of properties – tiny cottages,
farmhouses, converted mills, hunting lodges and even châteaux. There are
campsites along the Loire and simpler, quieter ones along the tributaries.
June and September are the ideal times to go: the châteaux won't be
packed with French and the weather is often at its best.

According to the novelist Henry James '...it is half the charm of the
Loire that you can travel beside it. A wide river, as you follow the road, is
excellent company.' With the growth of industry the Loire may not be such
good company as it was in 1882, but driving in the region generally is a
pleasant experience. Roads are lined with poplars and plane trees and are
often quite deserted.

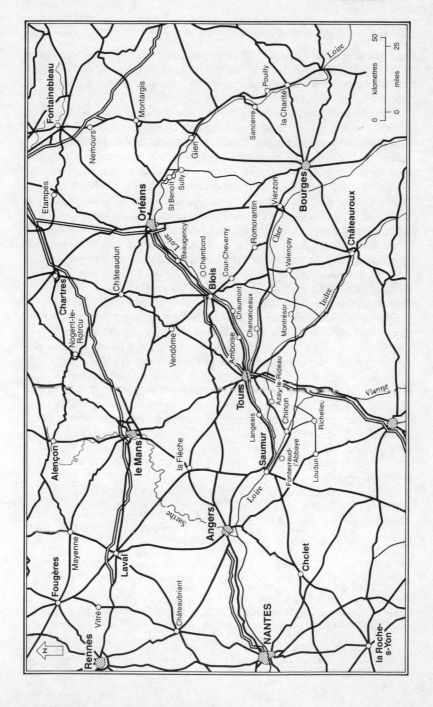

Food and drink

The nearness of the Loire to Paris (no more than a couple of hours by motorway) has ensured that it is liberally endowed with good restaurants; and although it is not in the first rank of wine-producing areas, there are lots of wine-tasting cellars.

With so many rivers, it's not surprising that the region has a wide variety of fish. There is *brochet* (pike) often served as *quenelles* or lightly poached dumplings, *sandre* (like perch), *alose* (shad), *turbot* (turbot) and *saumon* (salmon). The two sauces that commonly come with them are *beurre blanc*, a butter sauce similar to hollandaise, and *sauce à l'oseille*, sorrel sauce. Game is a speciality of the Loire; and each region has its own *rillons* or *rillettes* (potted pork). There are several regional cheeses, including goat's cheese and Olivet, a whole milk cheese, either blue or *cendré* (cured in wood ash). Mushrooms are another speciality of the Loire; near Saumur, large white ones are cultivated in the soft, chalky tufa caves. These same caves create ideal underground cellars for the sparkling Saumur wines.

The Loire has a wide variety of wines, among them crisp white Muscadets from Sèvre-et-Maine, fruity dry whites from Sancerre and Pouilly, dry or sweet sparkling wines from Vouvray, the rosé wines of Anjou and the soft red wines of Chinon. Tasting places range from tiny off-the-beaten-track vineyards to the cellars of big, efficient châteaux or *caves coopératives*, with guided tours (some in English). Look out for signs by the roadside saying '*dégustation*' (tasting). For free tasting one of the best places is Vouvray, east of Tours, where all the roads up the steep valleys are lined with cellars. Other centres are Pouilly-sur-Loire, which exists solely for the purpose of making wine, and the rather more attractive medieval village of Sancerre, with numerous wine shops where you can taste or buy. In Saumur there are guided tours of cellars and well organised *caves coopératives*.

Gazetteer

Amboise

Basking in the glory of its château, Amboise is a picturesque little town of narrow streets and leaning houses.

What to see

Château Best admired from across the river, the castle rises on a spur above the water, flanked by two enormous round towers. The hooks along the battlements are grim reminders of the bloody massacre in 1560 when over a hundred Protestant Huguenots, plotting to overthrow the Catholic de Guise family, were hung from the balcony and battlements or thrown into the Loire in sacks. The Renaissance wing is now the main feature of the castle, still furnished with some of the treasures that Charles VII brought back from Italy. Highlights are the Chapel of St-Hubert, a Gothic gem, and the Tours des Minimes – a massive round tower with good views from the top.

Clos Lucé A 15th-century manor house where Leonardo da Vinci, under the patronage of François I, spent the last three years of his life. It is full of models, made to his extraordinarily progressive technical designs.

Hotels

The **Hostellerie du Château de Pray** just outside Amboise £££ ☎ 47 57 23 67 is a real medieval château with the parkland, formal gardens and period furnishings that you might expect. There are lovely views across the valley, comfortable rooms and excellent, straightforward cooking – a fine place to stay if you can afford it. A much cheaper and simpler alternative is the **Lion d'Or** ££ ☎ 47 57 00 23, below the château of Amboise. Food here is particularly good and served in a hunting-lodge-style dining room. For a quiet night, ask for a room at the back. (Closed winter.)

Angers

The formidable fortress and the black schist stone and grey slate of the houses make a somewhat forbidding introduction to Angers. But the old city around the cathedral has some attractive old houses with wooden shutters and amusingly carved façades.

What to see

Château This mighty feudal castle, flanked with seven great towers, was built in the 11th century by the notoriously violent Foulques Nerra, Count of Anjou, as a defence against the neighbouring Count of Blois, but was rebuilt by Louis IX. Inside, the focus of attention is the Apocalypse tapestry, 100m long (originally 168m) – a remarkably vivid illustration of the Apocalypse of Saint John the Divine. (Audio guides available.)
Cathedral Impressive 12th- to 13th-century building with Romanesque façade, rose windows and superbly sculpted doorway.

Nearby

There are various châteaux in the vicinity worth visiting including two with moats – Serrant, a sumptuous mansion, and Plessis-Bourré, a slate-roofed fortress.

Beaugency

Often neglected in favour of the more famous towns and châteaux, Beaugency is a charming, characteristically medieval town with old houses and cobbled streets sloping towards the Loire. The 15th-century château, tucked behind the town walls, is modest by Loire standards.

Hotel

The **Ecu de Bretagne** ££ ☎ 38 44 67 60 is centrally placed, with simple rooms (some in an annex) and good-value food.

Blois

A bustling town on the Loire, with sloping streets and a few old timbered houses, dominated by its brooding château – a fascinating jumble of five architectural styles, from the feudal to the classical. The guided tour (with an English text) takes you through history, with a long pause for the gory details of the assassination of the Duc de Guise in Henry III's bedroom. Walls and ceilings are richly painted and there is a fine octagonal spiral staircase embellishing the François I wing, but furnishings are sparse.

Nearby

Chambord (18km E) Unquestionably the most colossal and extravagant château of the Loire, Chambord is crowned by a forest of chimneys, turrets, spires and pinnacles, and surrounded by limitless forested parkland. The impact of the château's great mass is extraordinary as you approach it along straight, tree-lined avenues. Inside there are 440 rooms, almost all bare of furniture and hardly indicative of the luxurious palace of pleasure that it once was. The focal point is the huge double staircase, designed so that one person could ascend and another descend simultaneously without seeing one another. There are are no guided tours here – you are free to roam around at leisure.
Chaumont (17km SW) Feudal, turreted castle on a hill high above the Loire. Three great ladies of France stayed here: Catherine de Médicis (wife of Henry II), Diane de Poitiers (mistress of Henry II) and, later in history, Madame de Staël, exiled from Paris by Napoleon, famous for her comment on Chaumont: 'Yes it's an admirable scene, but how much I prefer my gutter in the Rue du Bac.' The interior of the château is

elegant, with tapestries and furniture.
Cheverny (13km SE) Unlike most of the châteaux of the Loire, Cheverny has been in the same family for 300 years and is still inhabited; as a result the decoration and furnishings of this small, classical mansion have been beautifully preserved. The hunting museum with 2,000 stag antlers is included in a visit to the château.

Hotel

The **St-Michel** £££ ☎ 54 20 31 31 has an idyllic setting, right opposite the château of Chambord, on the edge of the huge forest. After the crowds have disappeared it is quiet, and there are beautiful views, but the rooms and food are nothing special. Game, still hunted in the park, is the speciality of the restaurant.

Bourges

Well to the east of the main highlights of the Loire, Bourges is a large town with enough sights to occupy at least a day. The industrial outskirts are unpromising but the core of the town is well preserved, with medieval houses, cobbled streets, a splendid palace and a cathedral which is among the finest in France. The most illustrious son of Bourges is Jacques Coeur, medieval shipping and trading kingpin, whose name still pervades the town.

What to see

Palais de Jacques Coeur Extravagant Gothic palace, built by the man himself. This is no less sumptuous than the châteaux of the Loire, from the outside at least. The interior is almost empty.
Cathedral Exceptionally fine edifice (built 1192–1324), dominating the surrounding landscape. Particularly beautiful are the carved doorways and the stained glass windows in the ambulatory and choir.

Chinon

The maze of cobbled alleys and the timber-framed riverside houses, wedged under the ramparts of the ancient fortress, give the impression that little has changed since the days when Rabelais lived here. Streets of the historic quarter are flanked by old houses and intersected by alleys which reveal glimpses of the castle.

What to see

Château Dilapidated fortress where Joan of Arc, as a peasant girl of 18, recognised the Dauphin hiding among the crowds. The château sits high above the town, its majestic ruins sprawling along a cliff. Guided tours are optional but there is not a lot to see inside. It was at Chinon that both King Henry II and his son Richard the Lionheart met their deaths. And in 1321 all the Jews in Chinon were burnt alive on the Ile de Tours, the island in the river Vienne.

Nearby

Abbaye de Fontevraud (23km W) One of the great curiosities of Anjou, this huge Romanesque abbey was run by a series of abbesses who received (in separate institutions) monks, nuns, lepers and aristocratic ladies who wanted to withdraw from worldly pursuits to a life of prayer. A visit to the château takes in the abbey church (with the tombs of Henry II, his wife Eleanor of Aquitaine, their son Richard Lionheart and Isabelle, wife of his brother King John), the quiet cloisters and the most unlikely feature of all – a Romanesque kitchen.
Azay-le-Rideau (21km NE) Heralded by a shaded avenue, surrounded by gardens and mirrored in the still waters of the Indre, this is one of the gems of the area. It is a tourist favourite, so be prepared for crowds and go as early as you can. The inside is less impressive than the façade: some fine tapestries, a few bits of furniture and a four-storeyed straight staircase – one of the first of its kind. The *son et lumière* performance is unusual, and worth catching – a troupe of young people lead you around the moat as they re-enact episodes from the history of the château.
Ussé (10km N) This is a classic picture-book château, said to have inspired the story of Sleeping Beauty. Set at the junction of the Indre and Loire, it lies amid thick forests, lakes and parkland. Guided tours are limited but the chapel, in pure Renaissance style, has remained almost intact with sculptures and

decorations. Don't miss the Virgin in enamelled clay by Luca della Robbia in the little south chapel.

Hotel

7km out of Chinon at Marçay, the **Château de Marçay £££££** ☎ 47 93 03 47 is a 15th-century fortress converted to a luxurious and expensive hotel. It has its own park with pool and tennis courts, and a Michelin-starred restaurant. The **Diderot** 4 rue de Buffon ££ ☎ 47 93 18 87 in Chinon itself is quite different – a small and friendly hotel, with simple rooms in a beautiful old stone house. (No restaurant.) 7km south-east of Azay-le-Rideau, in the tiny village of Saché (where Balzac lived), the **Auberge du XIIe Siècle** ☎ 47 26 86 58 is an outstanding restaurant. House and setting, high above the Indre, are both picturesque. (Closed Tue.)

Loches

A beautifully preserved medieval city, with the ruins of the château rising above its Renaissance houses.

What to see

Château The setting high above the Indre is serene, but the history of Loches is chilling. From the early 13th century the château became the prison of the kings of France. Under Louis XI prisoners were confined to small, iron cages which were often suspended from the roofs of the cells.

The grim dungeon and barred cells still survive (minus the cages) and you can see the sculpted tomb of Agnes Sorel, celebrated mistress of Charles VII, who lived here; but there's little else to see.

Hotel

Probaby the nicest place to stay and eat in town is the **George Sand** on the main road ££ ☎ 47 59 39 74 – attractive rooms and two restaurants but a bit noisy at the front.

In hotel and restaurant descriptions, D means dinner and L means lunch.

Le Mans

Well away from the mainstream of Loire sights (82km north-west of Tours) and renowned for the 24-hour car race above all else, Le Mans doesn't feature on the typical tourist itinerary of the Loire. But it is certainly worth seeing, with its churches, museums, Gallo-Roman remains, huge cathedral and a beautiful historic quarter.

What to see

Cathedral The city's show-piece, this is a beautiful Romanesque/Gothic church, rising above the market place. Among its finest features are a beautiful Gothic choir, superb stained glass, the Renaissance tombs of Charles IV of Anjou and Guillaume du Bellay (warrior and diplomat) and a sculpted porch.

Orléans

Badly damaged in World War II, Orléans is essentially a commercial rather than a tourist city. Joan of Arc, who miraculously lifted the eight-month English seige in 1429, is honoured throughout the city, and the *fête de Jeanne d'Arc* on 7 and 8 May is one of the main events of the year.

What to see

Cathedral Magnificent building spanning five and a half centuries of architecture. The constant theme is Joan of Arc, with monuments dedicated to her and stained-glass windows depicting events in her life.

Nearby

St-Benoît-sur-Loire, upstream from Orléans, has a beautiful Benedictine abbey – one of the most imposing Romanesque churches in France.

Saumur

Sparkling wine and mushrooms are the main source of income here, but tourists also come for the château, displays from its well known cavalry, and the little that is left of the old town. As a whole, though, Saumur has less charm and intimacy than other château towns of the Loire. Wine-lovers should head for the Maison du Vin next to the tourist office on Rue Beaurepaire.

What to see

Château Fortified bastion guarding the town, much remodelled but still quite authentic-looking; it houses the decorative arts museum (paintings, sculpture and tapestries, but particularly strong on pottery) and the horse museum.

Tours

In a region endowed with charming and intimate historic centres, Tours stands out as impersonal, noisy and industrial. But it has been an important metropolis since Gallo-Roman times, and old Tours in parts is very well preserved. During the peak holiday season, traffic through the town slows to a crawl.

What to see

Old town A labyrinth of little streets and squares, fine Renaissance sculpted façades and half-timbered houses. There are artisan workshops, pubs and night-clubs – quite trendy in places.
Cathedral Imposing because of its sheer size (about the same as Notre-Dame) and elaborate Gothic/Romanesque façade. Good views from the top of the south tower.
Musée des Beaux-Arts Interesting collection from the primitives to French 19th-century portraitists, housed in the former archbishop's palace. Paintings include a Rubens, Rembrandt, Delacroix and Degas.

Nearby

Chenonceau (35km SE) No tour of the Loire is complete without a visit to this fairy-tale château, built on arches spanning the river Cher. Its serenity belies a history of hostile jealousy between the *grandes dames de Touraine*. Built in the 16th century, it was given by Henry II to his mistress Diane de Poitiers, but after his death in 1559 it was snatched by his wife, Catherine de Médicis, who sent Diane de Poitiers to live in the lesser château of Chaumont.

The picture-book beauty of the château and its setting, the Italian gardens and the tapestries, paintings, ceilings and furniture that embellish the interior all contribute to make it the most popular château in the Loire. What's

more, there are no guided tours – so you can wander around the gardens and château at leisure (free leaflets in English available in each room).
Langeais (25km W) Not one of the most famous or beautifully sited châteaux of the Loire, Langeais is nevertheless remarkable for the fact that it was built in one single operation in the 1460s and has undergone no alterations since. A forbidding fortress from the outside, the inner courtyard façade presents a lordly mansion, and the interior is handsomely furnished. Flemish tapestries and Gothic furnishings give a good insight into aristocratic life in the 15th century. There are guided tours and commentaries through loudspeakers.
Montrichard (43km E) is an attractive small town, upstream from Chenonceau. Churches and half-timbered houses are huddled under the ramparts and ruins of its feudal castle, and there are wine cellars and cave-dwellings in the cliffs along the river Cher.
Villandry (20km SW) This is one of the few places where the gardens are more spectacular than the château. There is a glorious formal tapestry of ornamental hedges, shaded paths, herb gardens, kitchen gardens, flower-beds, fountains and cascades, all based on French gardens of the 16th century. The original château keep survives, and a classical building was added at the end of the 16th century. Part of it is open to the public – there are Spanish paintings and an elaborate Moorish ceiling which was brought from Spain.

Hotel and restaurants

The **Bon Laboureur et Château** £££
☎ 47 23 90 02, a low-lying vine-clad building only a short walk from the château of Chenonceau, is a justly popular hotel and restaurant. Rooms are pleasantly furnished, though far from luxurious. (Closed Wed L and Tue out of season.) Close to the gardens of Villandry, the **Cheval Rouge** ££
☎ 47 50 02 07 is an attractive place to eat. There is home-made *foie gras*, fish from the Loire and a good choice of regional wines. (Closed winter and Mon out of season.)

The Atlantic coast

In the last few years, this area has grown enormously in popularity with British holidaymakers. With the Mediterranean coast chock-a-block during the summer, the British who want to venture further than Brittany and Normandy are switching to the less developed and less crowded south-western region of France. The weather may not always be as good as on the Mediterranean coast, and the Atlantic is of course colder, but the beaches are much better. The area is particularly popular with the pre-erected campsite operators, who have a number of sites here; there is also a good supply of *gîtes*.

From the Gironde estuary, north of Bordeaux, down to the Pays-Basque region at the border with northern Spain, the only wrinkle along the coastline is the basin of Arcachon. Otherwise there is not a reef, not an inlet, not a promontory or cliff – just miles and miles of sandy beaches. Further north, between the sandy shores of Les Sables-d'Olonne and the port of La Rochelle, the more curvaceous coastline is low-lying and featureless. The coast as a whole has none of the scenic splendour of Brittany's deeply indented coastline to the north, nor the cachet of the Côte d'Azur in the south.

But this coast suits many visitors very well, for several reasons. First, the beaches are huge – which means paradise for bucket-and-spade enthusiasts and far fewer crowds than in the south of France. Secondly this is an unpretentious and unsophisticated coast – no celebrities, cocktail bars or St-Tropez trendies. Thirdly it caters for every pocket, unlike the south of France. The big exception is Biarritz, which had its heyday years ago but is still expensive and relatively fashionable. The majority of resorts along the Atlantic coast have been developed since World War II, though some of the larger and older resorts have preserved at least some of their old-fashioned seaside charm. La Rochelle and Arcachon make attractive bases, and St-Jean-de-Luz, close to the Spanish border, is probably the most picturesque place along the entire coast.

Behind the coast, Les Landes is a massive triangle of maritime pines, planted in the 19th century as a barrier to the sands that were being driven inland by giant Atlantic rollers. Originally a mosquito-infested marshland, Les Landes is now one giant forest, broken only by the occasional lake (and lakeside resort), patches of agriculture and the arrow-straight roads that cut through the woodland.

South of Les Landes lies the Basque country – a small pocket of France with a character all of its own. Less agressive than their Spanish neighbours in their desire for self-government, the French Basques are nevertheless actively independent. It is still a country of cults and crafts, song and dance, festivals and fast-paced games of *pelote*. The coast takes on a rather more interesting aspect here, with tamarisk-covered cliffs behind Biarritz and a backdrop of low hills. Inland lies a delightful landscape of flower-decked hill villages, neat red-and-white timbered houses and lush fields and valleys.

The main cultural diversions from the Atlantic coast lie in Bordeaux, a fine city of wine and sights, and in the inland region of Poitou-Charentes further north. Although familiar to many a pilgrim on his way to the Spanish city of Santiago de Compostela, this is a region which today is usually bypassed. But among its attractions are Romanesque churches which are some of the finest in France.

The marshes of Poitou, stretching west from Niort, have become something of a tourist attraction, with trips on punts along a dense network of canals. Going by boat is the only really satisfactory way of getting around – local farmers and even cattle travel in large punts along the canals. The best place to start a trip and hire a punt is Coulon, 10km west of Niort. The area has recently become a National Park and the landcape is one of marshes and fenland, poplars and beech trees – the French call it *La Venise Verte* (the Green Venice).

Bordeaux is the world's biggest producer of fine wines. Château country is worth exploring, not so much for the scenery or the actual châteaux (which are usually more practical than romantic) but for the cellars and vineyards of some of the finest wines in the world. See *Food and drink*.

What sort of holiday?

This is not ideal territory for touring. There are few picturesque historic towns and villages and not as many small, charming hotels as you find elsewhere in France. The coast is short of cultural interest, but Bordeaux, Saintes and Poitou inland are all rewarding historically and architecturally. Les Landes is a good choice for a quiet lakeside holiday. There are waterside campsites as well as self-catering holidays in rural cottages.

Miles of sandy beaches and shallow waters make the Atlantic a good choice for family seaside holidays. The drawbacks are murky waters (in parts), strong currents and the fact you may have to walk miles to get waist-deep in water. There are watersports both along the coast and on the lakes (windsurfing, sailing, pedaloes). Surfing in big Atlantic breakers is a major attraction of Biarritz.

Food and drink

Fish and seafood proliferate along the coast: oysters, mussels, prawns, tunny fish and sardines, all fresh from the sea. Look out for *mouclade* – a mussel stew with white wine and cream. Specialities inland include game from Les Landes: *perdreau* (partridge), *caille* (quail) and *ortolans* and

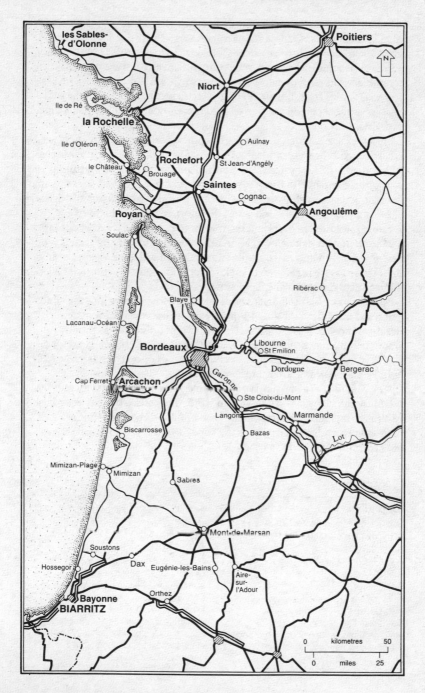

palombes (wood pigeons). The Bordeaux speciality is *sauce bordelaise*: red wine, bone marrow, shallots and tarragon served with steak or lamprey eels. *Chabichou*, a soft sweet cheese made from goat's milk, is a speciality of Poitou. Basque dishes tend to be piquant; specialities are *pipérade* (scrambled eggs with tomatoes, peppers, garlic and onions), *ttoro* (fish stew), *chipirones* (squid, usually cooked in their own ink). Bayonne is renowned for its cured ham – an excellent accompaniment to the melons from Charentes.

Bordeaux's reputation as a wine-growing region rests mainly on superior red clarets and the sweet white Sauternes. The main areas are the Médoc (full-bodied but elegant reds), St-Emilion and Pomerol (warm, full-bodied reds, often compared to Burgundies), Graves, Sauternes and Barsac (some fine reds and sweet white dessert wines), Entre-deux-Mers (mainly dry white) and Côtes de Blaye and Côtes de Bourg (mainly fruity reds).

Those interested in tours and tasting should go to the local tourist office or Maison du Vin (wine information office) for up-to-date information on the châteaux (or vineyards). While a few of them welcome visitors at any time, the majority prefer you to make an appointment or come with a letter of introduction from a wine merchant.

Bordeaux and St-Emilion are both good bases for forays into the wine country. The Maison du Vin in Bordeaux is well stocked with wine literature and will make appointments for you. Tours are nearly always conducted in French and, except at a few of the great châteaux, aren't very extensive or professional. You're shown the casks or hogsheads and vats and, at some châteaux, rows and rows of bottles collecting dust in the cellars. You may get a tasting if you're lucky – from the latest vintage.

Only some vineyards sell their own wine, but bottles bought at a Maison du Vin are no more expensive than those bought directly from the vineyard. The other alternative is the *cave coopérative*, which sells cheap wine from small-scale local producers.

Gazetteer

Angoulême

The old town of Angoulême, which is undergoing restoration, stands high on a steep-sided rocky promontory, with beautiful views over the valley of the Charente. The modern town is commercial and not particularly attractive.

What to see
Cathedral The 12th-century building remains beautiful despite heavy-handed 19th-century restoration. The square bell-tower looks Italian but the façade is pure French and embellished with beautiful sculpted scenes from the Last Judgement.

Arcachon

Golden sands and ridiculously cheap oysters lure the Bordelais here on summer weekends (it's a quick 65km from Bordeaux). The resort has been fashionable since the 1880s, when rich Europeans frequented Arcachon for the casino, cafés and beaches. There are still a few traditional hotels and 19th-century villas, as well as shops, cafés, oyster bars and oyster stalls. But the beaches are far from ideal, especially at low tide when weed and the stakes of oyster beds are exposed.

Nearby
Dune du Pilat Sand dunes are a prominent feature of this coast, and 8km south of Arcachon the Dune du Pilat rises up in a colossal pyramid – about 375ft high and still growing! There are great views from the top (staircase to the summit) and terrific slides down.
Boat trips to Cap Ferret (sprawling beach resort), to the Ile aux Oiseaux (island bird sanctuary) and deep-sea fishing trips.

Bayonne
Just inland from Biarritz, Bayonne is quite different in spirit and character. Typically Basque, it is lively and lighthearted – and for a whole week at the end of July the city becomes a frenzied scene of song and dance, fireworks and bullfights and matches of *pelote*. There's a busy port and a historic centre of cobbled streets, low arcaded houses and elegant cafés – drinking chocolate is the local speciality.

What to see
Musée Basque Lively display of the life and culture of the Basques including seafaring traditions, costumes, arts, crafts and the game of *pelote*.
Musée Bonnat Works of the local 19th-century portrait painter, Léon Bonnat, and the large collection of drawings and paintings he bequeathed to the city. Among the more famous names are Leonardo da Vinci, Rembrandt, Rubens, Botticelli and Delacroix.

Biarritz
One of the most elegant and fashionable resorts of the 19th century, Biarritz used to be 'the beach of kings and queens'. In 1854, Empress Eugénie persuaded Napoleon III to come here. Impressed by the place, he built the elaborate Villa Eugénie (now the Hôtel du Palais) which served as their holiday home for 13 years. Biarritz then became a focus for royalty from all over Europe, among them Queen Victoria and, later, the Duke

of Windsor. When the Côte d'Azur became a centre for high society, Biarritz fell into neglect. But it has recently had something of a revival, though more as a centre for young surfers than the cream of European society. It still has more to offer than the rest of the resorts along the Atlantic: wide sweeping beaches, superb Atlantic rollers, splendid cliffs, a grand flower-decked promenade, two casinos and hotels which are still reminders of its heyday. There are sports galore, smart shops with top designer names and night-clubs.

Biarritz is large, expensive and far from intimate: many British people prefer the more cosy and more typically Basque resort of St-Jean-de-Luz.

Hotels
Hotels in Biarritz are notoriously expensive. The **Hôtel du Palais** 1 av Impératrice ££££! ☎ 59 24 09 40, the villa where Napoleon III and Eugénie summered in the 1850s, is the most sumptuous and exorbitant. (Closed winter.) At the other extreme the simple **Edouard VII** 21 av Carnot ££ ☎ 59 24 07 20, uphill from the beaches and centre, is clean and friendly, with good home cooking. (Closed winter.)

Bordeaux
Primarily a port and a major wine, trade and cultural centre, Bordeaux isn't really a tourist city – which adds to its attraction for those tourists who do go there. Apart from the potent lure of flowing claret, Bordeaux has a well-groomed and very civilised 18th-century centre whose spacious tree-lined boulevards and classical façades give it a distinct air of prosperity and grandeur.

It is a city of luxury shops, antiques, elegant cafés and excellent restaurants. It also contains a more intimate medieval town of cobbled streets, small shops and galleries, where the grimy façades are gradually being restored to their former beauty. The show-piece sight of Bordeaux is the Grand Théâtre, which marks the heart of the city.

Bordeaux makes an excellent base for excursions into the wine country; details from the tourist office or Maison du Vin.

What to see

Grand Théatre Classical, colonnaded building exemplifying the city's unique 18th-century character. The sumptuous foyer and grand double staircase influenced Garnier's Opéra in Paris.
Cathedral Huge, elaborate edifice with soaring twin towers, built from the 11th to the 15th century. The 13th-century carvings on the south door are among the finest features.
Musée des Arts Décoratifs A particularly attractive collection of ceramics, silver, decorative paintings and furniture, in a delightful 18th-century house.
Musée des Beaux-Arts Mixed collection including works by Rubens and Delacroix and some fine Dutch paintings.
Musée d'Aquitaine Comprehensive collection of antiquities from paleolithic stone carvings and Gallo-Roman statues to 17th-century carved doorways.

Hotels

The big well-equipped hotels on the outskirts of Bordeaux cater for business travellers. Near the lakeside exhibition centre are various chain hotels offering functional, good-value accommodation – among them Novotel, Mercure, Ibis, Sofitel and Campanile. Hotels in the centre are smaller and more appealing, but very few have any real charm. A good plan is to keep costs to the minimum by staying at the **Bayonne** 4 rue Martignac ££ ☎ 56 48 00 88, which is simple but adequate – and quiet, considering its very central position close to the Grand Théatre.

In 1987 our hotel price ratings translate *roughly* into the following prices **for a typical double room for one night:**

£	up to £15
££	£15 to £25
£££	£25 to £45
££££	£45 to £70
£££££	£70 to £100
£££££!	more

Cognac

This is a proud, prosperous little town, with a distinctive smell of brandy distilleries. The warehouses are blackened by the fungi that thrive (no doubt very happily) on the vapours that emerge from the casks. Tourists come mainly for the free tours of the distilleries. Hennessy is the biggest name and tours include a visit to the barrel house, warehouse and bottling plant. The tourist office in Cognac has all the details of the various visits.

Poitiers

A major link between northern and southern France, Poitiers commands a great gap between the hills south of the lower river Loire and the Massif Central. It was near here that the Black Prince had his great victory in 1356 and won back Poitiers for England. But the city was back in French hands 13 years later, and gradually became a centre of great artistic wealth. This is not immediately apparent today as the sights are scattered all over town. Several fine churches lie within striking distance of the city.

What to see

Old town A maze of narrow, hilly streets encircled by boulevards that follow the line of the ancient fortifications.
Notre-Dame-la-Grande Most famous church of Poitiers, distinguished by a remarkable, profusely carved façade and unusual cone-shaped towers.
Cathedral Dating from the 12th to the 16th century, and built largely in the local Gothic style known as Angevin (after the counts of Anjou and their descendants). The carved wooden pews in the choir are among the oldest in France.
Baptistère St-Jean Dating from the 4th century and probably the oldest Christian edifice in France, the baptistry (south of the cathedral) now houses an archaeological museum containing a collection of very old tombs.
St-Hilaire-le-Grand Romanesque church (restored in the 19th century) built over the tomb of St-Hilaire, first known bishop of Poitiers.
Palais de Justice Impressive medieval

interior (former palace of the Dukes of Aquitaine) hidden by a 19th-century façade.

Nearby

Chauvigny In the attractive valley of the Vienne; the church of St-Pierre is distinguished by extraordinary gargoyles.

St-Savin The abbey church is very impressive, rising from the wooded banks of the river Gartempe. Superb frescoes (decorating the narthex, the ceiling of the nave and the crypt) and the overall beauty of the church combine to make this one of the finest Romanesque edifices in France.

Hotel

In Chauvigny, the restaurant of the **Lion d'Or** 8 rue Marché ☎ 49 46 30 28 is particularly good value for traditional dishes; quietest bedrooms are in the new annex. (Closed Sat out of season.)

La Rochelle

This is one of the liveliest and most picturesque places along the entire Atlantic coast. In its heyday it was a major port trading with Canada, but its prosperous era was put to an end in the early 17th century by Cardinal Richelieu, who was determined to see this wealthy Protestant stronghold come into line with Catholic France. He brutally laid siege to the port and after 15 months of heroic resistance and starvation the town was forced to submit. Only 5,000 of the 28,000 citizens were found alive. It was not until the 20th century that La Rochelle regained a little of its prestige, this time merely as a popular tourist/yachting centre. The busy port, quayside cafés, fishing boats and fish stalls around the harbour give it a distinctly cheerful air, while the arcaded streets, old stone houses and 14th-century solid towers are testimony to more illustrious times.

Nearby

Ile de Ré and Ile d'Oléron The queues for the ferry to the Ile de Ré in summer confirm the popularity of this long, narrow island, just 5km offshore. There are long, sandy beaches, backed by dunes and pines, salt marshes, oyster-beds and picturesque fishing villages. Hotels and campsites are packed in summer. The larger Ile d'Oléron, with more long sandy beaches and oyster-beds, is joined by a toll bridge to the mainland south of La Rochelle.

Hotels

Les Brises chemin de la Digue de Richelieu £££ ☎ 46 43 89 37, about 2km from the centre of La Rochelle, is modern and stylish with views of the islands and estuary. (No restaurant.) For a touch of real luxury and superb food there's no better place to stay on the Ile de Ré than the **Richelieu** at La Flotte ££££ ☎ 46 09 60 70; specialities of the restaurant are oysters and lobster. (Closed winter.)

Royan

A fashionable resort before World War II, Royan was almost entirely destroyed by bombs and is now modern and charmless – though quite lively. The main attractions are the beaches (though the waters are murky) and the dramatic 1950s church of Notre-Dame which rises above the town like the hull of a great ship.

Saintes

A market town on the river Charente, Saintes is rich in architecture and rewarding for any keen sightseer. Its oldest relics are a ruined 1st-century amphitheatre and an arch from a Roman bridge. There are two fine churches, several museums and a centre of medieval houses.

What to see

Cathedral of St-Pierre Huge flamboyant Gothic cathedral with a tall but unfinished bell tower.

Abbaye aux Dames 12th-century abbey, with a splendid tower topped by a 'pine-cone'. This was once a school for aristocratic young ladies, under the auspices of an abbess.

Amphitheatre Still used for open air performances, this is one of the earliest Roman arenas.

Les Sables-d'Olonne

A magnificent beach is the main focus of this lively, laid-back resort. Originally a fishing village, it has grown rapidly over the last few years as it has become more and more popular with Parisians; it now has abundant hotels, high-rise apartment blocks, boutiques and bars.

Nearby

Ile de Noirmoutier Popular island well to the north of Les Sables-d'Olonne, with good beaches, woods, salt marshes and oyster beds. Access is either over a toll bridge from Fromentine or by a road across the sands at low tide only.

St-Emilion

One of the more charming and intimate of the wine-country villages, St-Emilion makes an obvious base for lovers of claret. It lies on the edge of an escarpment, 39km east of Bordeaux, overlooking the green valley of the Dordogne. Mellow ochre houses, cobbled sloping streets, beautiful views and soft full St-Emilion wines are all good reasons for a visit.

What to see

Monastery Extraordinary medieval church entirely built out of the rock by monks from the 9th to the 11th century. Entry is via a grotto, said to be the 8th-century hermitage of St-Emilion. **Vineyards** See introduction to this chapter.

Hotel

Of the two hotels in town, the **Auberge de la Commanderie** ££ ☎ 57 24 70 19 is the better value. There are 15 small attractively furnished rooms, a rustic restaurant and a recently added *brasserie-crêperie*. (Restaurant closed Tue out of season.)

St-Jean-de-Luz

Popular and picturesque, St-Jean-de-Luz is still very much a fishing port, where trawlers land tunny and sardines to be sold on the quayside. It is also a charming beach resort with a fine stretch of golden sands, sheltered by breakwaters. Though buildings backing the beach are mainly modern, much of the resort is well preserved and typically Basque in character. Particularly picturesque is the square near the harbour, with its shaded cafes, bandstand and artists.

What to see

St-Jean-Baptiste Beautiful Basque church noted for its dark wood galleries which are traditionally reserved for men (the women sit in the nave) and the splendid altar-piece embellished with a gilded screen. In 1660 the church saw the sumptuous marriage of Louis XIV to Maria Teresa Infanta of Spain. The door which the Sun King passed through to meet his bride was sealed off so that no commoners could use it.

Hotel

The **Poste** 83 rue Gambetta ££ ☎ 59 26 04 53, close to the centre, is comfortable and pleasantly old-fashioned. (No restaurant, closed winter.)

The Dordogne

The Dordogne is a great favourite with British visitors – partly, no doubt, because it's easy to feel at home here. There's something quite English about the gentle wooded hills and the quiet, bucolic beauty of the whole area. But it is in any case one of the most visually delicious areas of France. Rivers, tributaries and valleys play a major role, providing picturesque sites for villages and castles. The Dordogne river itself is particularly beautiful, meandering seductively through quiet landscapes, under plunging cliffs, past sleepy hamlets and villages where the honey-coloured stone and russet-red roofs are reflected in its clear waters. The prettiest stretch of the river is from Souillac to Limeuil – further downstream the area gives way to the flatter lands and the vineyards around Bergerac.

The official *département* of the Dordogne occupies roughly the same area as the old province of Périgord – that's the area between Limousin and the valleys of Aquitaine. Despite the fact that the name changed nearly two centuries ago, the locals are still *Périgourdins* and as far as they're concerned the Dordogne is no more than a river. In this chapter we've concentrated on the area that most tourists cover – the Dordogne valley as far as Bergerac to the west, the Vézère valley in the north and the Lot valley and Cahors in the south.

The prehistoric caves of the Dordogne attract scientists and scholars from all over the world. They attract tourists too – you don't have to be a connoisseur to enjoy the natural and man-made curiosities they contain. It's hard to believe that the drawings and paintings, some of which are amazingly vivid and fluid, were done over 10,000 years ago. The greatest concentration of caves is around the village of Les Eyzics. Apart from the paintings and drawings, there are some amazing stalactites and stalagmites, and guides will draw your attention to rock formations resembling things such as mushrooms, butterfly wings and palm trees.

For years the Dordogne was one of the regions hotly disputed between the French and English and many castles and fortified towns (or *bastides*) remain from those times. Monpazier, with its attractive arcades, old houses and ruined fortifications, is the best-preserved of the *bastides*. There are isolated castles, too, often perched spectacularly on hilltops or rocky spurs. Usually there is not much to see inside, and some are no more than ruins. But there are exceptions, such as Castelnau: within its great red stone ramparts, high above the Dordogne and Céré rivers, is an interesting collection of art and furniture.

Tourism in the Dordogne mainly focuses on Périgord Noir – the area around the river Dordogne, which owes its name to the density of trees and the dark foliage of the oaks. Périgord Blanc to the north-west is an open, gentle landscape of orchards, wheat fields and outcrops of chalky limestone – hence its name. The whole region has witnessed major changes in the last 30 years or so. Foreigners, particularly the British, have been buying up and restoring ramshackle barns, and villages have been growing rich on tourism. But despite the foreign accents and proliferation of GB plates the region is still rural and relatively unspoilt.

What sort of holiday?

The Dordogne is an area where it's perfectly possible to have a wonderful time doing practically nothing but admire the view. But it is equally an area for sightseeing – of which the highlight is the caves. Sadly, access to the caves is becoming increasingly difficult. The finest cave paintings at Lascaux were sealed off several years ago, after it was realised that the warmth and carbon dioxide introduced by the of thousands of tourists going into the cave each day was destroying the paintings of bulls and bison. Tickets for some of the other well-known caves are now rationed to about 20 a day, which may mean queuing well before breakfast to get a look in. Where tickets aren't rationed the queues can be enormous, and the caves can be crowded and claustrophobic – chilly too.

No single place makes an obvious base for exploring the region, but you can't go far wrong by staying in or close to one of the beauty spots along the Dordogne. Les Eyzies makes an ideal base for cave enthusiasts but it's expensive and not particularly appealing as a resort. Probably the nicest town to stay in is Sarlat – an attractive, lively centre not far from the river, and with excursions available. There is no shortage of attractive, welcoming hotels in this area. There are also lots of *gîtes* to rent, and many campsites along the river – though inevitably over-subscribed in summer.

Activities are mainly centred on the water – fishing in rivers and ponds (known as *étangs*), swimming from river 'beaches' (the water is quite clear and fairly safe); there are also good pools in main towns. It's an excellent region for walks, with marked paths through woodlands.

Food and drink

The Dordogne has a liberal sprinkling of highly regarded restaurants, most of which are beyond the pockets of the average tourist. But there are also plenty of cheaper places where you can taste the local specialities. Truffles, the greatest delicacies, are known as black diamonds: they're sniffed out from the roots of young oaks (affected by a fungus disease) by trained truffle hounds or pigs and used as flavouring for pâtés and countless other dishes. They command very high prices, even when sold in tiny cans. More affordable specialities are duck and goose, often potted and preserved. Geese are force-fed to produce another local 'delicacy', fattened liver – *foie gras* – which is then made into pâtés.

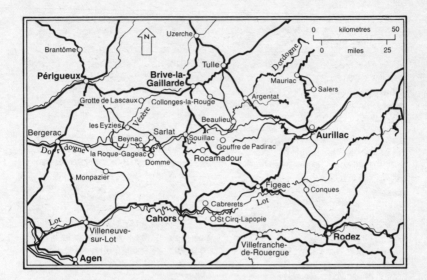

Wines to look out for are the *Appellation Contrôlée* Bergerac, similar to a light claret, and the 'black wine' of Cahors, so-called because of its deep red colour (it also has an appropriately full flavour). Monbazillac, well known for its intensely sweet white wines, is not far from Bergerac.

Gazetteer

Bergerac

A busy modern town beside the river Dordogne, Bergerac's main claims to fame are Cyrano de Bergerac (the romantic satirist and dramatist) and the sweet white wine of Monbazillac, served with dessert or *foie gras*. The château of Monbazillac is a handsome building in an elevated position south of the town, surrounded by carefully cultivated vineyards. In Bergerac itself a few old timbered houses and winding streets have survived, and there is the only tobacco museum in France – an intriguing collection of smoking paraphernalia. There's also a small wine museum.

Beynac-et-Cazenac

One of the showpieces of the Dordogne; its old houses huddle at the foot of a cliff face, and the amazing fortress above commands glorious views over the river valley. From here you can see the ruined fortress of Castelnaud (now being excellently restored with some fascinating exhibits and displays – well worth a visit), the château of Marqueyssac and the pepperpot towers of Fayrac, once an English stronghold.

Hotels

The homely and slightly old-fashioned **Bonnet** ££ ☎ 53 29 50 01 has been a British favourite for years; it has an attractive, popular restaurant, a small garden and lovely views. (Closed winter.) 2km south-east at Vézac, the more expensive **Rochecourbe** £££ ☎ 53 29 50 79 is a very peaceful small manor-house in a lush rural setting. (No restaurant, closed winter.)

Brantôme

This is justifiably one of the most popular spots in the area. The smiling river Dronne flows through the town, its banks lined by weeping willows, lime trees and pale stone houses with russet-coloured roofs. There are several good hotels and restaurants but it is is not a particularly convenient base for exploring the Dordogne valley.

What to see

Abbey This is one of the main landmarks of the town – an imposing, much restored Benedictine abbey with a beautiful bell tower and gardens. Pierre de Bourdeilles, chronicler of clever scandalous court stories, lived here in the 16th century.

Nearby

Bourdeilles (10km SW) A sleepy hamlet in the Dronne valley with a fine château built on sheer rocks above the river, and old houses clustering below. **St-Jean-de-Côle** (19km NE) A particularly pretty village. The Grottes de Villars, 8km away, have some fantastically skinny stalactites and some very early cave paintings.

Hotels

If cost is no object you can choose between two delightful mill hotels, both very comfortable and both renowned for good food. The **Moulin de l'Abbaye** ££££ ☎ 53 05 80 22 is beautifully set by the bridge in Brantôme. (Closed winter, restaurant closed Mon.) The **Moulin du Roc** ££££ ☎ 53 54 80 36 at Champagnac de Belair, 6km from Brantôme, is even nicer – a converted nut-oil mill by waterside gardens with two Michelin stars to its credit. (Closed most of winter, restaurant closed Wed L and Tue.)

Back in Brantôme, the **Chabrol** 59 rue Gambetta £££ ☎ 53 05 70 15 has one Michelin star and comfortable rooms beside the river. (Closed Sun and Mon out of season.) The very much cheaper **Auberge du Soir** £ ☎ 53 05 82 93 is not without simple charm. (Closed Mon out of season.)

In Bourdeilles, the **Hostellerie les Griffons** £££ ☎ 53 05 75 61 is an attractive riverside hotel with rustic furnishings, comfortable rooms and good food. (Closed out of season.) Much further away, 20km north at Nontron, the **Grand** 3 pl A-Agard ££

☎ 53 56 11 22 is excellent value, particularly for food. (Closed Sun D out of season.)

Cahors

This dignified old town lies within a loop of the river Lot, surrounded by wild green hills. A sleepy backwater noted for dark, heady wines, the town has all the warmth of southern France. The medieval tone is set by the Pont Valentré, a remarkably well preserved 14th-century fortified bridge with towers and crenellations. Timbered houses and a maze of narrow lanes lie close to the cathedral, near the tree-lined river walk.

What to see

Cathedral of St-Etienne A domed, rather severe church whose main features are a beautifully sculptured tympanum above the north door and fine, vaulted cloisters.

Nearby

Grotte du Pech-Merle (34km NW, near Cabrerets) A huge and refreshingly uncrowded cave (though still with big summer queues); interconnecting galleries contain spectacular stalagmites and stalactites and some splendid paintings of bison, mammoths and horses. The cave was discovered accidentally by two small boys in the 1920s. An explanatory film and museum are included in the ticket.

Along the Lot Places worth travelling to from Cahors include the large quiet village of Luzech (downstream) and the exceptionally pretty St-Cirq-Lapopie (upstream), whose half-timbered houses lining steep cobbled streets have beautiful views of the river and broad plains below.

Hotels and restaurant

There's not a very good choice of places to stay in town but the best bet is the **Terminus** 5 av Charles-de-Freycinet ££ ☎ 65 35 24 50, opposite the station, which is pleasantly and traditionally furnished. For the best food go to **La Taverne** 1 rue J B Delpech ☎ 65 35 28 66 whose specialities include dishes with truffles. (Closed Mon out of season.) The **Hôtel de la Pélissaria** at St-Cirq-Lapopie ££ ☎ 65 31 25 14 is a tiny, old hotel with six quiet, simple rooms. (Closed out of season.) The **Pescalerie** at Cabrerets ££££ ☎ 65 31 22 55 is one of the most seductive hotels in France – a beautifully furnished but unpretentious old house with gardens running down to the river, and a very inviting atmosphere – the food is good too. (Closed out of season.)

Collonges-la-Rouge

Originally a weekend retreat for the nobility, this 16th-century village is a unique blend of rose-red sandstone houses, mansions and small-scale castles with towers, turrets and pepperpot chimneys. There are no cars from June to mid-September, and life centres around a picturesque square and covered market.

Nearby

If you're planning to stay a day or two in the area, **Argentat** to the east and **Beaulieu** to the south-east are worth visiting – attractive old towns straddling the Dordogne; beyond Argentat, the **Tours de Merle** are the ruins of a stronghold, partly encircled by a narrow river and surrounded by wooded hills.

Hotel

The **Relais de St-Jacques-de-Compostelle** £ ☎ 55 25 41 02 is a small, picturesque red sandstone building with modest accommodation. The food is excellent value and there's a pretty terrace overlooking the garden. (Closed Wed out of season.)

Domme

Unquestionably the most popular hilltop village of the area, Domme has a superb setting on a rocky promontory, with a giddy drop down to the river and a breathtaking panorama of the wide Dordogne valley and rolling hills beyond. Day-trippers come in coachloads for the views, the cliff walks and the village itself – beautiful ochre stone houses and picturesque streets. There's a 17th-century covered market, and caves which served as refuge for locals in the Hundred Years' War and Wars of Religion. Domme is crowded by day but delightfully quiet at night.

Hotel

The **Esplanade** £££ ☎ 53 28 31 41 has beautiful views, typically French floral rooms and good food. (Closed Mon out of season.)

Les Eyzies

Go to Les Eyzies any time from spring to the end of September and you're bound to feel at home. The place positively seethes with British and Dutch visitors and, unlike a lot of French villages in the middle of the countryside, presents few language problems. The village is straggling and without much charm, entirely geared to tourism, but this is more than compensated for by the abundance of caves (see introduction to this chapter), the quality of food and the comfort of its hotels. Enthusiasts could happily spend two or three days here visiting caves in and around the resort.

Caves

Font de Gaume (just E of the centre) Only 20 visitors a day are allowed to see the cave paintings – generally reckoned to be the best after Lascaux. There are engravings and colour drawings of reindeer, horses, mammoths and a superb frieze of five bison.
Combarelles (3km E on Sarlat road) 300 pictures of animals are engraved along two cave tunnels – rather faint, but you can see how prehistoric man was already using the rock contours to convey the shapes of the animals.
Abri du Cap Blanc (6km E) A rock shelter with bison and a fine frieze of horses carved in high relief.
Grand Roc (on Périgueux road) Popular cave tunnels with illuminated stalactites, stalagmites and fascinating crystallisations.
Rouffignac (9km NW; take Périgueux road, then road signed to right) A small train carries you through 4km of chilly, dank corridors. There are dozens of drawings and engravings of stags, mammoths, bison and other beasts.
Lascaux (Close to Montignac, 25km NE up the winding Vézère) The caves themselves, containing the best of the prehistoric wall-paintings, are now closed to the public. But both caves and

paintings have been faithfully reproduced nearby at Lascaux II – very well done, and worth seeing despite the endless queues and tricky French commentary.

Other sights

National Museum of Prehistory A good place to start your sightseeing. It tells the story of the cave discoveries and illustrates the prehistoric eras through skeletons, tools, mammoth bones, drawings etc.

Gorge d'Enfer Forest trails lead through a wildlife reserve where the animals resemble those you see depicted in the local caves.

Hotels

At the top end of the market are two hotels renowned for their food. The elegant, modern and exceedingly comfortable **Centenaire £££** ☎ 53 06 97 18 specialises in *nouvelle cuisine* and has two Michelin stars. (Closed winter, restaurant closed Tue L.) The more old-fashioned **Cro-Magnon £££** ☎ 53 06 97 06 has large grounds and a pool. A cheaper, perfectly comfortable alternative is **Les Glycines £££** ☎ 53 06 97 07 – civilised, with a shady terrace and large garden. (Closed winter.) The **Moulin de la Beune ££** ☎ 53 06 94 33 is a converted mill next to the Museum of Prehistory, with the river Beune flowing through its garden. (Closed winter.)

Périgueux

With plenty of hotels, restaurants and exceptionally good markets, this might seem like a good base. But it's mainly modern, and not as appealing as many other towns in the region. There's an old quarter, dominated by the huge Basilica and some fragmentary Roman ruins.

What to see

Cathedral of St-Front A huge eccentric edifice with cupolas, colonnaded turrets and a towering belfry – remarkable more for sheer size and eastern flavour than elegance or harmony. Originally Romanesque, it was renovated by the 19th-century architect Abadie – otherwise known as 'The Wrecker'.

Périgord museum Prehistoric collection including a mammoth's tusk, plus Gallo/Roman mosaics.

Rocamadour

Known as the vertical village, Rocamadour clings spectacularly to the 1,500-foot cliff wall of the Gorge of Alzou. Since the 12th century it has been a place of pilgrimage, the faithful making their way up the Great Stairway to its seven sanctuaries. Nowadays it's also a mecca for tourists (approach roads are choked with cars in high summer) and the souvenir trade sadly detracts from the medieval charm of its buildings. You can pay to use a lift and avoid the steep climb to the chapels but access to the château, which commands stomach-churning views down on to the valley and village, is only by car or foot.

Nearby

Gouffre de Padirac (about 9km NE) One of the most dramatic natural phenomena of the Dordogne, the giant cave of Padirac draws the longest queues and demands the highest prices. Lifts take you down to caverns with pools, giant concretions, waterfalls and galleries, culminating in the enormous Hall of the Great Dome. There are no paintings. Some caves are reached on foot along steep paths, others by underground boats. Although it's well worth a visit, the high-season queues and crowds may persuade you to leave it until a quieter time.

Hotel

The best place to stay is the **Ste-Marie ££** ☎ 65 33 63 07 which lies in the old town, close to the sights. There are small comfortable rooms, a cosy traditional restaurant and lovely views; it's also quiet, standing above the noise and traffic. (Closed winter.)

La Roque-Gageac

An eye-catching village on the banks of the Dordogne, huddled against the foot of a steep cliff. Warm stone houses, steep alleyways and arches all give the place a picture-postcard charm, and it's not surprising that it frequently wins 'prettiest village' prizes and draws crowds of day-trippers.

Sarlat

Arriving in Sarlat by the the main Rive de la République can be a disappointment. This 'modern' street cuts insensitively through the medieval town; but the old quarters either side are charming, and the town as a whole is one of the most captivating in south-west France. Its distinctive architectural style has echoes of eastern Europe – indeed the town centre was recently used by a film company as a middle-European town in a remake of *The Bride of Frankenstein*. There are winding alleys lined with honey-coloured houses, quaint steeply pitched roofs, sculpted doors and stairways, towers and turrets, and a handsome cathedral with flying buttresses. There are few set-piece sights but it's a lovely town for ambling. It is also an excellent base for exploring Périgord Nord and for trying out the *foie gras* and walnuts which it supplies to the whole of France. There are good shops and an excellent, though crowded, market on Saturday mornings. Unlike most towns in the Dordogne, Sarlat is quite lively at night.

Hotels and restaurant

For a central hotel the **St-Albert** pl Pasteur ££ ☎ 53 59 01 09 is quite good value, particularly for food. (Closed Sun D and Mon out of season.) If you're prepared to stay just out of town, **La Hoirie** £££ ☎ 53 59 05 62 makes a quiet and comfortable base – a welcoming old house standing in its own grounds with a pool. (Closed winter.) The **Hostellerie de Meysset** £££ ☎ 53 59 08 29 is a small manor-house perched above two beautiful valleys, 3km out on the road to Les Eyzies, with pretty rooms overlooking a wooded park. (Closed winter.) The **Madeleine** 1 pl Petite-Rigaudie £££ ☎ 53 59 10 41 is a comfortable, traditional hotel with a friendly restaurant serving good, hearty regional fare. (Closed winter.)

Souillac

The redeeming feature of this rather dull town straddling the N20 highway is the old abbey, particularly the beautiful sculpted doorway which was mutilated by Protestants and rebuilt inside the church. Tourists come here mainly for the shops, hotels and restaurants.

Hotels and restaurant

There's a good choice of middle range hotels, but none of them stands out sufficiently to be recommended. The best restaurant is the **Vieille Auberge** pl de la Minoterie ££ ☎ 65 32 79 43 which serves excellent value regional dishes; it also has 20 quite attractive rooms, and a pool. (Closed winter.)

Provence and the south coast

Holiday tastes change over the years; resorts and whole regions come in and go out of fashion. Yet the south of France, particularly that stretch of coast from Monte-Carlo to St-Tropez, has held its place among the most stylish and most glamorous destinations in the world. For French and foreigners alike, the south (or the Midi as the French know it) is the favourite region of France. Its combination of culture, beauty and sheer hedonism is unrivalled. Added to the basic Mediterranean pleasures of sun, sea, food and wine are the glittering resorts, palatial hotels and ribbons of golden sand. White cliffs rise from sparkling seas, swaying palms line sea-front promenades and dazzling white villas bask in sunshine almost all the year round.

The Côte d'Azur (the coast east of Marseille, reaching to the Italian border) was once the exclusive playground of the rich and famous – monarchs, prime ministers, film stars, business tycoons and famous painters who were drawn by the intense quality of the light. And in the early part of this century the short stretch east of Cannes known as the Riviera was monopolised by moneyed British.

Today the coast belongs to no one and to everyone: campsites and high-rise apartment blocks have sprung up along the shore and in peak season the coastal road is almost one long traffic jam. Yet, despite the crowds and commercialism, there is still at least a whisper of those heady Edwardian days: the grand casino at Monte-Carlo, the Croisette boulevard at Cannes, the neo-baroque palaces and the wedding-cake hotels. The affluent and opulent still come here: if you doubt it, you need only look at one of the many marinas along the coast, packed with million-pound yachts.

The sleepy medieval villages of inland Provence provide a quiet contrast to the razzamatazz of the coast. Some of these villages are perched perilously on peaks, overlooking hillsides of silvery olive trees and vines baking in broad terraces. Slender cypresses, almond groves and the scent of rosemary, lavender and thyme – these are all as characteristic of southern France as the sea and beaches. There are ancient cities with Roman remains (the name *Provence* is derived from *Provincia Romana*), vibrant towns and villages where you can sit in the shade of a plane tree, sipping *pastis* and watching a game of *boules*.

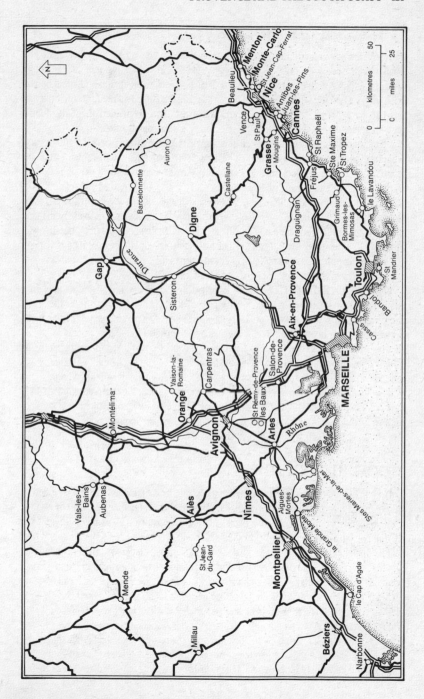

What sort of holiday?

The south provides an ideal combination of sea and sights. If you want to concentrate solely on culture, base yourself in Lower Provence: Nîmes, Orange and Arles are outstanding for Roman remains, Avignon and Aix are both vibrant cities with plenty of sights, colour and culture. If you don't want to stray from the Riviera, there are some superb museums of modern art along the coast, and Nice is particularly good for sightseeing.

The Côte d'Azur provides excellent opportunities for sports enthusiasts. Nearly every resort has a choice of sailing, windsurfing, waterskiing and tennis. There are golf courses at Cannes, Monte-Carlo and St-Raphaël, horse riding in the Camargue, and football, volleyball or badminton matches on some of the beaches. The less energetic can always join the locals and try their hand at *boules* or *pétanque*. West of Antibes nearly all the beaches are sandy; to the east (in Nice, for example) they tend to be shingle or pebble. The most immaculate beaches, usually in the centre of a resort, are almost inevitably controlled by restaurants and hotels who levy high prices for the privilege of using their facilities.

With so much to offer, the coast is popular and crowded, particularly in July and August. If you prefer a base in quiet countryside, opt for one of the perched villages inland, and drive to the sea. Or go in early June or late September when the French are all at home and the beaches, hotels and campsites are less crowded and the coastal road less of a traffic nightmare. The warmest area for an out-of-season holiday is the coast east of Nice, where mountains protect resorts from the cold northerly *mistral* wind.

The whole area is expensive and you're unlikely to find charming hotels at moderate prices. But eating out doesn't have to be exorbitant. It's a good idea to avoid the sea fronts and seek out the cheaper local places in the back streets or simple country *auberges* inland.

Food and drink

Eating in the south of France is enjoyable not because it is an area of great gastronomic subtlety or sumptuous individual dishes, but because garlic, fresh rosemary and thyme, olive oil and fresh mayonnaise can do wondrous things to simple fish, meat and prime, fresh vegetables.

The most famous Provençal dish is *bouillabaisse*, a classic fish soup with onions, tomatoes, garlic, olive oil and saffron – almost a meal in itself. Try *bourride* too, a creamy fish soup with *aïoli*, a Provençal garlic mayonnaise. Other fish dishes you're likely to come across are *loup de mer* (sea bass), often prepared with fennel, *daurade* (a tender white fish), *rouget* (red mullet), *scampi* (prawns, usually frozen), *langouste* (expensive spiny lobster) and *moules* (mussels). Fish and meat are often served with *sauce provençale* – a mixture of tomatoes, herbs, garlic and olives. Lamb is usually cooked with herbs and garlic; *daube de boeuf* is a traditional beef stew, cooked slowly in rich wine stock.

On the eastern side of the Côte d'Azur the Italian influence is strong and pasta is plentiful. But the finest products of southern France are fresh vegetables: plump tomatoes, gleaming aubergines, red and green peppers, asparagus and artichokes. *Ratatouille* (tomatoes, onions, aubergines, courgettes, green peppers) is practically a meal in itself. Abundant fruit, including luscious melons, wild strawberries, figs and peaches, makes for delicious desserts.

The south produces a great deal of wine and, although it does not pretend to rival the great wine-growing areas, offers a wide range of interestingly distinctive wines at good-value prices. The most prestigious wines are the heavy reds, rosés and dessert whites from the Rhône valley: the most famous name is Châteauneuf-du-Pape, a warm and full-bodied red. The light, slightly fruity whites of Provence are an ideal accompaniment to fish and shellfish. Bandol and Palette are two of the best Provençal reds, Cassis is the most interesting white, but the orange-tinted, light and fruity rosés of Tavel and Lirac probably have the most appeal.

Gazetteer

Aigues-Mortes

This remarkably well preserved medieval town stands among lagoons and misty marshes. It was built in the 13th century by Louis IX (St-Louis) and it was from here that he embarked on his Seventh Crusade in 1248. There are fine views from the ramparts and the Tour de Constance, but be prepared for crowds.

Aix-en-Provence

Lively, civilised and elegant, Aix is one of France's most desirable provincial cities. Capital of Provence for five centuries, its golden age was the 15th-century reign of 'great King René' who nurtured the arts and introduced the muscat grape. Aix today is a city of students, sights and culture. There is no better introduction than to have a coffee or *pastis* in a pavement café on the Cours Mirabeau – a graceful boulevard sweeping through the centre, lined on one side by 18th-century aristocratic mansions and hotels, on the other by shops and a string of cafés frequented by students and tourists alike. Old Aix, to the north, is a picturesque network of narrow alleyways opening on to sunlit squares, the prettiest of which is the cobbled Place d'Albertus.

For part of July and August, Aix is the venue for one of Europe's finest music festivals. The main events are formal concerts with first-rate singers and musicians, but it is also an excuse for lesser musicians and modern groups to strike up all over town.

What to see

Cathedral A curious hybrid, spanning 11 centuries of architecture, from the 5th-century baptistry to the 16th-century carvings on the west-door panels. The highlight is the triptych of the Burning Bush symbolising the virginity of Mary (you have to ask the verger to see it).
Granet museum A diverse collection of foreign and French paintings, including an excellent small self-portrait by Rembrandt and the outstanding portrait by Ingres of the 19th-century painter Granet. Also Roman relics.
Tapestry museum Exquisite collection of 17th- and 18th-century Beauvais tapestries in the old archbishop's palace beside the cathedral.

Most museums and historic buildings are closed on public holidays.

Cézanne's studio Turn-of-the-century studio where Cézanne worked until his death. A rather fusty place, with reproductions, mementoes and a few bits and pieces that Cézanne used in his still-life paintings.

Museum of Old Aix Folklore museum with a large collection of *santons* (local figurines).

Vasarély Foundation Collection of geometrical abstract art by the Hungarian-born painter, housed in a modern museum decorated with alternating black and white circles.

Hotels

Aix is a noisy and expensive place to stay and you may prefer to make your base outside the city, though even here prices are high. The **Mas d'Entremont** £££ ☎ 42 23 45 32 at Celony, 3km out of the centre, has quiet, attractively furnished rooms (some in the old Provençal house, others in bungalows), good food, a pool and tennis courts. (Closed winter, restaurant closed Sun D and Mon L exc public hols.) In Aix itself the quietest and most distinguished hotel is the **Pigonnet** 5 av du Pigonnet £££ ☎ 42 59 02 90, a typical Provençal house set in beautiful gardens with pool. (Restaurant closed Sun D out of season.)

Antibes

Narrow streets and squares within 17th-century ramparts form the heart of Antibes. It's a colourful, fashionable seaside town with smart galleries, sleek yachts moored in a picturesque port and a daily market of exotic fruit and flowers.

What to see

Grimaldi museum Château beside the sea where Picasso lived and worked in 1946. His works predominate: paintings, drawings, lithographs and sculpture, all displayed in cool modern galleries.

Except in *Channel ports*, we have not mentioned winter closing times of hotels and restaurants: if you are going out of season, do check first that hotels are open.

Arles

Capital of latter-day Roman Gaul and focus of early Christianity, Arles is a city with much to keep the sightseer amused. Compared with Aix and Avignon it seems quiet and unsophisticated, but it is a pleasant place to amble, with elegant streets and squares. The main sights are close together and one admission ticket covers the lot.

What to see

Amphitheatre Once the scene of fights between gladiators and wild beasts, this colossal arena is still used for bullfights. Though not as well preserved as its counterpart in Nîmes, it's still in a relatively good state. All that remains of the nearby theatre is a pair of soaring columns.

Cathedral Outstanding Romanesque edifice, with a beautifully carved western portal and delightful cloisters whose capitals are carved with Biblical scenes and local legends.

Arlaten museum Fascinating local folklore museum.

Christian art museum Impressive collection of richly-carved early Christian stone coffins housed in a former Jesuit chapel.

Musée Lapidaire Païen Mosaics, Roman stone coffins and statues from the theatre, set in a former church.

Musée Réattu Former 15th-century priory of the Knights of Malta, housing a large and eclectic collection of paintings. The tiny coloured sketches by Picasso stand out from the rest.

Avignon

Avignon is a lively and likeable city with lots to see and some very chic shopping. It lies at the very centre of Provence, the old city enclosed within ramparts that rise defiantly above the Rhône. Its richest epoch was the 14th century when Pope Clement V, threatened by political scheming in Rome, opted for a more peaceful residence at Avignon.

Papal rule lasted here until 1377, and Avignon became a place of decadence, crime and debauchery. When the papacy officially returned to Rome, a few cardinals selected a second pope who established a rival seat in Avignon. A succession of 'antipopes' followed and the Great Schism went on until 1417. The massive Palais des Papes still dominates the city, its towers and spires rising high above all else.

What to see
Palais des Papes Fortress-like Gothic building of huge proportions. It consists of two buildings: the austere Old Palace, built for the Cistercian Benedict XII; and the more elaborate New Palace, reflecting the lavish life-style of Clement V. The rooms of both palaces are grandiose but devoid of their former lavish furnishings. All you can see now are frescoes and tapestries. Guided tours are conducted in various languages including English.

Pont St-Bénézet Bridge across the Rhône made famous in the nursery song 'Sur le Pont d'Avignon' (though in fact the dancing took place *sous le pont* – under the bridge – on an island in mid-stream). Only four arches remain.

Petit Palais Outstanding collection of medieval painting and sculpture, mainly works of Avignon and north Italian schools, appropriately housed in the archbishop's palace across the square from the Palais des Papes.

Notre-Dame-des-Doms 12th-century cathedral, partly rebuilt from the 14th to the 17th century and topped by an incongruous 19th-century gilded statue of the Virgin. The main feature is the flamboyant Gothic tomb of John XXII, Pope of Avignon.

Rocher-des-Doms Rocky promontory with superb views over the Rhône; delightful terraced gardens with trees, lawns, flower beds and a duck pond.

Musée Calvet Interesting collection which includes paintings, antiquities and wrought ironwork. Particularly worth seeing are the 16th- to 20th-century French paintings.

> If a hotel has no restaurant, we say so at the end of the hotel description.

Les Baux
One of the most extraordinary sites (and sights) of Provence, Les Baux is an immense limestone spur, rising above dense scrub and crowned by a giant ruined château and a ghostly, semi-deserted, semi-ruined village. The castle used to be the residence of some of the most powerful *seigneurs* in the south of France, controlling as many as 80 towns and villages. The castle was famous as a court of love, though in the latter part of the 14th century it became the scene of less happy pursuits. Raymond de Turenne, known as 'the scourge of Provence' adopted the eccentric pastime of terrorising the locals by kidnapping innocents and pushing them off the clifftop.

The inhabited part of the village has restaurants, shops and studios. You can explore the deserted village beyond it, and clamber all over the castle ruins. Very good views.

Hotels and restaurants
In the valley below Les Baux are several good hotels and outstanding restaurants. The **Oustaù de Baumanière** £££££ ☎ 90 54 33 07 is the grandest place: three Michelin stars, pool, garden, terraces etc, and prices to match. (Closed mid-winter, Thu L and Wed out of season.) Still expensive but not so exorbitant is the **Cabro d'Or** ££££ ☎ 90 54 33 21, an elegant hotel with peaceful gardens and competent cuisine. (Closed Tue L and Mon out of season.) Much cheaper is the **Mas d'Aigret** £££ ☎ 90 97 33 54 – an old farmhouse below the castle, with lovely views. (Closed mid-winter, restaurant closed Thu out of season.)

Cannes
Until the 1830s Cannes was merely a fishing village. It was Lord Brougham, British Chancellor, who discovered the place by chance and built a villa there in which to escape the English winter. The English aristocracy followed suit, and Cannes blossomed into a fashionable resort.

Today Cannes is an all-year-round resort, packed with visitors not only in summer but also at certain other times of the year when it hosts several festivals. It is still a glamorous, expensive and sophisticated place, with grand hotels, dazzling white villas, smart yachts, art galleries, jewellers and fashionable cafés. The grandest architectural flourish is La Croisette, the elegant tree-lined boulevard which curves gently round from the old port past cafés, boutiques, galleries, gardens and palatial hotels to the Palm Beach Casino at the eastern end. The sands of Cannes are white and handsome – and you have to pay handsomely to make use of them.

Nearby
Iles de Lérins Boats leave regularly for the wooded islands of Ile St-Honorat and Ste-Marguerite, both providing quiet retreats from Cannes.

Cassis

It is not surprising that this enchanting fishing village, sheltered by limestone cliffs, became the favourite subject of artists at the turn of the century. Now self-consciously picturesque, Cassis is a small, popular and prosperous community with a centre of winding alleys and open-air cafés.

Nearby
Les Calanques Cassis makes the best starting point for a boat trip to these deep, fjord-like creeks of crystal-clear waters, fringed by steep, limestone cliffs.

Fréjus

Generally a rather dull town and resort, Fréjus can pride itself on its Roman relics and a cathedral with a charming cloister and 5th-century baptistry. The damaged amphitheatre is still used for bullfights and concerts.

La Grande Motte

Probably the most innovative resort in France, La Grande Motte is an extraordinary futuristic conglomeration of glass and concrete cones and pyramids, which on closer inspection turn out to be apartment blocks. The beach is good and there are excellent facilities for watersports enthusiasts.

Grasse

Grasse is the world capital of the perfume industry, but has little to offer apart from pleasant fragrances in the air, beautiful views and tours of the perfume factories. They claim that three out of four bottles of perfume sold throughout the world contain essences distilled here.

Juan-les-Pins

Fashionable resort of the 1920s and setting of Scott Fitzgerald's *Tender is the Night*, Juan-les-Pins is today a large, modern and rather brash place. Two of its luxury hotels echo the days of the elite; otherwise the beach and nightlife are the main attractions.

Marseille

Marseille is notorious as the 'French Connection' city of heroin, prostitutes, thieves and white-slave traders. Even if it is not as bad as people make out, it is still a fairly seedy place, with none of the sophistication or glamour of the popular resorts of the Côte d'Azur. The city's shipping links with the old French colonies of Algeria and Tunisia have given it a pronounced African atmosphere. Apart from a colourful, bustling port there's not much else to see: most of Marseille was destroyed in World War II.

Nearby
Château d'If Boats leave regularly to the prison island whence Dumas' hero the Count of Monte Cristo made his famous escape.

£	up to £15
££	£15 to £25
£££	£25 to £45
££££	£45 to £70
£££££	£70 to £100
£££££!	more

In hotel and restaurant descriptions, D means dinner and L means lunch.

Monte-Carlo-Monaco

If you tell people you are holidaying in Monte-Carlo, they still look suitably impressed. The name still conjures up images of high living – mink coats, Rolls Royces, Grand Prix racing, expensive jewellers, casinos and millionaires' yachts. And although the elegance of the *belle époque* before World War I has largely given way to high-rise concrete blocks, it is still undeniably a smart and affluent place – generous tax concessions retain the loyalty of the very wealthy. The heart of the town is the casino, a lavish, late 19th-century rococo building – worth a look even if you're not a gambler (you don't have to be dressed up, as long as you don't mind disapproving looks).

The principality of Monaco (which is distinct from France) is tiny and you can see all of its attractions in a fairly short time. The old town of Monaco, perched on a cliff, is the place to wander: narrow winding streets, glorious views of the sea and the palace of Prince Rainier (you can watch the changing of the guard every day, but the state apartments are open in summer months only). Other sights include an oceanographic museum under the direction of Jacques Cousteau, and a fine tropical garden of exotic plants and flowers.

Hotel

Staying in Monte-Carlo is outrageously expensive, and if you merely want a taste of the place you should go for the day only. The ultimate in luxury is the **Hôtel de Paris** pl Casino £££££! ☎ 93 50 80 80. The foyer of gilded pillars, marble ceilings and the affluent clientele will give you some idea of the prices to expect.

Montpellier

Montpellier's university was founded in the 10th century and the town is still very much a student stronghold. Life focuses on the Place de la Comédie, a paved piazza with a fountain, 19th-century opera house and elegant cafés. Parts of the old town have been expertly restored and there are some plain but elegant 17th- and 18th-century palaces; other quarters remain shabby and totally neglected.

What to see

Musée des Beaux-Arts (or Fabrée) The best of Montpellier's museums, including a fine collection of 19th-century paintings (several by Courbet)

Menton

While Monte-Carlo draws the jet set, the slower-paced, quieter Menton has become a favourite place for the retired. One good reason is the climate, which is the mildest of the Côte d'Azur. Tropical vegetation flourishes and lemon trees line its streets. Old Menton is charming and distinctly Italian in style (the border is only minutes away).

Nice

One of the most famous resorts of the 19th century, Nice still has a lot to offer. It is large and lively, with a good choice of hotels, restaurants and shops, a picturesque old town, a famous festival and flower market, various good museums and a superb setting below hills and mountains. It is no longer a focus of high society, and in comparison with places like Cannes or Monte-Carlo it feels pleasantly down-to-earth, with a bustling life of its own. This is best seen in the old town – a teeming scene of shops, bistros and markets lining narrow lanes. But Nice is also very cosmopolitan, and grand hotels still stand behind its palm-lined Promenade des Anglais. The beach is no more than shingle.

What to see

Cimiez Once a Roman settlement, this is now the elegant residential area, with grandiose villas and *belle époque* hotels. Matisse lived here for many years, and you can see a collection of his work at the Musée Matisse in a villa beside the Roman arena. Also in Cimiez is the Musée National Marc Chagall, with works donated by the artist including paintings, sculptures, mosaics, drawings and lithographs.
Musée des Beaux-Arts Jules Chéret A varied and interesting collection of

paintings displayed in a dark but impressive turn-of-the-century palace. Works include those of Italian and Flemish primitives and impressionists, some of whom worked here.

Masséna museum Souvenirs of Nice's history and of the city's two illustrious sons, Garibaldi and Masséna, appropriately housed in a fine Empire-style building.

Nîmes

Nîmes claims to be the Rome of France. A slight exaggeration, perhaps, but it is one of the oldest and most important towns of Roman Gaul and has some of the finest Roman remains in Provence. Apart from the old town around the cathedral, Nîmes today is largely industrial.

What to see

Amphitheatre One of the best-preserved Roman arenas in existence. The Romans used it for chariot races, gladiatorial contests and fights between wild beasts; today it's still a scene of bullfights.

Maison Carrée The 'square house' (distinctly oblong in fact) is the best-preserved of all Roman temples, showing strong Greek influence.

Jardin de la Fontaine Ornamental 18th-century gardens outside the centre: a large expanse of lawns, balustraded paths, flowers, pines, cedars and the ruins of the Temple of Diana. Good views from the Tour Magne if you can manage the climb to the top.

Nearby

Pont du Gard One of the great wonders of the Roman world: an aqueduct of three graceful tiers of arches, still spanning the river Gard. Built 2,000 years ago to supply water to Nîmes, this is one of the best-preserved Roman structures in existence. Walking along the roof of the aqueduct is strictly for those with no imagination or abundant nerve.

Most museums and historic buildings are closed on public holidays.

Orange

The outstanding features of this ancient town are Roman monuments: the elaborately carved triumphal arch heralding the north of the city, and the Roman theatre – one of the finest in existence, with the main wall behind the stage still standing, complete with decorations. It is still used as a theatre and has excellent acoustics.

St-Jean-Cap-Ferrat

Cap-Ferrat is a pine-covered peninsula where villas of the wealthy hide behind gates and gardens. St-Jean, at the tip, is a small fishing port with a a big marina and plenty of cafés.

Hotel

The **Clair Logis** £££ ☎ 93 01 31 01 is a 19th-century villa in beautiful gardens with palms and fig trees. Rooms are quite simple; the best are those in the main building. Good value for this area. (No restaurant.)

St-Paul-de-Vence

Perched on a hill north of Antibes, St-Paul is a superb example of a hill village. Its feudal walls rise above green terraces of vineyards, bougainvillea and mimosa – a setting which has long attracted artists. The narrow pedestrian streets are lined with mellow stone houses containing art and craft galleries, and there are two outstanding collections of modern art.

What to see

Maeght Foundation An outstanding collection of contemporary art. Works by Matisse, Chagall, Bonnard, Giacommetti, Kandinsky and others are beautifully displayed in the house, courtyard and garden.

Hotels

St-Paul has some very pleasant hotels but they are pricey. The most interesting is the **Colombe d'Or** pl des Ormeaux ££££ ☎ 93 32 80 02, a small luxury hotel famous for the collection of paintings by artists who stayed here in its less luxurious days – Matisse, Bonnard, Dufy and Utrillo among them – which is normally open only to those who eat or stay at the hotel. **Le Hameau** £££

☎ 93 32 80 24 is a delightful hotel with a series of old villas amid gardens of fruit trees which yield home-made jams for breakfast. (No restaurant, closed winter.) **Les Orangers** £££ ☎ 93 32 80 95 is a tiny hotel in a quiet garden setting. (No restaurant.) It is cheaper to stay in Vence, the less visited but nevertheless attractive hill town 4.5km away. Good value here is the **Auberge des Seigneurs** ££ ☎ 93 58 04 24, a delightful, old-world restaurant with equally charming rooms. (Closed Sun D out of season and Mon.)

St-Rémy-de-Provence

A sleepy market town at the foot of the rocky Alpilles hills, St-Rémy makes a good base for sightseeing. It is roughly equidistant from Avignon and Arles, and is a relaxing place to stay. Sights in or close to St-Rémy include a folklore museum, an archaeological museum with relics from the Roman site of Glanum (just south of the town) and the former monastery of St-Paul-de-Mausole, converted to a mental home: this was where Van Gogh stayed for a year after cutting off his ear and handing it to a prostitute in an Arles brothel.

Hotels

St-Rémy is well endowed with hotels, mainly on the edge of town. The **Soleil** ££ ☎ 90 92 00 63 and the **Van Gogh** ££ ☎ 90 92 14 02 are reasonably priced: both are fairly quiet and have a pool. More expensive and more atmospheric, but further out, are the **Château de Roussan** £££ ☎ 90 92 11 63, an 18th-century house in a park, and the **Mas des Carassins** £££ ☎ 90 92 15 48, a beautifully converted farmhouse. (None of these hotels has a restaurant, and the first three are closed in winter.)

Don't assume that a sight you want to see will be open: many museums and historic buildings close for a couple of hours over lunch, and often one or two days a week as well. Check with a *Syndicat d'Initiative*.

St-Tropez

Unlike many of the major resorts of this coast, St-Tropez wasn't discovered by the British. The first people to make the place fashionable were the artists who came in the late 19th and early 20th century, inspired by the setting and the coloured houses reflected by the deep blue sea. But it was not until the 1950s and 1960s that St-Tropez really became synonymous with glamour. Roger Vadim's film *And God Created Woman* (with Brigitte Bardot) started it all off and established St-Tropez as the resort of the jet set – famous for celebrities, topless beaches and people who came to be seen at the 'in' cafés on the waterfront.

The reputation has waned a little but St-Tropez is still undeniably chic and extremely popular. Under the huge onslaught of summer tourists it manages to retain something of its picturesque fishing-village charm. There are still a few fishing vessels among the sleek yachts, and modern development has been relatively restrained. Beaches in the town are small and shingly, but there are excellent sandy ones further out.

Ste-Maxime

A modern, sophisticated resort with plenty of life, Ste-Maxime takes a lot of the overflow from nearby St-Tropez. It doesn't have the same cachet but there are more hotels, plenty of watersports, and a good beach in the resort itself. A busy palm-lined promenade is the main focus, while behind it streets with cafés and shops rise steeply up through the old town.

What to see

Musée de l'Annonciade A deconsecrated chapel housing a small but outstanding collection of paintings by impressionists and post-impressionists, many of them closely associated with St-Tropez.

Hotels

Accommodation in St-Tropez is predictably expensive. If you've reconciled yourself to high prices, the place to head for is the **Mas de Chastelas** ££££ ☎ 94 56 09 11, a beautifully converted old farmhouse

which retains the feel of a private home.
It is quiet and secluded, 4km from St-
Tropez, with gardens, pool and tennis
courts – celebrities come here for
peace, not recognition. (Closed winter.)
If you're feeling particularly rich you can
always stay at the **Byblos** £££££!
☎ 94 97 00 04 – the ultimate in luxury,
with the atmosphere of a Provençal
village. (Closed winter.)

Les-Saintes-Maries-de-la-Mer

The Camargue is a national park of
lagoons and marshes where bulls and
white horses roam, and this is its main
resort – a popular but slightly scruffy
beach community. The most interesting
thing about it is the fortress-like church
which houses the relics and statue of
Sarah, patron saint of gypsies. Every
year on 24 May gypsies come from all
over Europe to pay respects to their
patron saint and to make merry the
following day.

Hotel

The **Etrier Camarguais** chemin bas des
Launes £££ ☎ 90 47 81 14 is 3km north
of town – a ranch-like hotel with a herd of
white horses which are hired out to
guests. A good family place, with a
friendly, casual atmosphere, large
helpings of plain food and a good-sized
pool. There is a disco in a separate
building. (Closed winter.)

Neglected France

Picardy and the north

Apart from the obvious attractions of the ferry ports, this area doesn't sound like a particularly rewarding one for the tourist as it offers unspectacular scenery, heavy industry and weather depressingly like our own. But there are good reasons for detours, both east and west of the motorway: the great Gothic cathedrals of towns such as Amiens, Beauvais and Laon, the monuments and battlefields of World War I and the historic centres of Lille, Arras, St-Omer and Compiègne.

North-east of Paris, the Ardennes is a pleasant area of woods, rivers and lakes, renowned for the pâté made from the wild boars still to be found in the forests. The Champagne district further south has obvious sparkling attractions, with free tasting and guided tours in the underground cellars of Reims and Epernay. Both towns are surrounded by a charming landscape of sloping vineyards. Reims has other attractions including a glorious cathedral, abbey church and two excellent museums. The other centre worth visiting is Troyes, in the south, whose numerous medieval buildings include half-timbered houses, a cathedral and several other outstanding churches.

On the coast, Le Touquet-Paris-Plage is not the exclusive playground of 50 years ago, but is still more appealing and lively than its neighbours. Montreuil-sur-Mer is no longer on the sea, despite its name, but is nevertheless one of the most attractive resorts, well endowed with hotels and restaurants – a good choice for a short break.

Alsace and Lorraine

Alsace is distinctly German in character – not surprising, since Germany lies just across the Rhine and the region has changed hands countless times. Few Brits come here despite the attractions of picturesque villages, glorious mountain drives and famous white wines. It's a lovely area for walking in summer: the gentle green Vosges mountains are easy going for hikers, and there are plenty of spotless country inns and campsites.

Strasbourg, capital of Alsace and seat of the European Parliament, has a beautiful but touristy old centre with timber-framed houses, narrow streets, a superb cathedral and several museums. The smaller town of Colmar, further south, is beautifully unspoilt, with a large and exceptionally rich art museum. The most popular drive in the region is the Route du Vin (wine road); it takes you through orderly ranks of vines and pretty villages, with cobbled streets full of half-timbered houses – all set against a backdrop of wooded mountains crowned by ruined fortresses.

Neighbouring Lorraine has less charm. The north is full of heavy industry, the south is greener and more peaceful. Between the two lies Nancy, an outstandingly beautiful 18th-century town.

Burgundy and the Jura

Known as 'the belly of France', Burgundy is chiefly famous for food and wine. There are wine fairs, wine auctions, wine museums and some of the most prestigious wine villages in the world. Shops and markets are a feast for the eyes and nose, and restaurants are renowned for the quality of their food. It's here that you get the best beef and snails in France. But Burgundy has a wider appeal than wine and food. This is also a province of glorious abbeys and châteaux, mellow towns and earthy villages. The landscape is a rich tapestry of rolling fertile plains, wooded hills, broad valleys and vineyards – a beautiful and very civilised region for touring.

Burgundy's boundaries once stretched as far as Flanders and the Low Countries; today the medieval treasures of Dijon and Beaune testify to the days of that great Burgundian Empire. The 12th century saw the construction of some of the finest cathedrals in France: Vézelay, Autun, Tournus and the Cistercian monastery at Fontenay are particularly fine, but there are many others which are worth a detour; there are also a number of beautiful towns. Attractive bases in Burgundy are Beaune, Dijon and Auxerre (see *Getting to the south*).

The Jura, also known as Franche-Comté, is a quiet and untamed region where tourism has made few inroads. There are wild mountains, forests of black spruce, lakes and swift-flowing rivers. The highest region, near Geneva, is good for cross-country skiing in winter and for walks, pony trekking and water sports in summer. On the lower slopes the Jura is gentler, with orchards, stone villages and vineyards.

Besançon, on a big loop of the river Doubs, is the only large town of the region. The imposing citadel with four museums, the cathedral and fine arts museum are good enough reason to go there, though the city itself lacks charm.

The Alps

The snowy peaks, lakes and glaciers of the French Alps provide some of the grandest and most spectacular scenery in Europe. The northern Alps are well geared to both winter and summer holidays, with mountain and lake resorts catering for skiers, hikers and other sports enthusiasts. High passes take you right into the mountains (along with dozens of cyclists training for the Tour de France). The Alpine pastures are a rich hunting ground for botanists, with an amazing variety of colourful flora. But there is little of the chocolate-box charm that you find in Austria and Switzerland: most of the ski resorts are modern, with big apartment blocks – though there are a few exceptions. Chamonix is a lively town, long established as a mountaineering centre; it lies in the shadow of Mont Blanc – at 15,780ft, Europe's highest mountain. The prettiest area is south-west of here, in the lower Aravis mountains around the pleasant village of La Clusaz.

At the foot of the mountains are the glacial lakes, with deep azure waters, which also attract tourists. The loveliest of the natural lakes is Annecy, surrounded by beautiful mountain scenery and fringed on its northern shores by the pretty town of the same name. On the larger and less beautiful lake of Le Bourget, Aix-les-Bains is a major spa and fashionable resort. Larger still is Lake Geneva, more properly called Lac Leman – 13km wide, and more like an inland sea. There are beaches along the French shore and the main resort is the lively spa of Evian.

The capital of the Alps is Grenoble: a large, lively and cosmopolitan centre. Also worth visiting is the elegant old centre of Chambéry to the north-east of Grenoble. The Alps south of here are harsher and less developed, but still worth exploring.

The Massif Central

Relatively few tourists find their way to the mountainous and remote Massif Central. This is principally a place for an active adventure holiday or a real away-from-it-all break. Occupying a huge chunk of central France, it is a mysterious and spectacularly diverse land of dead volcanoes, rugged walls of lava, deep ravines, caves and plateaux.

The south is the wildest region, with the magnificent Cevennes mountains and the neighbouring, impressively desolate Causses – great arid limestone plateaux with gorges, chasms and caves. Communities in the south are small, rural and self-contained, and the only tourist resorts are those around the breathtaking gorges of the Tarn and Ardèche.

The north and eastern part of the Auvergne are the most populated areas, with the industrial city of Clermont-Ferrand, and the spas of Vichy – whose healing springs bring thousands seeking a health cure – and of Le Mont-Dore and La Bourboule. To the south-east corner is the extraordinarily located city of Le Puy, where jagged volcanic pinnacles loom above the red-roofed buildings. For sightseers the Auvergne has beautiful Romanesque churches, many of them built of the red, black, white and yellow local stone.

The Pyrénées

The Pyrénées stretch in an almost unbroken line from the Atlantic to the Mediterranean, forming a natural border with Spain. The landscape is varied, with the lush mountains of the Basque country in the west, the silent massifs of the centre and the harsh dry mountain plateaux of Catalonia in the east.

The mountains never reach the spectacular heights of the Alps, but they constitute excellent walking and climbing territory – cheaper than the Alps, with plenty of accommodation available in mountain refuges, unsophisticated village inns and campsites, and more cultural interest including the paintings in the caves of the Ariège, beautiful Romanesque churches and spectacular ruins of fortresses built to withstand cross-border invasions.

The peaks are not confined to expert hikers: some mountains, like the towering Canigou, are very easy going. The scenery is beautiful and seldom spoilt by development; one of the loveliest areas is the National Park in the Hautes Pyrénées, with its lakes, granite peaks and flourishing array of wild animals and wild flowers. The valleys of the Hautes Pyrénées are dotted with small spas which serve as ski resorts in the winter, many of them in beautiful settings. Luchon, a lively and fashionable spa, makes one of the most attractive bases.

On the western side, the coastline of cliffs, creeks and jagged rocks is short but beautiful and very popular (see *Atlantic coast*): the main resorts are the once highly fashionable Biarritz and picturesque St-Jean-de-Luz. Just inland lies the Basque country, with its green rounded hills, villages of flowery timbered cottages and lush green pastures crossed by fast-flowing rivers. Bayonne is the typically Basque capital of the area and St-Jean-Pied-de-Port is the prettiest of all the villages.

North of the mountains, Toulouse is rich in art and architecture, but is a big city lacking in charm. Lourdes has 400 hotels to accommodate the millions of pilgrims who go there each year, many of them in search of a cure. In Pau, the Boulevard des Pyrénées provides beautiful views of the snowy peaks.

Languedoc-Roussillon

The coast from Montpellier down to Perpignan on the Spanish border lacks the cachet of the Côte d'Azur to the east, but the combination of sandy beaches, sports, activities and long hours of sunshine is hard to beat. We have covered a small part of this area in *Provence and the south coast*.

Once a series of mosquito-infested swamps, the coast now offers some of the most modern and most colourful holiday complexes in France. The main resorts are the futuristic La Grande Motte, Cap d'Agde (in neo-Provençal style with a huge nudist section) and Argelès-sur-Mer, with a big beach and endless campsites.

Approaching the Spanish border the coastline changes abruptly from flat sands to a rocky shoreline, heralding 'the wild coast' of the Costa Brava. Along this stretch, Collioure is easily the most picturesque resort.

Various towns just inland provide cultural diversions from the coast – the well preserved walled town of Aigues-Mortes, Montpellier, Béziers, Narbonne and Perpignan. About an hour's drive west of Narbonne is the immaculately restored hilltop town of Carcassonne, one of the most popular excursions of the region.

Part III
En route

This part of *France Without Tears* is crammed with information to help you make important decisions about your trip – which way to cross the Channel, where to break your journey if you're heading for the south, and so on. The chapter on *Driving* offers reassurance as well as vital information for those new to Continental motoring. And the *Factfile* is a mini-encyclopaedia covering all aspects of travel in France.

Crossing the Channel

There can't be much doubt that motoring holidays on the Continent would be cheaper, less complicated and more popular if Britain were not separated from France by water. But they would be less fun, too. It's the Channel which has kept the French and British ways of life as distinct as they still are, and for us that's a key part of the appeal of travelling in France. The Channel crossing also gives the trip a sense of adventure and romance which simply does not arise at your average Continental frontier post. And it's only because the crossing involves spending some time at sea in 'no man's land', between here and there, that the Chancellor of the Exchequer makes you a present of the tax and duty on a carrier-bag-full of booze and tobacco.

Choosing your crossing

Deciding which cross-Channel service to use is blissfully simple for someone who is starting from a housing estate just outside Dover and aiming for a campsite just outside Calais. For most travellers to France, it isn't nearly that simple. The table of cross-Channel services over the page shows that there are 15 ways to get you and your car to France, and the pros and cons of each vary widely. There are basically six factors to take into account: crossing time, total travelling time, cost, fatigue, comfort and flexibility.

Crossing time matters only to those who are worried about seasickness and boredom; if you want to keep the risk of either to the absolute minimum, you will plump for one of the short crossings to Calais or Boulogne. The choice between travelling by hovercraft or conventional ferry is tricky: hovercraft are clearly quicker than ferries – 30 minutes for the crossing rather than 75 minutes or 90 minutes on the ferry – and are also less prone to unloading delays once you've arrived, because they hold relatively few cars and no trucks. But the constant up-and-down motion of hovercraft can induce seasickness in people who normally consider themselves immune.

The short crossings also have the advantage in flexibility: because of the high volume of traffic across the straits of Dover, there are over 50 ferry sailings a day between the English ports of Dover and Folkestone and the French ports of Calais and Boulogne – plus 20 hovercraft 'flights'. On most longer crossings there are only two or three crossings a day, on some only one. Provided you have a booking and get to the departure port well ahead of time, how many other sailings there are the same day is a matter of no concern; but it becomes relevant if you want to turn up at the port without a booking, or if you think you'll have difficulty keeping to schedule.

If you want to take into account the matter of comfort – by which we don't mean seasickness but the question of how civilised your surroundings are on-board – you've got a problem. Two problems, in fact: first that the ships used on a single route can vary quite a bit, and secondly that the introduction of new ships can radically change the picture. Up to 1986, for example, most travellers would agree that the Townsend Thoresen boats on the short crossings took some beating. But then up came Brittany Ferries with the smart *Duc de Normandie* on their new service from Portsmouth to Caen, and suddenly that was the comfortable way to cross the Channel. Other companies have plans for new ferries in the next few years – though they will be doing well if they can better the very civilised *Duc*.

For most people, the crunch comes with the final three factors – total travelling time, fatigue, and cost. How the different crossings compare will depend crucially on where you are starting from and where you want to end up. When thinking about cost, the key thing is to remember that the ferry fare is not the whole story. (If it were, the short crossings would naturally have the edge – though by a smaller margin than you might expect, particularly on peak-season crossings.) It's obvious that petrol needs to be taken into account, and the amount you will use in driving from Calais to Brittany, say, is not insignificant. But there may be other costs to weigh in the balance too. Motorway tolls may play a small part in the equation, but what is likely to be more important is overnight stops on the road. It is often possible to cut out the need for a stop in France by taking an overnight crossing which puts you on the quay early in the morning with the whole day ahead of you.

A common mistake beginners make when planning a trip to Paris or the south is to ignore the Normandy ports, thinking that they are only of interest to people heading for western France. Not so: Le Havre and Caen are both very sensible arrival points for such a trip (and Dieppe is only slightly less convenient), so the main question to ask yourself is whether Newhaven or Portsmouth are sensible ports of departure, given your home location.

At the port

As you approach your chosen departure port you will find signposts to the ferry. In most British ports access is fairly straightforward, although some of the signposted routes (very sensibly) take a roundabout way to the docks in order to keep traffic out of the town. If you have distant memories of getting lost in Dover and are planning to travel that way again, you may be relieved to know that a direct road into the eastern docks was built a few years ago, making access there as simple as could be.

There is always a terminal building at the port, through which passengers on foot are funnelled. But car passengers need not leave their cars, and

The table below shows, for each cross-Channel route, the operator, the approximate number of sailings per day and the crossing time.

Route	Operator	Daily sailings	Journey time
Plymouth–Roscoff	Brittany Ferries	1 to 3	6hr
Weymouth–Cherbourg	Sealink	1 or 2	4hr
Poole–Cherbourg	Truckline	1 or 2	4hr 30min
Portsmouth–St-Malo	Brittany Ferries	2	9hr
Portsmouth–Cherbourg	Townsend Thoresen	4	4hr 45min
Portsmouth–Caen	Brittany Ferries	1 or 2	5hr 45min
Portsmouth–Le Havre	Townsend Thoresen	3	5hr 45min
Newhaven–Dieppe	Dieppe Ferries	4	4hr 15min
Folkestone–Boulogne	Sealink	6	1hr 50min
Dover–Boulogne	Townsend Thoresen	8	1hr 45min
Dover–Boulogne	Hoverspeed	6	30min
Dover–Calais	Townsend Thoresen	15	1hr 15min
Dover–Calais	Sealink	16	1hr 30min
Dover–Calais	Hoverspeed	20	30min
Ramsgate–Dunkerque	Sally Line	5	1hr 45min

indeed at some ports are not really encouraged to do so. If you do make for the terminal in search of refreshment or relief, don't leave your car for too long. The ferry is unlikely to go without you, but unattended cars can cause jams if the queue starts moving.

Even after years of cross-Channel travel, it's difficult to quell the anxieties of the ferry queue. Why have we been put in this lane when everyone else is in that one? Why is that lane moving forward before ours? Will we get off sooner if we board first, or if we're last on? Why is there no sign of movement when it's only 30 minutes to sailing time? How do we know this is the right ferry? There is no answer to any of these questions, and all you can do is try to distract yourself by rehearsing a few French phrases or imagining the first lunch of the trip.

On the ferry

All Channel ferries these days are equipped with various ways for you to spend your time and money – provided by the ferry operators partly in the interests of keeping customers content, partly in the interests of adding to their fare revenues. You'll usually find a currency exchange office; a shop or two selling papers, a few books, maps, photographic film, sun-cream and so on; bars where the drinks are cheap because the alcohol is free of duty and tax; a self-service restaurant and usually a table-service restaurant as well; and possibly a variety of entertainment, mainly aimed at children, from space invaders to discos. There will also be open-air decks, from which you can watch the hectic sea traffic of the Channel, and (back inside) large areas of simple seating, usually arranged in rows, aircraft-style. Hovercraft contain only this sort of seating, to which you are confined (apart from trips to the loo).

Long crossings are much more civilised if you opt for a cabin. On night sailings, if you're lucky you'll get a good few hours' sleep; on day sailings, cabins are very cheap and it's comforting to know that you can have a snooze in peace or lie down to combat seasickness.

Finding your way around a large ship with all these different areas (which will be spread over two or three decks) can be confusing. Look out for drawings which show the ship in cross-section.

Arriving in France

If you're arriving in a particular French port for the first time, don't be put off by the fellow Brits who evidently know it inside-out and race off the dockside as if life itself depended on crossing the Dordogne before noon. The opposite is true: life itself depends on taking things very calmly at first. Be sure you have a plan of the port and a map of the surrounding area, and that you know quite clearly what towns you are heading for, so that you can make the most of the local signposting. In some ports, you can't go far wrong if you head the same way as all the other GB plates; but don't be surprised if you end up in a hypermarket car park.

Channel ports

Derek Allen

Whether you're planning a three-week holiday in southern France, a long weekend in Normandy or a quick hop across the Channel for lunch and a bit of shopping, it's well worth getting to know a bit about the French ports. For a short trip across it's vital to weigh up which port will suit you best – they vary widely. And on a longer holiday you can take a lot of the stress out of getting home if you plan to spend a few hours (or even a night) in the Channel port before embarking, avoiding the usual mad dash for the ferry. This chapter tells you what you need to know about shops, sights, hotels and restaurants; it takes the ports in alphabetical order.

Boulogne

If you're thinking about a day-trip to France, Boulogne is unquestionably a better proposition than Calais, even though the crossing takes about half an hour longer. There's a wider range of shops, the town is more compact and accessible, and the fact that the old upper town was largely unscathed in World War II certainly makes it more pleasing on the eye. Whereas Calais has a largely functional appearance, Boulogne is a port with at least some aesthetic charm.

Like Calais, Boulogne has always had close (but not always amicable) links with Britain. It was Julius Caesar's base for the conquest of England; and in 1803 Napoleon, who hoped to follow in Caesar's footsteps, also chose Boulogne for his planned invasion.

Shopping

The range of shops in Boulogne is excellent, from a huge, well-stocked hypermarket out of town to tiny specialist food shops in the centre. These central shops are only a short walk from the ferry terminal – coming from the hoverport, take the free bus.

The best shops are centred on the Grande Rue (which leads up to the Haute Ville, the upper town) and the Rue Thiers which runs off it. In the Grande Rue is **Derrien**, the best *charcuterie* in town, with sausages, cold meats, *foie gras*, stuffed snails and so on. **Idriss** has a superb display of crystallised fruits, nuts and spices. **Lugand** sells luscious home-made chocolates – all beautifully wrapped – and excellent *pâtisseries* which you can eat there. **Comtesse du Barry** has luxury foods including tins of *foie gras*, exotic jams, top-quality preserves and small hampers with meals for two.

In Rue Thiers, **Cornet d'Amour** is named for its mouthwatering speciality – cream-filled *choux* pastries. Perhaps the best known of all Boulogne's shops is **Philippe Olivier** at 43 – an essential experience for any lover of cheeses. With a choice of over 200 varieties, this is undoubtedly the best *fromagerie* in northern France – so be prepared to queue. Also available are farmhouse butter, yoghourts, walnut bread and creamy desserts in pots. If you're taking cheese back home, ask which ones will keep a day or so. On the same street, **Nouvelles Galeries** is Boulogne's largest department store – good for children's clothes, kitchenware and food.

Every Wednesday and Saturday (until about 4.00pm) the market is held in Place Dalton (off Grande Rue), taking over the square and spilling into the side streets. This is a scene with plenty of local colour: farmers' wives with baskets of eggs, stalls with herbs and spices, nuts and dried fruits, hot roasted chickens, cream and goat's cheeses, pumpkins, artichokes, garlic and chicory.

The **Champion** hypermarket, right on the front, is convenient but uninspiring. A far broader range of food, drink and kitchenware is stocked by **Auchan**, a few kilometres out along the road to St-Omer. It is particularly good for wines, beers, spirits and liqueurs.

What to see

The medieval centre or *Haute Ville* is surrounded by grassy ramparts and crowned by the grandiose domed cathedral of Notre-Dame. There are medieval gateways, cobbled streets, a 13th-century castle and fine views from the top of the ramparts.

Hotels and restaurants

The **Plage** 124 bvd Ste-Beuve £ ☎ 21 31 45 35 has cheap rooms and excellent food – a good place to pick if you want to eat and sleep under one roof close to the docks. (Closed Dec to Jan and Mon, restaurant closed Sun D out of high season.) The **Metropole** 51 rue Thiers ££ ☎ 21 31 54 30 is the most comfortable hotel in Boulogne; but, being in the centre, it can be noisy.

Boulogne is a major fishing port and there are plenty of places, in all price ranges, which serve good straightforward fish dishes. The **Matelote** 80 bvd Ste-Beuve ☎ 21 30 17 97 (opposite the casino) is one of the best restaurants in France, combining traditional and *nouvelle cuisine*. (Closed Dec to Jan, Sun D and Tue.) The central **Liégeoise**, in the centre at 10 rue Monsigny ☎ 21 31 61 15 is the next best restaurant in town. (Closed Sun D and Fri.) For something more down-to-earth, **Hamiot** 1 rue Faidherbe ☎ 21 31 44 20 is a café with a cheap upstairs restaurant, popular with both locals and day-trippers for fish; a good place to take children. On Place Dalton, the **Brasserie Alfred** and **Welsh Pub**, despite their names, are reliable restaurants for seafood.

South-east of Boulogne, 5km out in the uninspiring suburb of Pont-de-Briques, the **Hostellerie de la Rivière** ☎ 21 32 22 81 has a superb restaurant serving both *nouvelle* and *bourgeoise* cuisine. (Closed Aug, Sun D and Mon.)

Calais

For the British, Calais is no more than a functional ferry port, useful for stocking up with food and wine. Virtually the entire town was wiped out in World War II (ironically by British bombers) and with a few exceptions its buildings are modern and drab.

Shopping

Calais has a wide range of shops but they are not a patch on those of Boulogne. It's also less compact, with two shopping centres about 15 minutes apart – Place d'Armes in Calais Nord, and Calais Sud. The town is fairly spread out and you'll probably need to take the free bus service or a taxi from the port to either centre.

In Calais Nord the main street is Rue Royale. **Bellynk** is an excellent *charcuterie*, stocked with sausages, pâtés and vinegars. **R Cousin** has a tempting selection of fruit tarts and chocolates. **Coffea** sells coffee beans and exotic teas. For chocolates, head for **Au Royal**, **Outtiers** and **Leonidas** (which has wickedly extravagant fresh-cream chocolates from Belgium). **Descamps** has beautiful bed-linen and towels.

North of Rue Royale is the Place d'Armes, a car park surrounded by shops, and the scene of a market every Wednesday and Saturday. On the square is the **Gro** supermarket, two wine shops and, close by, the **Maison du Fromage**, with a comprehensive selection of cheeses – though nothing to compare to Philippe Olivier's shop in Boulogne. At **Caprice** you can sit and rest your feet for coffee and excellent cakes or chocolates. One of the best bakeries and *pâtisseries* is **JC Delahaye** in Rue des Thermes.

Calais Sud is generally better for shopping, and is more popular with the locals. A market (better than the one in Place d'Armes) is held every Thursday and Saturday morning at Place Crêvecoeur. The main shopping streets are Boulevard Lafayette leading off Place Crêvecoeur, and Boulevard Jacquard; this is the seedier side of Calais but the quality of the *charcuterie*, *pâtisserie* and fish should delight any food lover. Starting from the market place, the shops to head for are: **Gastronomie Sud-Ouest** for tins of *confit* and *foie gras*, **Eug Davélou** for *charcuterie*, **Cupillard** for kitchenware, **Ducard** for delicious cakes, chocolates and home-made ices, **l'Huitrière** for oysters, fish and prepared platters of freshly caught seafood.

The **Continent** hypermarket, about 3km from the ferry port on the Dunkerque road, is well signposted from the port, and there are buses from the station. But more enticing is the huge new **Mammouth** on the west side of Calais, out on the road to Boulogne. It is excellent for wines as well as food. As at a number of other hypermarkets, you are required to use a 10 franc piece in order to release a trolley, but a 2p piece will do the job just as well. Be prepared for long checkout queues at either hypermarket if you go at a busy time.

If a hotel has no restaurant, we say so at the end of the hotel description.

What to see

Calais is something of a cultural backwater, but the town museum provides at least some diversion from gluttonous pursuits. There are Rodin studies, some fine views of early Calais by leading British watercolourists and a section devoted to the Calais lace industry, which was imported from Nottingham. Calais also has a War Museum with a sobering record of the Nazi occupation.

The most distinctive and eccentric building in town is the 20th-century *hôtel de ville* (town hall) – built in Flemish Renaissance style. In front of it stands Rodin's moving memorial to the heroic burghers of Calais who were prepared to sacrifice their lives if Edward III spared the rest of the city (but were saved by the intervention of the king's French wife, Philippia).

Hotels and restaurants

The **Meurice** 5 rue Edmond Roche ££ ☎ 21 34 57 03 is the smartest and quietest hotel in town; furnishings are pleasantly old-fashioned – a good base, but ignore the restaurant. The slightly cheaper and smaller **Richelieu** 17 rue Richelieu ££ ☎ 21 34 61 60 is clean and comfortable; the **Sole Meunière** 53 rue de la Mer ££ ☎ 21 34 36 08 is a small, friendly hotel and the only one in town with sea-view rooms; the **Bellevue** 23 pl d'Armes ££ ☎ 21 34 53 75 is clean, reasonably priced and convenient for the ferry.

Calais offers an easy transition to French cuisine, with dishes like chicken and chips widely sold alongside a good range of more sophisticated and typically French fare. There are cafés, brasseries and plenty of fish restaurants serving the catch of the day. There are no outstanding restaurants but plenty that are good value.

The **Channel** 3 bvd de la Résistance ☎ 21 34 42 30 is generally regarded as the best restaurant in town and its traditional *cuisine bourgeoise* is excellent value, particularly if you opt for the cheap menu. (Closed Dec to Jan, Tue, Sun D and public hols D.) Next door, the **Sole Meunière** 1 bvd de la Résistance ☎ 21 34 43 01 is, as its name might suggest, strong on fish. (Closed Dec to Jan, one week Jun, Mon and Sun D out of season.) One of the best places to eat is the **Hôtel des Dunes** at Blériot-Plage ☎ 21 34 54 30 – about a 20-minute walk west of town along the sea front – offering imaginative food in plush surroundings. (Closed Mon.)

Back in the centre, inexpensive restaurants include the very popular but not always reliable **Coq d'Or** 31 pl d'Armes ☎ 21 34 79 05. (Closed Wed). Also worth a try is the **Côte d'Argent** plage de Calais ☎ 21 34 68 07, where the emphasis is on fish. (Closed D out of season, exc Fri and Sat.) Out of Calais, at Les Attaques, 9km south-east, the **Restaurant de la Gare** ☎ 21 36 32 28 is a small, amazingly good-value station restaurant. (Closed Aug and Mon.)

Caen

The newly-established Brittany Ferries service from Portsmouth to Caen has opened up this relatively unknown city and its surroundings, both to weekenders and those *en route* to Paris and the south. You arrive on the sands of Ouistreham, a popular beach resort and yachting harbour north of the city and not far from the fashionable resorts of the Côte Fleurie.

Caen's history goes back to the days of William (Conqueror-to-be) who founded the Abbaye aux Hommes as a penitence for a marriage frowned on by the Pope. The city of Caen was virtually wiped out in 1944 in the days following the D-Day landing, but miraculously its two beautiful abbeys survived, along with other churches and a handful of half-timbered houses. Otherwise the town is functional but dignified, with new buildings faced in pale mellow stone, spacious streets with stylish shops and tree-lined river walks. It's an excellent place for a winter break, with lots to see, excellent shopping and plenty of good restaurants. There are châteaux and manor-houses in the surrounding countryside and no less than three Michelin-starred restaurants in or near the town.

Shopping

Caen is one of the best shopping centres in northern France. The pedestrian streets and abundance of cafés make shopping easy and pleasurable. The best time to be there is Sunday morning when the colourful stalls of the main market spread from the Place Courtonne along the quayside.

The main shopping area is around the church of St-Pierre. This is where the main department stores are – Le Printemps, Nouvelles Galeries, Bon Marché etc – as well as a lot of smaller shops and elegant boutiques. An amazing *charcuterie* is Poupinet in the Rue St-Jean. Further along the same street Luet is another good *charcuterie*, also selling cheeses. *Pâtisseries* and chocolate shops abound, but the outstanding one is Heiz Legrix in the Place St-Pierre, which also sells bread.

What to see

Abbaye aux Hommes Striking, lofty-towered Romanesque church, perched on a hill in the city centre. The inside – a blend of Gothic and Renaissance – is remarkably simple. Duke William, the founder, was buried here but his body was pillaged in the French Revolution and only a thigh bone survives; a marble plaque marks the place of the tomb. The abbey buildings beside the church date from the 18th century.

Abbaye aux Dames A smaller, less pure version of the Abbaye aux Hommes, but interesting nonetheless. It was founded by William's wife, Matilda, who lies under a marble slab at the entrance of the choir. Don't miss the carvings on the capitals in the apse, including a surprising one of an elephant.

Château Attractively restored castle at the heart of the city, built by William and now housing the fine arts museum (including one of Manet's water lily paintings) and the local history museum.

> Most museums and historic buildings are closed on public holidays.

Church of St-Pierre A richly carved Gothic church at the foot of the castle; the elaborate ornamentation is striking after the relative simplicity of the great abbey churches.

Hotels and restaurants

At the port of Ouistreham, restaurants and hotels have been gearing themselves up to make the most of the flood of potential customers brought to their doors by the new Brittany Ferries service from Portsmouth. Already in the area there are some excellent eating places. The Normandie ££ ☎ 31 97 19 57 has clean, bright, reasonably priced bedrooms, and its restaurant is a good introduction to the region, offering Norman dishes (including lots of fish) cooked with flair. 5km south of Ouistreham at Bénouville the Manoir d'Hastings ££££☎ 31 44 62 43 is a perfectly delightful old priory with extravagant menus and highly competent cuisine; also 11 luxury rooms. Booking is essential. (Closed Sun D and Mon out of season.)

The best place to eat in Caen itself is La Bourride 15 rue Vaugueux ☎ 31 93 50 76. A small, elegant restaurant in a picturesque old house, with a very high standard of cooking and prices to match. (Closed two weeks Aug, Sun and Mon.) Another up-market restaurant is Les Echevins 36 rue Ecuyère ☎ 31 86 37 44, a former hotel converted into an intimate bistro. (Closed two weeks Jul, Mon L and Sun).

The Relais des Gourmets 15 rue Geôle £££ ☎ 31 86 06 01 is a small, elegantly furnished hotel opposite the castle. Its restaurant is among the best in town – and the most expensive. The Moderne 116 bvd Mar-Leclerc £££ ☎ 31 86 04 23 offers a reasonable standard of accommodation and its Quatre Vents restaurant is competent, but you need a degree in map-reading to find the hotel in Caen's labyrinthine one-way system. (Closed Sun D out of season.)

Caen lacks cheap and cheerful hotels but the modern Quatrans 17 rue Gemare ££ ☎ 31 86 25 57 is clean, central and relatively inexpensive.

Cherbourg

Big, busy and industrial, Cherbourg does not have much to detain British tourists keen to head south. The best thing about it is the shopping.

Shopping

The best food shops are in the Grande Rue, near the old fish market. There are three excellent *charcuteries*: **De Poittevin**, **Collette** and **A La Renommé**, superb *pâtisseries* at **L'Huilley** and top-quality coffee from **Caffea**. The main market is held on Tuesday and Saturday on the Place du Général de Gaulle. The more permanent attraction of the square is the *charcuterie*, **Laulier**, with a wide range of meats, salads, ready-made dishes and barrels of olives.

The best bet for wine is the **Caves du Roy** in the Rue Tour Carrée, where you can taste before you buy. The **Continent** hypermarket is just behind the town centre and not far from the ferry terminal.

Hotels and restaurants

The best hotel is the comfortable, modern **Mercure** Gare Maritime £££ ☎ 33 44 01 11. The cheaper **Louvre** 2 rue H-Dunant ££ ☎ 33 53 02 28 is better value. (No restaurant.)

There is not a wide choice of highly regarded restaurants and only one manages to get itself into Michelin. This is the **Grandgousier** 21 rue de l'Abbaye ☎ 33 53 19 43, a charming small restaurant with a garden. (Closed two weeks Apr, three weeks Sep, Sat L and Sun.) Just down the road at 27 the **Pêcherie** is excellent value for fish, but probably the best restaurant in town is the **Plouc** 59 rue au Blé ☎ 33 53 67 64, a smart rustic restaurant serving sophisticated dishes. Booking is essential. (Closed two weeks Aug, Sat L and Sun.)

> If a hotel has no restaurant, we say so at the end of the hotel description.

Dieppe

Lively and civilised, with a distinctly French character, Dieppe is far more than a simple ferry port. The range of shops and restaurants is excellent, and the town itself, despite substantial damage during the last war, retains some old quarters which have a certain old-fashioned charm. There's a fine long pebble beach (a great attraction for the English in the early 1900s), and behind it a massive medieval castle.

The deep, narrow harbour pierces the heart of the town, and once on the quayside you're only a minute or two away from the main shopping street, the Grande Rue. On a Saturday morning, the market spreads over the whole area, stalls spilling into side streets, stacked with all the fruits of the land. It is one of the best and biggest markets in Normandy. Food is fresh from the farm: there are huge slabs of butter, big bowls of cream, fresh curd and cream cheese. There are barrows of glistening fish, and a vast variety of vegetables from pumpkins and artichokes to baby leeks and blanched dandelion leaves.

Shopping

Access from the ferry terminal is easy as most shops are concentrated in the central, pedestrianised streets close by. The best shopping streets are Grande Rue, Rue de la Barre and Rue St-Jacques, all of which meet at the famous and much-photographed Café des Tribunaux. Once the haunt of literati and leading famous French impressionists, even now it tends to attract aspiring artists as well as foot-sore tourists.

The Grande Rue has the best of all the shops. **A Eurieult**, **J Buquet** and **Rôtisserie Parisienne** are good *charcuteries*. **Grisch** is the best *pâtisserie* and good for chocolates, too. When you reach the Café des Tribunaux, you'll see opposite in the Rue de la Barre the **Duchesse de Berry** with *pâtisseries*, chocolates and 30 different types of ice cream. In Rue St-Jacques there are good cake shops, and super cheeses at **Claude Olivier** (the father of Philippe

Olivier of the amazing cheese shop in Boulogne) – you also find good wine offers here. For fish, head for the **Municipal Poissonnerie** on the quay where fish is sold straight from the boats, or **Crustaces** just opposite.

The **Mammouth** hypermarket is on the outskirts of town, on the Rouen road.

What to see

Castle Medieval stronghold of massive proportions overlooking the sea front. The lofty rooms house the Museum of Dieppe – marine relics, Peruvian pottery and fascinating carved ivories which were made by local craftsmen in the Middle Ages. Other exhibits are the paintings by turn-of-the-century British artists and about a hundred prints of the cubist Braque, who used to spend his summers in Dieppe.

Hotels and restaurants

The best hotels in Dieppe are along the sea front, behind the beach. The old-fashioned **Windsor** 18 bvd Verdun ££ ☎ 35 84 15 23 is a bit sedate but comfortable and serves competent food. (Restaurant closed Sun D out of season.) The **Select** 1 rue Toustain ££ ☎ 35 84 14 66, near the castle and casino, is a clean, quite elegant base – but beware of some noisy rooms. (No restaurant.)

The working fishing fleet based at Dieppe means lots of good fish restaurants, from tiny oyster bars on the quayside to smart restaurants serving more sophisticated fare. The majority of places serve large helpings of good, plain fish and seafood, and most of them are very good value. The best of the fish restaurants along the Quai Henri-IV is **L'Armorique** ☎ 35 84 28 14. (Closed first two weeks Jun, last two weeks Oct, Sun D and Mon.) **La Marmite Dieppoise** 8 rue St-Jean ☎ 35 84 24 26 is a small, cheerful restaurant serving the dish of the same name – a big bowl of seafood in a creamy sauce – plus other Norman specialities. (Closed late Jun and early Jul, Thu D, Sun D and Mon.) Others worth trying include the **Normandy** 16 rue Duquesne ☎ 35 84 27 16 for fish

and Norman specialities in rustic surroundings. (Closed Mon).

At Martin-Eglise, 6.5km south-east on the D1, the **Auberge du Clos Normand** ££ ☎ 35 82 71 01 is a delightful rustic restaurant with 9 rooms in converted stables. Good provincial cooking, but rather high prices. (Hotel closed winter, restaurant closed mid-winter, Mon D and Tue.)

Dunkerque

The ferry service to Dunkerque actually pitches up a good 20-minute drive west of the town centre and the main beach. This is less inconvenient than it sounds for day-trippers intent only on pillaging the nearest hypermarket, which is only a five-minute bus-ride from the port. Those who venture further into Dunkerque find there isn't an awful lot for them to see or do. With big refineries, chemical plants and a vast port (the third biggest in the country), it's not a very promising introduction to France.

For those travelling further south, Dunkerque's principal attraction is that it offers a quick and easy access to the French motorway system (much more rapid than Calais).

Shopping

Dunkerque isn't one of the best ferry ports for shoppers, though you will find a range of shops specialising in *charcuterie*, cheese, *pâtisserie* etc and the **Codec** supermarket in the centre is very good. The Grande Synthe shopping complex west of the town includes a well-stocked **Auchan** hypermarket.

What to see

Dunkerque's show-piece is its harbour and shipyard. Enthusiasts can take a 90-minute boat tour around the docks. The city still has a handful of old buildings, including the Town Hall and Church of St-Eloi; there's also a museum of contemporary art where over 7,000 canvases and sculptures are displayed in a futuristic museum and the gardens around it.

Hotels and restaurants

There are no very charming hotels in Dunkerque and the good restaurants lie out of the centre. **La Meunerie** ☎ 28 26 01 80, close to Teteghem, 6km south-east, is a modern Michelin-starred restaurant with elegant décor serving first-class food at highish prices. (Closed mid-winter, Sun D and Mon.) At Cappelle-la-Grande, 9km south of Dunkerque, **Le Bois de Chêne** ☎ 28 64 21 80 is good for regional dishes and has excellent-value menus. (Closed two weeks Aug, Sun D and Sat.)

Le Havre

It's hardly surprising that ferry passengers make a quick dash out of this grey, gargantuan seaport. Virtually the whole town was wiped out in September 1944, and only a tiny fraction of the old town survives. Today Le Havre is France's second largest port, largely thanks to Auguste Perret, pioneer of reinforced concrete construction, who rebuilt the entire city with giant blocks, towers, big squares and streets giving wide perspectives. The hotels are look-alike tower blocks, the restaurants rarely open at the times you want to eat and there's a notable dearth of open-air cafés.

Shopping

The town is very spread out, but if you have a car you can do all your shopping under one roof by heading for the Halles Centrales, behind Place Gambetta. Parking is easy here and you can push a trolley around the covered market. You can get fruit, vegetables, fish, bread, groceries – and the best cheeses in town at **Cheinisse**. **Nicolas** usually have special wine offers.

The Place Gambetta has specialist shops like **Lefèvre**, the best *charcuterie* in town – there are always queues here for the superb selection of cold meats, pâtés and ready-made dishes. It sells wine, too. In the same area are other specialist shops (Belgian chocolates etc) and the big department stores.

There are two good hypermarkets:

Mammouth at Montivilliers (about 8km north-east on the D925 to Fécamp) and the even better **Auchan** in the Haute Ville. This is a vast complex with a huge range of foods and wine.

What to see

Musée des Beaux-Arts Very close to the ferry terminal (handy if you've got a few hours to kill) – a remarkable building, made entirely of glass and metal, with the emphasis on space and light. The works of impressionists and post-impressionists include Normandy scenes by Raoul Dufy (who was born here) and a collection by Boudin.

Hotels and restaurants

Hotels are fairly dull and functional. The most comfortable is the modern, efficient **Bordeaux** 147 rue L-Brindeau £££ ☎ 35 22 69 44. The much cheaper **Charolais** 134 cours de la République £ ☎ 35 25 29 34 is not very impressive from the outside, but pleasant enough inside, and conveniently placed for the ferry.

If time is not pressing, there are pleasant alternatives to staying in Le Havre itself – Honfleur, Caudebec and Pont-Audemer, all of which are within reasonable reach of the port, offer much more attractive accommodation (see *Normandy*).

There are plenty of cheap eating places in the town but not many with a lot of character. For good value, try the restaurants in the Quai Michel Féré. The best place to eat used to be the **Petite Auberge** 32 rue Ste-Adresse ☎ 35 46 27 32 – a small rustic restaurant; but it has changed hands and standards may have dropped. (Closed Aug, Sun D and Mon.) In the same area **Le Beau Séjour** 3 pl Clemenceau, Ste-Adresse ☎ 35 46 19 69 is useful to know about if you're in Le Havre on a Sunday when practically everywhere else is closed; good fish is served at tables overlooking the water-front. Another good place for fish is the **Cambridge** 90 rue Voltaire ☎ 35 42 50 24. (Closed mid-Jul to mid-Aug, Sat L, Sun and public hols.)

Roscoff

Roscoff has links with Britain that go back far further than the founding of the ferry service. In 1387 the English endeared themselves to the locals by burning down the town, and in 1548 the five-year-old Mary Queen of Scots landed here, on her way to Paris to be engaged to the Dauphin.

Today Roscoff is one of the most attractive ferry ports, with a bustling centre of flower-decked streets flanked by grey, granite houses. Apart from being a ferry port, it's a popular seaside resort, a fishing harbour (lots of lobster and crayfish) and a major centre for vegetables – particularly onions, a lot of which get shipped to Britain by Brittany Ferries (which is part-owned by a co-operative of Breton farmers). The local beach isn't wonderful but Roscoff is a good base for excursions to the adjacent coastlines with their wide, sandy bays.

Shopping

The town has a reasonable selection of small specialist shops, mainly concentrated in the Rue Gambetta, the Rue Revéillère and Rue Jules-Ferré where you'll find two outstanding charcuteries, Inizan and Le Duc. There are no hypermarkets in Roscoff itself, but motorists need not worry – there are branches of Rallye and Codec (and other big stores) 4km away at St-Pol-de-Léon.

What to see

Charles Perez aquarium Extensive collection of fish and other sea creatures, plus an exhibition of marine biology.
Notre-Dame-de-Kroaz-Baz Gothic church with a remarkable Renaissance belfry and an elaborate high altar piece.

In hotel and restaurant descriptions, D means dinner and L means lunch.

Le Grand Figuier (6 rue des Capucins) Giant fig tree planted by monks in about 1625. One year's crop of figs from its branches, propped up by granite columms, can amount to as much as 400kg – over a third of a ton.
Ile de Batz Boats leave hourly in summer for this flat, sandy island of fishermen and farmers.

Hotels and restaurants

The Gulf Stream rue Marquise-de-Kergériou, Roskogoz ££ ☎ 98 69 73 19 is a modern, comfortable and quiet hotel lying just outside the centre behind a beach, with huge windows overlooking the garden. Rooms are very good value, and its restaurant, specialising in fish, is the best in the immediate area. (Closed winter.) The Brittany bvd Ste-Barbe £££ ☎ 98 69 70 78 is smaller and slightly more expensive, but again quiet and comfortable and with the advantage of a pool; there are lovely views of the garden and sea. (No restaurant, closed winter.) In the centre of the town, between the church and the sea front, is the Talabardon pl Eglise ££ ☎ 98 61 24 95 – larger and cheaper, with a welcoming dining room. (Closed winter, restaurant closed Sun D.)

There are several attractive restaurants in the town which are of no great culinary distinction but offer good value – from the cheap and very cheerful crêperie of Les Korrigans to the more proper Chardons Bleus near the church. But for excellent cooking with more atmosphere than the Gulf Stream can offer, head down to St-Pol-de-Léon and the Auberge de la Pomme d'Api 49 rue Verderel ☎ 98 69 04 36 – a charming 16th-century house in the town centre, with log fires and candles.

St-Malo

It is hard to believe that this citadel, with its sturdy 13th-century ramparts and grey granite houses was almost entirely destroyed in the closing stages of World War II. The city walls rise dramatically out of the sea; within them, the twisting cobbled streets are inevitably commercialised, but they still retain a beguiling charm. From the ramparts there are beautiful views, with the bay on one side and the town on the other. You can climb down on to the beach and, at low tide, walk across to the tiny deserted islands of Petit Bé and Grand Bé, where the writer Châteaubriand (chiefly remembered, at least by the British, for the way he liked his steak) is buried.

Just inland from the citadel lies the new town of St-Malo, which has spread to join with the resorts of St-Servan and Paramé – both of which have good beaches.

Shopping

Shopping may not be the big business in St-Malo that it is some more easterly ports – the potential for day-trip shopping raids is rather limited by the crossing from Portsmouth, which at 9hr is the longest on the Channel – but there is no shortage of good shops. Near the centre of the new town is a big **Continent** hypermarket, while in the old town are countless specialist shops including some excellent *charcuteries* and *pâtisseries* – several of the latter also operating as attractive *salons de thé*. There is a good market, dominated by fish and seafood, in the old town every day except Sunday.

What to see

Castle Massive fortress housing the city museum (history of the port, covering the privateers and other great sons of the city) and the Quic-en-Groigne wax museum.

Cathedral Dating from 12th to the 18th century, with some stunning stained glass.

Hotels and restaurants

Two of the most attractive small hotels are in the quiet suburb of St-Servan-sur-Mer, about 2km from the old town. **La Korrigane** 39 rue le Pomellec £££ ☎ 99 81 65 85 is an elegant old house. (No restaurant, closed winter.) The **Valmarin** 7 rue Jean XXIII £££ ☎ 99 81 94 76 is an extremely civilised modern hotel, converted from an 18th-century house, with lovely gardens. (No restaurant, closed mid-winter.) There are plenty of good-value fish restaurants in the area.

Within the town walls, too, there are plenty of reasonably priced eating places, most of them serving straightforward fish dishes. Of the more sophisticated restaurants, **L'Astrolabe** 8 rue Cordiers ☎ 99 40 36 82 serves good fish, with the emphasis on *nouvelle cuisine*. (Closed mid-Jan to Mid-Feb and Tue out of season.) In contrast the Michelin-starred the **Duchesse Anne** 5 pl Guy La Chambre ☎ 99 40 85 33 is solidly traditional, both in décor and food. (Closed Dec to Jan and Wed.) A cheaper alternative to these two is **Le Chalut** 8 rue Corne de Cerf ☎ 99 56 71 58, a small lively restaurant in the centre with good fish. (Closed Oct and Wed.)

Getting to the south

Michael Long

For people heading for the south without time to spare – or with young
children – motorway travel is a necessity which unhappily means
bypassing most of inland France. If you're in this hard-pressed category,
it's still worth trying to make the journey to the south an enjoyable affair of
two or three days, stopping *en route* at quiet country inns to absorb the
pleasures of rural France.

Most people get well south of Paris before detouring. If you make an
early start from the ferry and don't linger over lunch, you'll probably get
well into Burgundy and maybe as far as Beaune for an overnight stop. The
places we've recommended in this section all lie within reasonable striking

distance from the main motorways going south: historic sights, outstanding or good-value restaurants, wine-tasting routes, small charming hotels, and towns and areas which are particularly interesting – such as Beaune or Beaujolais. You'll find most of the motorway information, including how to cope with the tolls, in *Driving in France*.

Getting past Paris

For the newcomer to Continental motoring, getting past Paris is a daunting prospect. In principle it's easy: the centre is bypassed by a motorway ring-road called the Périphérique, equivalent to London's M25 orbital motorway. But the Périphérique is very close to the city centre, which means that the junctions where it meets roads out of Paris are very close together. Add to this the fact that the traffic goes extremely fast (except in the rush hour, when it barely moves), and the net result is like something out of a Mad Max movie.

What the Périphérique requires above all else is confidence; if you have it (and preferably a competent navigator to spot your exit, too) you will have no problem; if you lack it, you should arrange to bypass Paris altogether.

Gazetteer

This section, unlike other gazetteers in this guide, is arranged geographically – from north to south.

Melun

The sumptuous château of **Vaux-le-Vicomte** stands some way north-east of the town, among immaculate gardens and fountains. It was built by Nicolas Fouquet, Louis XIV's finance minister, and so impressed the king that it became the model for his palace at Versailles. It's less crowded than nearby Fontainebleau, and rather more relaxing to visit. There are no guided tours, but hand-outs in English are available.

Fontainebleau

One of the grandest châteaux of France, Fontainebleau is built in an enormous variety of rich styles. It was established by François I in the 16th century as a magnificent court and lavishly decorated by leading Italian artists. For years it housed kings, queens and mistresses; the boudoir of Marie-Antoinette is one of the most exquisite

rooms. Guided tours are optional – you can wander around independently.

Hotel
The **Moulin** ££ ☎ (1)60 96 67 89 at Flagy, 22km east of Fontainebleau, is well worth the longish detour from the motorway. It is a beautifully converted old mill, with a dining room (excellent food) overlooking gardens and a stream, and ten very attractively furnished rooms. There's a friendly atmosphere, and a warm welcome from the English-speaking owner. (Closed two weeks Sep, Sun D and Mon.) See also hotels under Barbizon.

Barbizon

With hotels, restaurants and expensive antique shops, Barbizon bears little resemblance to the original bohemian hamlet of 19th-century landscape painters; and Millet's favourite view is now cut through by the A6 motorway. Nevertheless it's still quaint with its galleries and small museums; a good place to stay overnight and also to enjoy a meal.

Hotels and restaurants

Hotels range from simple places without restaurant to the very expensive **Bas-Bréau £££££ ☎** (1) 60 66 40 05, whose Michelin-starred restaurant specialises in wild duck and Scottish grouse. (Closed mid-winter). The best bet for food and lodgings is the **Hostellerie Clé d'Or £££ ☎** (1) 60 66 40 96, a charming old inn. (Closed Sun D and Mon except hols.) If this is full (which it usually is), try the **Alouettes ££ ☎** (1) 60 66 41 98 in quiet gardens close to the centre: a slightly eccentric place but reasonably priced.

Nemours

Nemours is these days only worthy of note for its service station – one of the best along the A6, with good catering facilities, a restaurant, shop selling regional specialities and a tourist office which will provide you with pamphlets on the area, book hotels (for a fee) and change foreign currency.

Sens

The pride of this Burgundian town is St-Etienne: the oldest Gothic cathedral in France. Begun in 1130, it is still has a Romanesque look. The highlight inside is the medieval stained glass, parts of which illustrate scenes from the life of Thomas-à-Becket who spent several years of exile at nearby Pontigny.

Auxerre

This beautifully sited town (pronounced 'orsaire') extends along the tree-lined left bank of the river Yonne, its churches rising majestically above the medieval timbered houses. Outstanding among its sights are the fine cathedral, with a Romanesque crypt and beautiful stained glass, and the Abbaye Saint-Germain, the oldest monument of Auxerre with a 9th-century crypt and frescoes.

Restaurant

6km out of Auxerre, on the D163, **La Petite Auberge ☎** 85 53 80 08, is in a quiet spot by the River Yonne, and serves some of the best food in the area; the emphasis is on simple, light dishes – it serves excellent local wines. (Closed early July, Sun D, Mon and public hols.)

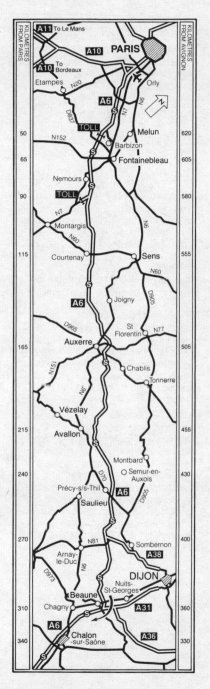

Noyers

This wonderfully picturesque village 15km SE of Chablis is overlooked by most guidebooks (and so tourists). It is a beautiful cluster of crooked, half-timbered houses, arches and arcades, flanking narrow cobbled streets.

Mailly-le-Château

An unremarkable village, 30km S of Auxerre, with an excellent hotel.

Hotel

Le Castel pl Eglise ££ ☎ 86 40 43 06 is a *Relais du Silence* with a warm welcome (excellent English spoken), good classical food and modest prices. Rooms are quiet apart from the chimes of the Town Hall clock. (Closed winter and Tue evening and Wed off-season.)

Vézelay

Of all the churches in Burgundy, the Basilica of Ste-Madeleine on the hilltop of medieval Vézelay is perhaps the finest, with its view over the sweeping forests of the Morvan and extraordinarily powerful interior. The journey across the rolling Burgundian hills and down the delightful valley of the Cure is worthy of a detour in itself. The village itself is beautifully preserved and very attractive despite the heavy emphasis on tourism.

Hotels and restaurants

For a true gastronomic experience you can't do better than the Espérance ££££ ☎ 86 33 20 45 at St-Père (3km from Vézelay at the foot of the hill) generally agreed to be one of the finest restaurants in France. The dining room is elegant and light, overlooking beautiful gardens and there are 17 stylish rooms. (Closed four days June, restaurant closed Wed L and Tue.) The Poste et Lion d'Or £££ ☎ 86 33 21 23 at the foot of old Vézelay is a comfortable and traditional hotel with restaurant. (Closed winter.)

Avallon

This area is known as '*une bonne étape*', a good stopping off place for food, hotels and sights. The most attractive part of Avallon is the old centre with cobbled streets and lime-lined ramparts which give splendid views over the terraces and wooded hills around the town.

Hotels

The most distinguished hotel is the Hostellerie de la Poste ££££ ☎ 86 34 06 12 in the centre of town. There are 24 exceptionally comfortable rooms and an elegant Michelin-starred restaurant; you pay handsomely for both. (Closed winter.) About 5km outside Avallon there are two particularly quiet, secluded hotels, both converted mills, tucked away in the leafy Vallée du Cousin. The Moulin des Ruats £££ ☎ 86 34 07 14 is the smarter of the two. (Closed winter, Tue L and Mon.) The Moulin des Templiers ££ ☎ 86 34 10 80 is cheaper and more intimate; rooms are very small but the atmosphere and the delightful riverside setting make up for that. Good breakfasts but no restaurant. (Closed winter and Sat.)

Semur-en-Auxois

Semur is a particularly fine town, set on a promontory above the River Armançon and dominated by the massive medieval towers of its castle. Steep streets lined with medieval houses lead up to the church of Notre-Dame and there are beautiful views of the valley from the lime-lined ramparts.

Saulieu

For centuries, Saulieu's reputation has rested on gastronomy. Nowadays the excesses of the past (thick cream-and-butter sauces and the speciality of a pâté made with 16 types of game) have given way to lighter fare. The Côte d'Or ££££ ☎ 80 64 07 66, with two Michelin stars, places emphasis on fish and vegetables – and serves snails with nettles, rather than butter and garlic. (Closed Wed L and Tue out of season.)

£	up to £15
££	£15 to £25
£££	£25 to £45
££££	£45 to £70
£££££	£70 to £100
£££££!	more

Châteauneuf-en-Auxois

You can see this exceptionally picturesque medieval village from the motorway: it stands high up on a hill about 7km from Pouilly-en-Auxois.

Hotel

The **Hostellerie du Château** ££ ☎ 80 33 00 23 is an ex-presbytery, attached to the village château. Downstairs it is rustic and charming, with old stone walls, a big fireplace in the bar and a beamed dining room. Bedrooms are small and rather simple. Exceptionally popular place, despite the fact it is not in Michelin. (Closed winter, Mon evening and Tue out of season.)

Fontenay

The superb Cistercian abbey at Fontenay (6km NE of Montbard) narrowly escaped demolition during the Revolution. The revolutionaries chased off the last monks, and the purchaser of the abbey in 1791 had the bright idea of transforming it into a paper-mill, and saving at least the shell. Paper was churned out until 1906, when remodelling of the building led to the rediscovery of the abbey, intact.

Dijon

The capital of Burgundy and the former seat of the great Burgundian dukes, Dijon is today a particularly attractive city, with a lot more to offer than mustard. You can see almost everything on foot: there are cobbled streets, timbered houses, Gothic churches (don't miss the gaping gargoyles on the façade of Notre-Dame church) and gleaming tiled roofs. It's an excellent centre for shopping, with attractive pedestrian streets and smart shop-windows.

The main sight is the **Ducal Palace**, off the graceful Place de la Libération. The palace houses the Museum of Fine Arts, a magnificent collection of paintings, and claims to be France's second largest museum after the Louvre; but the crowning masterpieces are the tombs of the great dukes, Phillip the Bold and John the Fearless, with their exquisitely carved processions of hooded alabaster mourners.

Hotels

The **Hotel du Nord** 2 rue de la Liberté ££ ☎ 80 30 58 58 is a convenient stop, west of centre. Rooms are on the whole comfortable and civilised, but those without bath are more noisy and basic. The cuisine of its Restaurant de la Porte Guillaume is more than competent, and there are plenty of Burgundian specialities. For a quiet, rural base not far from the city there is the **Hostellerie du Val-Suzon** ££ ☎ 80 35 60 15, 15km north-east of Dijon at Fontaine-les-Dijon, Val-Suzon. It is peacefully set in a tiny village and has a friendly, rural atmosphere. Food is good and the emphasis is on Burgundian specialities. (Closed Wed.) If the hotel is full, as it often is, you can always try the spruce, modern little **Chalet de la Fontaine aux Geais** ££ ☎ 80 35 61 19 up the road, which is even quieter, but with less atmosphere. (No restaurant; closed winter and Wed.)

Beaune

An important wine town and a beautiful city, it is not surprising that Beaune has become one of the favourite stopping-off places on the way to the south.

Behind Beaune's daunting traffic-choked circle of ramparts lies one the most exquisite town centres in France. The city's showpiece is the Hôtel-Dieu, a medieval hospital which still functions as a home for the aged and is maintained with proceeds from the yearly Beaune wine auction. Inside the courtyard, the beautiful polychrome-tiled roof, pointed gables and spires, wooded galleries and ancient well combine to make a picturesque ensemble. A guided tour covers the 'paupers' ward', the medieval kitchens, the pharmacy, a museum with beautiful tapestries and the Last Judgement – a superb painting by Roger van der Weyden.

The town has many wine-tasting cellars and a profusion of lavishly stocked food shops. Such are the temptations of the place you are unlikely to come away empty-handed or sober-headed: particularly if you discover the Maison du Vin, very close to the Hôtel-Dieu, where you can sample as many as

37 wines, among them some of the finest Burgundies, all for less than a fiver. You can stay as long as you want – though the lack of toilets imposes its own time limit!

You may well be tempted to follow two of the greatest wine routes in Europe: the Côte de Beaune and the Côte de Nuits. The names of the villages read like a prestigious wine list – Gevrey-Chambertin, Vosne-Romanée, Vougeot, Nuits-St-Georges – but the small and rather modest villages hardly live up to the fame of the wine they produce. Various châteaux are open to the public, among them Clos de Vougeot and Corton-André at Aloxe-Corton, Meursault and Pommard.

Hotel
Unfortunately there is an acute shortage of reasonably priced hotels in Beaune. Unless you want to spend a small fortune on accommodation it's wise to stay outside the town. The obvious place is **Hotel Parc** £ ☎ 80 22 22 51 at Levernois, 5km south-east of Beaune, which is pleasantly rural, friendly and simple. There is no restaurant so you can eat in Beaune itself. Reserve early as this one features in practically every guidebook.

Tournus
Lying between the motorway and a sleepy stretch of the river Saône, Tournus is a pleasant town of cobbled streets, dominated on all sides by the twin towers of its beautifully preserved abbey church. The interior of the church is remarkably beautiful – bathed in warm light and supported by vast pillars of pink stone.

Cluny
Founded in 910, Cluny became the most illustrious and powerful abbey in the Christian world, its abbots wielding more influence than that of popes and kings. Today only the ruins of the main southern transept remain, dominated by a lonely belfry. It was the monks of Cluny who planted the first vines of the Mâconnais. Today there are plenty of small, friendly tasting places in the area; there is usually a small charge for each glass

you drink but there is no compulsion to buy larger quantities.

Hotel
The place to stay in Cluny, if you can afford it, is the **Bourgogne** £££ ☎ 85 59 00 58, almost opposite the abbey. The atmosphere is civilised, the rooms comfortable and the food is consistently good. (Closed winter, Wed L and Tue out of season.)

Service area
Aire de St-Albain-la-Salle This is one of the best-equipped service areas along the motorway, with a tourist office which will reserve a hotel, 24-hour money changing facilities, various restaurants (one with a *routier* menu), a hotel with a pool and a wide choice of regional crafts and food for sale.

Beaujolais region
The rolling green vineyards of Beaujolais rarely detain motorists heading south along the motorway – a pity, as this is lovely countryside. The joy of the vineyards lies not only in the pleasure of wine-tasting but also the views from the steep twisting roads of gloriously green hillsides carpeted in unbroken rows of vines. With its earthy life and ruddy-faced locals clad in overalls and caps, Beaujolais is the essence of rural France. You can taste and buy everywhere, from cooperatives, cellars, wine estates and even private houses by the road.

Lyon
Lyon, the third biggest city in the country, is often referred to as the Manchester of France. Its size and industrial sprawl deter most tourists but the old quarter on the right bank of the Saône has distinct Parisian charm. Narrow streets are lined with beautiful Renaissance houses; there are galleries, shops of old books and antiques, art nouveau cafés and bistros crammed with old world atmosphere. Less elegant is the Basilique de Notre-Dame on a steep hill above the old town: a great 19th-century pilgrimage basilica with all the vulgarity but none of the unity of Montmartre's Sacré-Coeur. The original town of Lyon

was set on top of this hill and you can still see the remains of two Roman theatres and a museum devoted to Gallo-Roman Lyon. The motorway goes into the heart of Lyon, and passing through can take anything from 10 to 90 minutes, depending on the traffic.

Restaurants

The Lyonnais region is world-famous for its good food; memories of a meal in one of its smart restaurants may well linger a lifetime. The region is peppered with Michelin stars but there are four restaurants with the highest accolade of three stars, and two are close to Lyon itself – **Paul Bocuse** ☎ 78 22 01 40, 12km north at Collonges-au-Mont-d'Or, and **Alain Chapel** ☎ 78 91 82 02 at Mionnay, 20km north-east. (Closed Tue L and Mon exc public holidays.)

Pérouges

This impeccable medieval village is set on a hilltop north-east of Lyon. It has picture-postcard beauty, with medieval houses, arcades and steep, roughly cobbled winding streets.

Hotels

The **Hostellerie Vieux Pérouges ££££** ☎ 74 61 00 88, *the* hotel of Pérouges, is comfortable but expensive (the annex is cheaper). It is famous for *galettes*, served either with drinks (to bar customers as well as guests) or with lashings of cream as a dessert. (Closed Thu L and Wed out of high season.) Better value than the hostellerie is **Claude Lutz ££** ☎ 74 61 06 78 at neighbouring Meximieux. The emphasis is on food, both regional and classical (it is Michelin-starred), but there are also 16 reasonably priced rooms. (Closed ten days July, Sun D and Mon.)

Vienne

The industrial outskirts of the town are off-putting, so it's not surprising that most people drive straight past Vienne and its ancient sites. It has a strategic position commanding a gorge of the Rhône, and from the days of the Roman conquest until the early Middle Ages it was a more important city than Lyon. A Roman theatre, Roman temple, and the

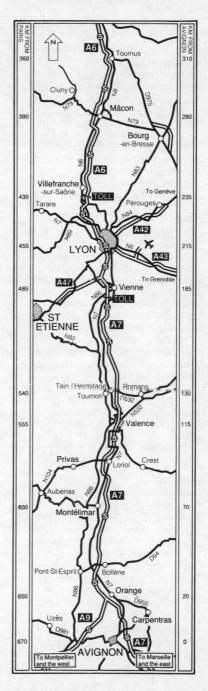

'pyramid' – a sort of obelisk – are the main remains. There is also a handsome cathedral and two very early churches.

Hotel and restaurant

The **Domaine de Clairefontaine** ££ ☎ 74 58 81 52 at Chonas l'Amballan, 9km south, is an old mansion with extensive gardens, simple rooms and reasonable prices. (Closed mid-winter and Sun D out of season.) In Vienne itself is the **Pyramide** blvd Fernand Point ☎ 74 53 01 96, run by the widow of Fernand Point (pioneer of *nouvelle cuisine*), and blessed with three Michelin stars. (Closed Mon D and Tue.)

Tain-l'Hermitage

The steep terraced slopes of vineyards which dominate Tain-l'Hermitage produce some of the best wines of the Côtes du Rhône. The red is robust, dark and ruby-coloured, the white is golden and dry. There is an excellent *coopérative* just outside the town. Entrance is free and there are generous quantities to be tasted, even of the better wines. Leaflets in English explain the character and quality of the wines and there is usually an English speaking employee behind the bar.

Across the Rhône from Tain-l'Hermitage lies Tournon, a town with cool quaysides, perched ruins and terraces stretching out below its old château. The dramatic Corniche du Rhône starts here and stretches down to Valence.

Valence

The only attractive parts of this market town on the Rhône is the area immediately around the cathedral – and a fine esplanade and park which provide excellent views of the mountains across the Rhône. Art-lovers should not miss the lovely collection of sepia drawings by the French landscapist, Hubert Robert – 96 scenes of Rome and the Italian countryside on view in the old bishop's palace.

Restaurant

The Menu Rabelais at **Restaurant Pic** ££££ 285 av Victor-Hugo (south of the town) ☎ 75 44 15 32 is probably the longest menu in the south of France. There are seven or eight courses, all of them house specialities, served in small enough helpings to let you enjoy the last mouthful of the seventh or eighth course. There are also five very expensive rooms. (Restaurant closed most of Aug, Sun D and Wed.)

Montélimar

Synonymous with nougat, Montélimar has been producing confectionery since the first almond trees were planted here over 300 years ago. The town is full of nougat shops, selling nougat with fruit, nougat truffles, chocolate nougat – you name it. But there's also a nougat shop at the Aire de Montélimar on the motorway, between the north and south exits for the town.

Hotel

22km east of Montélimar near Dieulefit lies the tiny medieval hill village of Poët-Laval and the beautifully converted **Hôtel les Hospitaliers** ££££ ☎ 75 46 22 32. It has a delightful position, with wonderful views of the Drôme hills, an excellent restaurant (service on the terrace in summer), comfortable rooms and a pool. (Closed winter; restaurant closed Tue out of season.)

Ardèche gorge

The exit after Montélimar, marked Bollène, takes you to the most breathtaking natural phenomenon of the region: the Ardèche gorge. You can either shoot the rapids in a canoe or drive through the mountains, way above the slow-flowing Ardèche river. Whichever way you choose the scenery is spectacular.

Orange

Orange is the first name on the holiday route that truly evokes the spirit of Provence. This is where the Autoroute du Soleil splits into two, one branch going south-east to the Côte d'Azur and eventually to Italy, the other heading south-west towards the Spanish border. For information on Orange itself, see *Provence and the south coast*.

Driving in France

Michael Long

Watching the jumbo ferries disgorging GB-plated cars on to the Calais dockside in August, you could be forgiven for thinking that at least half the population of Britain have packed their bags in the boot of the family car and set off across the Channel. But you'd be wrong: the proportion of UK-registered cars which cross the Channel in any one year is surprisingly low – around five per cent.

Many of those who stay at home, or stick to packages in Spain, are filled with unreasoning terror by the very idea of taking their car to France. The fact that the French drive on the wrong side of the road is only the start; they go the wrong way around roundabouts, everyone knows that the

French drive like lunatics – and isn't there some sort of curious rule which gives farm carts emerging from dusty side-roads the right of way over thundering juggernauts?

But in fact the French rules of the road are not difficult to master. And once you're over that hurdle you soon discover that driving in France is on the whole a more pleasant experience than it is in Britain. A lot of the roads (even minor ones) are fast, straight and uncrowded (for most of the time anyway) and they take you through some of the most striking scenery in Europe. As long as you steer clear of the notorious traffic blackspots on high-summer weekends (when the Paris ring-road and the motorway to the south of France have jams to beat the M25 and the M1 at their worst) you should experience no problems. Motoring is the most relaxed and rewarding way of seeing the country, and those who succumb to unjustified fears about the difficulties of driving in France are depriving themselves of one of life's great pleasures.

Anyone who has taken holidays by car knows its numerous advantages. First and foremost, it's convenient – particularly if you have a family. Travelling on the ferry, you can more-or-less take what you like: extra toys for the children, picnic gear, sports equipment, camera and video equipment – as much as your car will hold. Everything is loaded at your front door, and unloaded at the door of your tent, *gîte* or hotel. On the way back home you can stop at the hypermarket and load up with tins of pâté, cheese, bottles of olive oil, your full allowance of 50 litres of beer and 8 litres of wine.

British drivers are slowly learning to avoid the urge to dash down to the south as fast as possible. There is no longer the same mad rush of 'les Gee-Bees', as the French like to call them, who shoot down through the inland provinces in pursuit of the sun, invariably bypassing all the beauties of central France. You quickly discover that France is a big country (the biggest in Europe), and that distances are long – it's 500 miles to the Dordogne, 650 miles to the south, and it's all too easy to underestimate how long such journeys will take, even if you're on a fast motorway. The most sensible and most pleasurable way of travelling south is to take a couple of days over it, spending the night in a quiet rural *auberge*, many of which lie unexpectedly close to the motorway. (See *Getting to the south*). Each day, punctuate the journey with coffee breaks and of course a lunch-time picnic (perhaps the supreme pleasure of driving through France).

There is some truth in the notion that French drivers can be unpredictable, particularly after a boozy lunch, or when they've set themselves the target of reaching their holiday destination with a 12-hour non-stop drive from Paris. There are twice as many fatal road accidents in France as there are in Britain, and the high alcohol consumption is the major cause. This is perhaps not surprising in a country where wine is the price of mineral water and lunch is a national institution. Compensate for this state of affairs by driving only when completely sober.

Rules of the road

Driving in France is quite straightforward provided you remember the two main rules: drive on the right, and give priority to traffic coming from the right except where otherwise indicated.

For the first few kilometres of your journey from the main ferry ports, there are roadside reminders (in English) to keep to the right; and it's surprising how quickly you get used to the idea of hugging the right-hand kerb. The real danger comes when you stop, usually for petrol. If you drive out from the petrol station on to a deserted road, your instinct may be to begin driving on the left-hand side of the road. Even after several days of successfully keeping to the right, it's surprisingly easy to make this mistake – so remain vigilant. Another danger point is at a T-junction, turning on to a main road – again there is an overwhelming temptation to begin driving on the left. It's quite easy to make these mistakes even if it's your umpteenth time driving in France. If there are passengers, encourage them to keep an eye on your driving. Any amount of back-seat driving is better than one fatal accident.

Overtaking other vehicles – particularly slow-moving lorries – is of course tricky. You will often have to depend on the front-seat passenger's advice on whether or not it is safe to overtake. But use this technique with care; 'yes, go now, no hang on a minute, all right, OK, go but you'll have to be quick' can result in a broken marriage even if it doesn't cause an accident. It's best to hang back from the vehicle in front, push out gently when your passenger recommends it, and see for yourself if the road ahead is clear. Lorry drivers are usually very helpful when it comes to waving you on (a flashing right-hand indicator is usually a sign that it's safe to overtake, a left-hand indicator will mean 'wait'). It's a good idea to blow your horn as you're overtaking to indicate your presence.

Priorité à droite is the second golden rule. This means giving way to traffic coming from your right at junctions and crossroads – unless there are road-signs to tell you otherwise. The rule dates back to the days when there were comparatively few cars on the roads in France, and happily for the British the system is now well on the wane. Most main roads have priority, indicated by a succession of yellow diamond signs with white borders; when you lose priority the yellow sign has a black bar across it. Even if priority is officially yours, it's still wise to watch out for errant French drivers shooting out of side roads without a second glance, and forcing cars on the main road to come to a sudden stop – old habits die hard, particularly in rural areas.

Until 1984, cars approaching a roundabout had priority over those already on it, which meant total confusion for unsuspecting British tourists accustomed to exactly the reverse rule and who were already baffled by having to go round the roundabout anti-clockwise. When the system was changed to give priority to cars already on the roundabout, it was made fairly obvious by the signs saying **Vous n'avez pas la priorité** – you do not have priority. Even so, you still have to watch out for tiny roundabouts – perhaps going round a village monument – where the old rules still apply (and, of course, you still travel round the roundabout anti-clockwise).

Traffic lights operate in the same way as in Britain, except that the lights (or *feux*) change from red to green without the red-and-amber stage. The lights themselves are not as bright as British ones, and can be difficult to spot in sunlight. With green and amber filter lights, you can carefully turn right to join the main traffic, but beware of getting into the filter lane if you want to go straight on.

Motorways

France has developed an impressively comprehensive motorway system. 'Serious' travellers to France tend to be sniffy about motorway travel, implying that real travellers stick only to back-roads. But if time is short and you're anxious to spend as much of it as possible at your ultimate destination, the French motorways provide a rapid and efficient route to the sun (except during peak times when you really would be better off on the back-roads). The motorways are built to a high standard, though most have only two lanes per carriageway. Tolls are charged on almost all of them, and these can mount up to considerable sums – around £50 to travel to Nice and back. There are often free stretches around cities, and the other notable exception is the Dunkerque–Lille stretch of the A25.

All of the French motorways provide at least some relief from the monotony of driving. Motorway service areas are a far cry from their British equivalents, where you stop reluctantly to use the toilets or to bolt down a hamburger and soggy chips. Catering facilities in a single motorway service area can range from a snack-bar, serving fresh-ground coffee and croissants, to a waiter service restaurant with four-course menus. In addition there will invariably be a cafeteria with hot and cold dishes which range from things like steak and chips to *andouillettes* or *cassoulet*. The best-value meals are the *routier* (truck-driver) menus, where you can get a four-course meal with beer, mineral water or a quarter-litre of wine for under a fiver. The only hitch is that these meals are reserved for lorry-drivers or for holders of the up-to-date issue of the Relais Routier Guide. But since they are by far the cheapest full meals along the motorway, and there are also recommendations in the guide for the rest of France, it could be a worthwhile investment (see *Factfile*).

Arrive any weekday at Mâcon service area on the Autoroute du Soleil (A6) and you are likely to find hordes of British lorry-drivers tucking into the *routier* meals. Other facilities in this huge and amazingly well equipped service area are a hotel with pool, a tourist office with hotel booking facilities, a 24-hour currency exchange office and a shop selling regional food specialities. On the same motorway, Beaune service area has a shop with tins of snails and terrines, pots of *boeuf bourgignon* and a host of Burgundy wines – so even if you're dashing through 'the belly of France' you can at least have a sampling of some of its delicacies.

French service areas are not only more appealing than their British equivalents, they also appear with more frequency – you won't find a motorway like the M11 with 50 miles of road and not one petrol station or loo, let alone a proper service area. The simplest service area in France will have at least petrol, a shop with maps, food (including pâtés, wine and cheeses), drinks from a machine, WCs and telephones. And about every 10km you'll find an *aire de repos* – a rest area with parking, loo (not always too salubrious) and probably a picnic area with a rustic bench or two.

Something you certainly won't have seen on British motorways are the brown picture-signs, pointing out features of local interest. It might be a château that you can see on the hillside, a famous abbey in a town that you bypass, a mountain visible in the distance or the fruits of the land such as apples, cherries or grapes – an excellent way of keeping you entertained.

Other roads

There are two main types of road: a *route nationale* (national road), prefixed with an N, and a *route départementale*, ('county' road), prefixed with a D. Many of the N roads have become D roads in the last few years, and although you'll find the new numbers indicated on up-to-date maps, a lot of the signposts haven't yet been changed and some maps are still out of date. The more important N roads – the country's major arteries before the motorways were built – are best avoided. They are often straight and fast, but present all sorts of hazards: they often have only two lanes or (just as dangerous for overtaking) three; they go straight through villages and towns; they're used by local farm carts as well as through traffic; and you have to be constantly on your guard for vehicles turning into or out of side-roads and cafés.

French motorways are notorious for horrendous traffic jams at peak holiday times. But most holiday routes can be duplicated along the less crowded alternative routes or *Itinéraires Bis*, indicated by green arrows on white (north to south) and white on green (south to north). The alternative network, 'marketed' under the name *Bison Futé* (crafty bison) was the brainwave of the French Ministry of Tourism; there are free maps available at toll booths, information centres and some service areas. Watch for the *Bison Futé* signs – a red Indian in full headgear who is supposed to know when the palefaces (tourists) will be on the warpath. The English version of the *Bison Futé* brochure is available from the French Tourist Office, ferry ports and the AA and RAC; it contains very useful motoring information, as well as maps of the alternative itineraries. Watch out also for yellow arrows on blue, labelled *itinéraires de délestage*, showing shorter alternative routes for avoiding traffic jams at peak periods.

Paying tolls

The toll system sometimes varies, but normally when you join a motorway on a slip road you'll be confronted by a number of gates: head for one of the gates with a green light, press a button and take the ticket that emerges. (This is obviously a job for the passenger if you're in a right-hand-drive car.) The ticket records where you joined the motorway, and determines how much you have to pay at the exit booth when you leave it. There are occasional toll barriers across the main motorway – usually as you approach a city, where there may be short stretches which are free, or for which you pay on entry rather than exit. Where this happens, there are big signs saying what the payment is, and if you have the correct change you can opt to go through an automatic gate where you toss your coins into a chute as you drive through.

At manned booths you can pay by Eurocheque if you've run out of French francs, and on some motorways Visa credit cards are accepted – the billing is done electronically, and you don't have to sign a docket. We've known the cashiers to accept foreign currency, but only when it's clear that there is no alternative.

There are varying price ranges according to the vehicle you're driving, but the two main categories you need to know about are (1) an ordinary car and (2) a car with a trailer or caravan (which works out about 50 per cent more expensive).

Maps

Studying maps and planning your routes in advance can save a lot of time and frustration. The Michelin route-planning map, sheet 911, covers dozens of alternative routes through France, using the extensive network of secondary roads (as well as motorways and major roads, of course). In addition there's information on distances and driving times between towns, and the peak holiday times to avoid. The new map 915, in booklet form, covers the major routes for the whole of France.

For touring once you've arrived in a particular area, you face a difficult choice, with three good series of maps available. The yellow-covered *Michelin* maps, which have a scale of 2km to 1cm, have the advantage that they link with the Michelin Red Guide, identifying towns and villages which have an entry in the guide and so greatly simplifying the job of finding a good hotel or restaurant when you're on the road (the Red Guide to France, unlike the one to Britain, does not contain a map showing all entries). The two other series both have a scale of 2.5km to 1cm, covering a bit more ground in a given area of map. The excellent maps published in France by Recta Foldex have in the past been difficult to get in Britain, but are now published here under the *Telegraph* name and widely available; these maps have the advantage of an index of place-names printed on the back. The maps published by the *IGN* (the French equivalent of our Ordnance Survey) are also well worth considering – though in Britain you will find them only in fairly specialist shops.

Even if you *don't* plan to do much eating out, the Michelin Red Guide is worth buying if you plan to navigate many sizeable towns – it provides many invaluable town plans. The regional Michelin Green Guides (for sightseeing) also have some town plans. The plans in both types of guide are linked to the yellow-covered maps by a common system of numbering the main roads into each town.

Regulations

Speed limits are slightly higher than in Britain (they're listed in the *Factfile*), except when it's wet. They are now quite strictly enforced. One ruse is to time your progress on the motorway to see if your average speed over a distance exceeds the limit.

Drinking and driving is being more vigorously policed too. Evidently the breathalyser has proved so effective that restaurateurs have had to put up their prices to make up for lower sales of wine. Random testing is widespread and fines can be high; pleading ignorance will get you nowhere. Drinking and driving can't disqualify a foreign driver, but a conviction can affect your insurance rating in Britain and can result in a prison sentence in France. It's worth remembering that a spirit measure in French cafés is twice as large as those in British pubs.

The other main rules to bear in mind are:

▶ seat belts are compulsory for the driver and front-seat passenger; children under ten are not allowed to travel in the front seat of a car which has a back seat;
▶ after overtaking on a multi-lane road you must return to the inside lane; the French are very good at keeping to this rule – probably since failure to do so can incur heavy on-the-spot fines.

On-the-spot fines, also imposed for speeding and drinking and driving, have to be paid in francs (in cash – credit cards are not accepted). If you don't pay on-the-spot you may be in for additional costs plus the fine at a later stage.

Parking rules are fairly similar to those in Britain – don't park where there are yellow marks on the kerb. On some roads in built-up areas there's a rather confusing system whereby you park from the 1st to the 15th of each month on the side of the road where the numbers of the buildings are odd, and from the 16th to the last day of the month on the side with even numbers. In most towns there are short-term parking areas or blue zones where you can park up to one hour if you display a special disc – you can get one free from the local tourist office or buy one from the police station. In grey zones, parking meters are used from 9am to 7pm.

Road signs

your right of way

priority to right

one-way street

give way

motorway

Road-sign symbols are more-or-less international these days, but there are a lot of written signs in France which you might not be familiar with. At the end of this chapter we've given the ones you're most likely to come across, such as *chaussée déformée*, which can mean anything from a tiny bump in the road to a huge, gaping chasm.

Direction-signing to cities and towns on motorways presents no problems. On other types of road, it isn't perfect. Driving through Nantes, for example, *en route* for Bordeaux, it is most infuriating when the Bordeaux signs suddenly come to an end, leaving you to retrace your steps or to ask directions. At a junction out in the country, you might see a tiny village signposted but no sign to the main town you're heading for. But Paris is signposted all over the country, so at least you can vaguely get your bearings from that. If you're going through a town and there are no signs pointing to the destination you want, follow signs saying *autres directions* (other directions) or *toutes directions* (all directions), meaning routes for through-traffic.

Breakdowns and accidents

It's easy to attach too much importance to the risk of breakdowns abroad.
The proportion of cars which break down is not high, and most are easily
fixed locally. The main attraction of the breakdown and accident insurance
sold by the AA and others is that it helps you deal with the very occasional
serious difficulty – an accident which immobilises your car, or the lack of a
crucial spare part which has to be obtained from Britain. (Naturally, the
latter is likely to arise only with British-made cars!)

In the case of a breakdown, move the car to the verge of the road and
either switch on the hazard warning lights or put the red warning triangle
about 30m behind the car (100m on a motorway). On a motorway, call the
police from an emergency telephone – there's one every 2km. On other
roads, it will normally be best to find the nearest garage, though you can
ring the police if necessary (☎ 17). The crucial phrase to remember is *je
suis en panne* – 'I've broken down'. The local *garagiste* is often a friendly
and highly competent mechanic who will charge you very modest prices.
Main dealers of major brands of car are listed for each town in the Michelin
Red Guide. If you have breakdown insurance, remember that in order to
make a claim you will need a receipt for any work done. The AA publish a
useful *Car Components Guide*, translating nearly 500 parts with
illustrations – from AA offices, free with AA breakdown insurance.

In the case of an accident, inform the police particularly if someone is
injured (☎ 17 from any telephone). Motorists involved in an accident must
complete a *constat à l'amiable* (accident statement form); if one or other
party refuses to sign, then the case is taken to a local *huissier* (bailiff) who
prepares a written report called a *constat d'huissier*. This may take several
days and costs about £40.

Motorail

If you don't fancy the idea of driving the whole way to the south of France,
you can use the French Motorail services: drive your car on to a rail
transporter and let the train do all the work while you sleep. The French
car-carrying train network has around 130 routes, carrying 320,000 cars
and 1 million passengers every year; in 1986 30,000 cars and 100,000
passengers were from Britain, a 50 per cent increase over the previous year.
The main hub of the network is Paris, but there are also extensive services
from the Channel ports to cities as far apart as Lisbon and Milan but
mostly to popular destinations in France – mainly in the south-west, the
south and the Alps. Most of these services run only in summer, operating
two or three times a week; a notable exception is Calais–Nice, which
operates daily year round.

Fares are quite high. A return trip from Calais or Boulogne to Nice for a
car and two adults, with a two-bed sleeper for each leg of the journey, costs

nearly £600 in summer 1987. French railways argue that using their services does not necessarily cost much more than driving, if you compare the cost of staying in hotels, restaurant meals, motorway tolls, petrol, and wear and tear on the car. You would have to stay in some very expensive hotels *en route*, and run a very fuel-inefficient car, to match that sort of spending if you made the same journey by road.

But there's no doubt that Motorail saves time and fatigue. The Calais–Nice service, for example, leaves Calais at 7pm every night, and arrives in Nice at 10.39am the following morning. Coming back, the train leaves Nice at 7.20pm, reaching Calais at 7am the following morning. There's more about Motorail in the *Factfile*.

Petrol

Pétrole in French means crude oil or paraffin; *essence*, graded *normale* or *super*, is the stuff you put in the car – though the word *essence* alone will often be taken to mean *normale*. If you want the tank filled, the French expression is '*Faites le plein, s'il vous plaît*' or simply '*le plein*' – but make sure you don't get charged for more than you've had. It's safer to specify how much you want, and if you prefer you can do so in francs rather than litres – eg '*pour cinquante francs*' (50 francs' worth). Self-service stations (which are not very common in France) are invariably cheaper than those with pump attendants, and petrol costs quite a lot more on motorways than at garages on normal roads. The most useful credit card for French filling stations is Visa, but acceptance of this is far from universal – look for *Carte Bleue* signs. Acceptance of Access cards is slowly improving.

Children

Since most children get fairly irritable on long journeys, it's as well to try to keep them amused by thinking up games you can play in the car and, if you're on the motorway, stopping frequently at service areas to relieve boredom. At least there will be the novelty of new drinks coming in different-shaped bottles, and the knowledge that chips are ubiquitous. The French are fairly well equipped for feeding children; in the motorway service areas, for example, there are small portions, children's menus, high chairs and, at the larger service areas, breast-feeding/changing rooms and playgrounds.

Being in a foreign country means that you have some chance of amusing the children on long drives without having to fall back on the games and cassette tapes you may employ at home. Even when you're travelling on the motorway, you can try to get the children to spot things typically French, such as the plain white Charolais cattle and the Montbellard, which are the ones with the black spots; or get them interested in the brown picture-signs (see above) or French words along the motorway.

Driving tips

Don't be surprised if...
- you get your windscreen cleared at petrol stations; it's common practice, and doesn't necessarily warrant a tip
- you find French drivers (particularly in Paris) occasionally ignore traffic lights
- your excuses for breaking French law are met with a Gallic shrug and an on-the-spot fine
- roads to the south are jammed on peak summer weekends (roads to the Alps on peak winter weekends, too)

Watch out for...
- roundabouts where (in the absence of signs to the contrary) the old *priorité à droite* rule still applies
- traffic lights suspended in mid-air, high over junctions
- unmarked crossings in towns, where locals will rely entirely on the *priorité à droite* rule
- slow-moving traffic on fast country roads
- petrol attendants who overcharge when you ask for a tank-full; watch the pump meter closely, or specify how much petrol you want

Remember that...
- petrol isn't *pétrole*; and most cars need *super* not *essence*
- the time when there's the greatest risk of finding yourself driving on the left is when you join a quiet road after stopping or at a junction
- decisions about overtaking are the driver's responsibility, not the passenger's
- a panic dash for the ferry and home (on roads crowded with other 'Gee-Bees') is asking for trouble

Useful phrases

Faites le plein, s'il vous plaît – Fill her up, please

Pour cinquante francs, s'il vous plaît – 50 francs'-worth, please

Vérifiez l'huile/l'eau/la pression des pneus – Check the oil/water/tyre pressure

Acceptez-vous les règlements avec carte de crédit/Eurocheques? – Do you take credit cards/Eurocheques?

Y'a-t-il des toilettes ici? – Is there a lavatory here?

Ma voiture est en panne – My car has broken down

Il y a quelque chose qui ne va pas avec ma voiture – There is something wrong with my car

Où se trouve le garage le plus proche? – Where is the nearest garage

Je prends quelle route pour Toulouse? – Which road do I take for Toulouse?

Combien de temps faut-il pour y aller? – How long will it take to get there?

Road signs

absence de marquage – no road markings

accôtements non stabilisés/consolidés – soft verge

agglomération – a built-up area

aire de service/aire de repos – service/rest area

autoroute à péage – toll motorway

attention aux travaux – danger, road works

autres directions – other directions

betteraves – mud and sugarbeet on the road

bifurcation – road fork

Bison Futé – Red Indian chief displayed on a poster where free road maps with alternative routes are available

bouchon – bottle neck

boue – mud

cédez le passage – give way

centre ville – town centre

chantier (or *travaux*) – roadworks

chaussée déformée – poor road surface

chute de pierres – (possibility of) falling stones

défense de stationner – no parking

déviation – diversion

dégustation gratuite – free wine-tasting

éboulement – landslide

entrée interdite – no entry

essence – petrol

éteignez vos phares/feux – switch off lights

feux – traffic lights

fin de – end of

flèches vertes – green arrows (alternative routes)

gravillons – loose chippings

interdit sauf aux livraisons/riverains – no entry except for deliveries/residents

itinéraire bis – alternative route

passage protégé – your right of way

péage – toll

poids lourds – heavy vehicles

priorité à droite – priority to right

préparez votre monnaie – get your money ready

prochaine sortie – next exit

ralentir – slow down

route barrée – road closed

sens unique – one-way street

serrez à droite – keep to the right

sortie – exit

stationnement – parking

syndicat d'initiative – tourist office (often marked with a small 'i')

toutes directions – all directions

travaux – roadworks

un train peut en cacher un autre – (frequently seen at level crossings – one train can hide another coming the other way).

véhicules lents – slow vehicles

vendange – grape harvest

verglas – ice on road

virages – bends

voie sans issue – no through road

Factfile

In this final section of *France Without Tears* we bring together a mass of detailed practical information to help with planning your trip and dealing with problems you might encounter *en route*. It is organised alphabetically under the following headings:

Bed and breakfast
Breakdowns
Camping
Car hire
Channel ferries
Currency
Customs regulations
Cycling
Electricity
Emergencies
Festivals and other events
Guidebooks
Health
Hiking
Hotel chains and groups
Insurance
Local time
Maps
Metric conversions

Motorail
Motoring regulations
Opening hours
Package holidays
Packing
Parking
Passports
Petrol
Postal services
Public holidays
Public transport
Radio and TV
Self-catering
Speed limits
Taxis
Telephones
Tipping
Tourist offices
Weather

Bed and breakfast

The UK contact for the *Café-Couette* organisation (you have to join if you want to make a booking through them) is Bed and Breakfast (France), PO Box 66, Symot House, Henley on Thames, Oxon RG9 1XS. For information on the b&b places available under the *Château Acceuil* and *Chambres d'Hôte* umbrellas, contact the French Tourist Office.

Breakdowns

Spare parts Your home garage should be able to supply lists of Continental dealers for your make of car (and there may be one already sitting in the glove-box). The Michelin Red Guide lists main dealers for each town in France. The AA hires out kits of the most frequently needed spare parts for most popular cars.

Motorways There are emergency telephones every 2km, which are connected to the police; they will contact a garage for you. There are 24-hour petrol stations and service areas about every 20km.

Insurance If the idea of breaking down abroad haunts you (and it really shouldn't) you can buy some peace of mind by taking out insurance against some of the costs which may arise – mainly, the cost of hiring a replacement car if a quick repair is impossible, and the cost of shipping spares out from Britain if they are not available locally. You also normally get the services of an emergency assistance office on the Continent. You can buy such insurance as part of a wider package of cover from a number of sources including the AA, the RAC, Mondial Assistance, Europ Assistance and American Express.

Camping

The national camping organisation is the Fédération Française de Camping-Caravaning, 78 rue de Rivoli, 75004 Paris. Bookings with campsites in the *Castels et Camping Caravaning* group can be made through Select Site Reservations, 55 Avenue Road, Cranleigh, Surrey, GU6 7LJ ☎ 0483 277777.

Package holidays

One of the fastest-growing types of holiday to France are packages which offer Channel ferry tickets and camping accommodation in pre-erected tents. The sites run by the main operators are impressive. The tents are new or nearly new, and are fitted out with double beds, electric lights, fridges, double burner stoves – and even a chemical toilet in its own tent, if you want one. The campsites they use are normally very well run: toilets are regularly cleaned, dustbins are regularly emptied. Most campsites offer a take-away food service which means you don't have to cook. Many sites also have their own restaurants and regular campers' barbecues. An increasing number also have their own swimming pool.

There are normally 'animateurs', employed by either the site or the holiday company, to organise fun and games for children. The holiday company will have a rep on the site (often a university student on vacation) to advise on sightseeing and local restaurants – and they are usually available to baby-sit for a small fee.

Prices are roughly the same as for a *gîte* holiday. Most operators offer very attractive rates for children. Two weeks for two adults and two children under 14 costs from £200 in May 1987 up to £600 during July and August.

Operators

Canvas Holidays Bull Plain, Hertford SG14 1DY ☎ 0992 553535
Carefree Camping 41-43 Stephyns Chambers, Bank Court, Hemel Hempstead, Herts HP1 1DG ☎ 0442 48101
Eurocamp Edmundson House, Tatton Street, Knutsford, Cheshire WA16 6BG ☎ 0565 3844

Keycamp Holidays Palmerston Road, Sutton, Surrey SM1 4QL ☎ 01-661 7334
Sunsites Sunsites House, Dorking, Surrey RH4 1YZ ☎ 0306 885000

Car hire

Car hire can be arranged before departure through Avis, Budget, Godfrey Davis or Hertz or through the airlines. Most companies offer weekly rates with unlimited mileage which work out cheaper than paying per kilometre driven.

Channel ferries

Services There is a table in the chapter on *Crossing the Channel* which shows, for each route, the operator, the approximate number of sailings per day and the crossing time.

Operators

Brittany Ferries Millbay Docks, Plymouth PL1 3EW ☎ 0752 221321; The Brittany Centre, Wharf Road, Portsmouth PO2 8RU ☎ 0705 827701.
Caen ☎ 31 96 80 80
Cherbourg ☎ 33 43 43 68
Roscoff ☎ 98 61 22 11
St-Malo ☎ 99 82 41 41
Dieppe Ferries Newhaven Harbour, Newhaven BN9 0BQ ☎ 0273 516699
Dieppe ☎ 35 82 57 01
Hoverspeed Maybrook House, Queens Gardens, Dover, Kent CT17 9UQ ☎ 0304 214514; Birmingham ☎ 021-236 2190; Manchester ☎ 061-228 1321; London ☎ 01-554 7061.
Boulogne ☎ 21 30 27 26
Calais ☎ 21 96 67 10
Sally Line 81 Piccadilly, London W1V 9HF ☎ 01-409 0536.
Dunkerque ☎ 28 68 43 44
Sealink PO Box 29, Victoria Station, London SW1 1JX ☎ 01-834 8122.
Boulogne ☎ 21 30 25 11
Calais ☎ 21 96 70 70
Dieppe ☎ 35 82 24 68
Townsend Thoresen Enterprise House, Channel View Road, Dover CT17 9TJ ☎ 0304 203338; London ☎ 01-734 4431 or 01-437 7800.
Boulogne ☎ 21 31 78 00
Calais ☎ 21 97 21 21
Cherbourg ☎ 33 44 20 15
Le Havre ☎ 35 21 36 50.
Truckline as Brittany Ferries.

Currency

The golden rule is to equip yourself with several ways of paying for things, so that you can deal with any eventuality.

Cash You're bound to need *some* French francs, even if you pay all your major bills in other ways (as you now can in France). You can exchange travellers' cheques and Eurocheques for cash in all sorts of establishments – but see *Exchange rates*, below. (Note that you can no longer cash ordinary British cheques abroad with the help of a Eurocheque card.)

Travellers' cheques These are almost as useful as cash (bigger shops, hotels and restaurants will take them in settlement of the bill) but safer – you're covered if the cheques are lost, stolen or destroyed. Cheques come in a range of fixed face values, either in pounds sterling or other major currencies (including French francs). You pay the face value when you get the cheques from your bank, building society or travel agent; there is usually a commission to pay too.

Credit cards Visa cards (*Carte Bleue* in France) are much the most widely accepted credit card; fewer hotels, shops and restaurants accept American Express, Diners Club or Access. Although Visa is now quite widely accepted by petrol stations, you still can't entirely rely on it.

Eurocheques These are special cheques available from your bank which you use, together with a special cheque guarantee card, in the same way as ordinary cheques at home – except you write them in local currency. They are now quite widely accepted by hotels, restaurants and shops as well as banks, but don't count on it in small places. The cheque card costs £3.50, and there are charges of 1.25 per cent plus 30p for each cheque you write.

Postcheques If you have a National Girobank account and cheque card you can use these to get cash at post offices. You write the cheques in francs; the sterling equivalent and a quite high commission is debited from your account. Look for the counter signs *Paiment des mandats*, *Mandats à encaisser*, or *Retraits à vue*.

Exchange rates Banks are the safest bet for a good exchange rate; railway stations, airports and tourist offices are likely to give you a better rate than hotels, shops, or restaurants. There are no hard and fast rules about whether you will get a better rate of exchange at home or abroad, and comparisons are complicated by the passage of time. If you're backing a strong franc, buy francs and franc travellers' cheques well ahead of departure. If you're backing a strong pound, pay all your bills by credit card.

Customs regulations

It's worth taking a bit of time to understand the rules about importing and exporting things – not only to avoid trouble, but also to make sure that you make the most of the import allowances.

Travelling out
You can take personal possessions (including your car and so on) into France with no particular problem, provided they're for your own personal use and you intend to take them out again when you leave. If the French Customs think you're importing stuff to sell, which is most unlikely, you may have to pay duty (which you'd get back when you actually took the goods out again), or they may catalogue the items in your passport. You can take as much cash as you like into France, but you should declare it if you expect to take a lot of it back out (see below).

There's a whole host of things you can't take out of Britain, or that you can take out only if you've been through certain formalities – including controlled drugs (anything from LSD to heroin, and including barbiturates and morphine), animals and birds, some plants, firearms, computers and antiques.

If you take any drugs, or have to use hypodermic syringes and so on, it's sensible to carry an explanatory letter from your doctor. If your French isn't too good, have a copy translated into French as well.

Coming back
Unless you declared your cash when going into France, you can't take out of

the country more than 2,000 francs, or more than 5,000 francs-worth of other currencies. If you've had items catalogued in your passport on the way out, allow plenty of time for the corresponding cancellation process on the way back – and make sure you get it done. If you've paid duty deposits, now's the time to negotiate their return – you'll be able to do this *only* if you leave through the same Customs point you arrived at.

There's another list of things you can't *bring into* Britain – all the things you couldn't take out, and more. Most importantly, you are not allowed to import many foodstuffs, including meat (cooked or uncooked) and meat products.

If you're taking with you any expensive and new-looking items (a camera you've bought for your hols, say) it's a good idea to make sure you have the UK receipt with you – on your return, it will prove you didn't buy it abroad.

Import allowances

Tobacco	Bought duty-paid	Bought duty-free
either		
Cigarettes	300	200
or		
Cigarillos	150	100
or		
Cigars	75	50
or		
Tobacco	400g	250g
and		
Strong alcoholic drinks over 22% vol	1.5 litre	1 litre
or		
under 22% vol	3 litre	2 litre
and		
Still table wine	5 litre	2 litre
and		
Perfume	75g	50g
and		
Toilet water	375ml	250ml
and		
Other goods into Britain	£207	£28

Spirits and strong liqueurs have more than 22% alcohol by volume; fortified wines such as sherry and vermouth have less.

These allowances – amounts of goods you can import permanently without paying import duty or VAT – are much the same for France and Britain. You get higher import allowances if the goods were bought in an ordinary shop in Britain or France (so that you've already paid the duty or VAT of that country) than if you bought them in a duty-free shop (on the boat, or at the airport).

Under the bold headings **tobacco** and **strong alcoholic drinks** you can make up your allowance from a mixture of the goods shown; for example, you can have 100 duty-free cigarettes, plus 25 duty-free cigars. But within each bold heading in the table, goods must be either all duty-paid, or all duty-free. For example, you can't import 2.5 litres of duty-paid wine plus 1 litre of duty-free.

If you don't want to import any spirits or fortified wines, you can add the allowance for those drinks to your wine allowance, making a total allowance of 8 litres of wine (bought in France) – 11 bottles at 72cl. The **other goods** allowance includes beer – but you are limited to 50 litres.

Over the limit If you're bringing back to the UK more than your allowances in other goods, you'll have to pay UK duty (if there is any) *and* UK VAT.

If you make a major purchase in France, you may be able to avoid paying French VAT in the first place provided you have proof that you are not resident in France (for example, by showing a UK driving licence). Failing that, make sure you get a formal receipt for the goods and the VAT, and get it stamped by French Customs to show that you have in fact exported the goods. You can then reclaim the VAT later. More information from HM Customs & Excise, Dorset House, Stamford Street, London SE1 9PS ☎ 01-928 0533; French Customs Information Centre, 192 rue St-Honoré 75001 Paris ☎ (1) 42 60 35 90.

Cycling

Two of the main operators of cycling package holidays are *Susi Madron's Cycling for Softies*, 22 Lloyd Street, Manchester M2 5WA ☎ 061-835 2400 and *Velo Bleu, Velo Vert*, offered in association with Brittany Ferries, The Brittany Centre, Wharf Road, Portsmouth, PO2 8RU ☎ 0705 751833.

Electricity

The electricity supply in France (even in camping sites) is very similar to that in Britain, and most appliances will work satisfactorily. In some areas, the voltage may be half that of Britain – your equipment might not work so well, if at all, unless it is designed for the purpose. Many travel irons, for example, can operate on lower voltages (they have a switch to select the appropriate voltage).

French sockets and plugs are quite different from British ones, and practically everything will need either a replacement plug or an adaptor. For appliances fitted with a two-pin plug, you can get sets of simple adaptors which will allow you to plug into any normal socket in Europe. For appliances with a standard 13-amp three-pin plug you can get an adaptor called a TravelPlug which will fit French sockets.

If the appliance needs an earth connection – that is, if it has three cores in its flex, as well as three pins on its plug you should not be tempted to power it from a two-pin socket. This is possible in France, because the earth connection takes the form of a hole in the plug and a corresponding pin sticking out from the socket, rather than a third pin on the plug.

Emergencies

Police ☎ 17, throughout France, to get the *police secours*.
Fire brigade ☎ 18, throughout France, to get the *sapeurs-pompiers*.
Ambulance Both the police and fire brigade deal with medical emergencies.

In Paris Emergency medical service: SAMU (*Service d'Aide Médicale d'Urgence*) – ☎ (1) 45 67 50 50.
All-night chemist: Dhéry, 84 av des Champs-Elyées, 75008
☎ (1) 45 62 02 41.
24-hour visiting doctor service: (*SOS Médecins*) ☎ (1) 47 07 77 77;
Emergency dental service: (*SOS*

Emergency dental service: (*SOS Dentistes*) ☎ (1) 43 37 51 00.
Car accidents Police are usually called to car accidents only if someone is hurt, one of the drivers is drunk, or if you're holding up the traffic. Before you move your car, you and the other driver should fill in a European Accident Statement Form or the French equivalent *constat à l'amiable*. (The two are laid out in exactly the same way, so you can translate the French one by reference to the English one – get a copy from your insurers before setting off.) If there's a dispute or confusion about the *constat*, don't sign it, and don't call for the police – instead, in a large town, call out a *huissier* (bailiff) who will prepare an independent report called a *constat d'huissier* for a fee of about 400F.
Lost passports Report to the police, and inform a Consulate so that they can issue you with temporary papers.
Lost credit cards Report the theft to the police, and phone the credit card company:
Access ☎ (1) 43 23 42 49
American Express ☎ (1) 47 08 31 21
Diners Club ☎ (1) 47 23 78 05
Visa ☎ (1) 42 77 11 90
Consulates There are Consulates in most large cities and major Channel ports. They are limited in what they can do, and will help you only in cases of serious trouble. The Consulate in Paris is at 109 rue du Faubourg-St-Honoré, 75008 Paris ☎ (1) 42 66 91 42 (the British Embassy is at number 35, and shares the same phone number).

Festivals and other events

The French Tourist Office produces a full list of events, which it is worth having as much for avoiding events you don't want to catch as it is for tracking down those you do. Among the events which dominate the French calendar are countless festivals of music, dance, theatre and film; traditional merry-making ranging from wine-harvest festivals to carnival processions; religious celebrations; and sports events, including the famous Tour de France cycle race (of which motorists should steer well clear).

Guidebooks

We list here details of the main guidebooks referred to in the text; for camping and self-catering guides, see those sections of the *Factfile*.

Michelin France (in our terms, the *Michelin Red Guide*) Published annually in March; huge selection of the better hotels and restaurants throughout France; very detailed, dense entries giving facilities, closing dates, costs and so on. £7.45 in British bookshops.

Gault Millau Guide France Published annually; whimsical descriptions (in French) mainly of selected restaurants (but some hotels), plus details. £15.50 in specialist bookshops in Britain, and widely sold in France.

The Good Skiing Guide Published annually in August; edited by Chris Gill; described by the Financial Times as 'the best buy of the skiing winter'. £8.95

Routiers Guide to France Published annually in March; simple but sound eating places, some with cheap rooms, but mostly on main roads. From 354 Fulham Road, London SW10 9UH; £5.95

Michelin Tourist Guides (in our terms, *Michelin Green Guides*) Updated irregularly; detailed regional guides for sightseeing, with some historical and geographical background; 16 volumes in French, covering whole country, 7 of them also available in English. £4.50 in British bookshops.

Health

Health precautions You don't need any special vaccinations for France. As in Britain, some beaches are polluted and it can be dangerous to bathe from them; from some you're not allowed to bathe (look out for *Défense de se baigner*, or *Il est défendu de se baigner*).

Drugs If you take drugs regularly, make sure you have enough to keep you going throughout your holiday. And check with your doctor whether you need to change what you're taking, or alter your habits at all to cope with the different conditions in France. A chemist's shop (*une pharmacie*, denoted by a green-cross sign) can often be a good source of first aid and medical advice.

Medical costs While in France, UK citizens are entitled to be treated for illness and accidents on the same terms as French citizens. This does not mean that attention from a doctor or drugs from a pharmacy will be free. It does mean that you will get back some of the cost in due course, but for complete cover you still need to buy medical insurance (see *Insurance*).

If you wish to be able to call on the French equivalent of the National Health Service, you should take with you a 'Certificate of Entitlement' (popularly known as a Form E111). And you get an E111 by filling in form CM1 which in turn you'll find in the back of leaflet SA30 ('Medical costs abroad'), which you can get from your local DHSS office, or Citizens Advice Bureau. (If you think this is a bureaucratic farce, you are not alone.) The leaflet SA30 explains in detail what treatment you are entitled to.

Hiking

The national hiking organisation is the Fédération Française de Randonnée Pédestre, 8 av Marceau, 75008 Paris.

Hotel chains and groups

While family-run, privately owned hotels are normally better run and better value, the chains of modern hotels and motels such as Ibis shouldn't be ignored. They are not among the cheapest of French hotels, but are particularly good for family groups who can squeeze into one room (complete with private bathroom and other mod cons) which will cost around £30; many of the chains also offer generous buffet breakfasts where you can eat as much as you want for around £2 per head. Other attractions of most chain hotels is that they accept payment by credit card, are easily accessible from *autoroutes* and city ring-roads and have ample car parking, often in secure garages.

Main chains

Several of the chains listed are booked through one agency – *Resinter* Hotel Novotel, Shortlands, Hammersmith, London W6 ☎ 01-724 1000.

Campanile 110 modern 2-star hotels.

Paris office: 58 bvd Gouvion-Saint-Cyr
75017 Paris ☎ (1) 47 57 11 11.
Climat de France Over 130 modern two-
star hotels. The Reservation Centre, 19
Catherine Place, London SW1E 6DX
☎ 01-630 9161.
Ibis/Urbis Over 130 mostly 2-star hotels,
including seven in Paris. Book through
Resinter.
Mercure Over 50 3-star hotels in main
French cities, with 10 in Paris. Book
through Resinter.
Novotel Over 80 3-star hotels, mostly
near motorways, on city outskirts and
near airports. Book through Resinter.
Sofitel Over 30 luxury 4-star hotels
throughout France. Book through
Resinter.

Main marketing groups
These consist of privately-owned hotels,
some of which have to be booked direct.

Inter-Hotels Over 180 2- and 3-star
hotels, including six in Paris. Bookings:
Hotels in France, Suite 310, 26-40
Kensington High Street, London W8 4PF
☎ 01-938 2222.
Logis and Auberges de France More
than 4,000 family-run hotels, most of
them 1- and 2-star, throughout France,
except none in Paris. A free guide is
available, published each March, from
the French Tourist Office in London; send
50p in stamps for postage. (On sale in
bookshops in France.) Book direct with
the individual hotels.
Les Petits Nids de France Over 120
hotels, mostly 2-star. Bookings: Inter
France Reservations, 3 Station Parade,
London NW2 4NU ☎ 01-450 9388.
Mapotel 150 3 and 4-star hotels, with 31
in Paris. Bookings: Best Western Hotels,
26 Kew Road, Richmond, Surrey ☎ 01-
940 9766.
Relais du Silence 140 2,3 and 4-star
hotels chosen for their peaceful setting.
Bookings: Relais du Silence, 38640
Claix ☎ 76 98 35 79.
Relais et Chateaux Over 115 splendid
and expensive independent hotels, 2-
star to 4-star, many of them in
outstandingly beautiful and historic
buildings. For the latest guide write to
the French Tourist Office in London

enclosing 50p in postage stamps. Book
direct with the individual hotels.

Insurance
Medical insurance for a trip to France is
not essential (see *Health*) but it is well
worth having. Apart from the security of
knowing that medical bills will be
covered, most insurance policies now
offer a 24-hour 'hot-line' to an
emergency assistance company in the
UK which will offer whatever help and
advice you may need if you or one of
your party becomes ill or has an
accident. If necessary, they will even
arrange an air ambulance to bring the
sick or injured person home to the UK.
    A travel insurance package (including
medical insurance) will also cover
various other risks – loss of pre-
payments if you are forced to cancel
through illness, loss of valuables while
you are abroad, and so on. Get details of
several policies, and study them to see
which covers your circumstances.

Local time
France is normally one hour ahead of
Britain. The French have a 'daylight-
saving time' when the clocks are put
forward an hour, as in Britain; this now
starts in the spring at the same time as
British Summer Time, but it finishes
sooner – so there is a period in the
autumn when the time in France is the
same as that in Britain. In 1987 this is
from 27 September to 25 October.

Maps
France is mapped very thoroughly.
Route-plannning and touring maps are
discussed in the *Driving* chapter. For
exploration of back-roads and walking
on well-marked paths, the 1:100,000
maps produced by the IGN (the French
'Ordnance Survey') are adequate, but
for exploration off the beaten track you
need their 1:50,000 series or their very
detailed maps at a scale of 1:25,000,
which is the same as the familiar 'two-
and-a-half-inch-to-the-mile' maps the
OS produces in Britain. These, and other
walking maps from other publishers, are
available only from specialist shops in
Britain and France.

Metric conversions

Length/distance

Exact conversions
One millimetre (mm) = 0.039 inch
One centimetre (cm) = 0.033 foot
One metre (m) = 1.09 yards
One kilometre (km) = 0.621 mile
One inch = 25.4mm
One foot = 30.5cm
One yard = 0.914m
One mile = 1.61km

Rough and ready
A metre is one-tenth more than a yard
A square metre is a fifth more than a square yard
10cm is 4 inches
30cm is 1 foot
8km is 5 miles
10km is 6 miles
A map scale of 1:1 million is just under 16 miles to the inch;
1:250,000 is just under 4 miles to the inch
1:200,000 is just over 3 miles to the inch

Volume

Exact conversions
One millilitre (ml) = 0.061 cubic inch
One litre (l) = 1.76 pints
One cubic inch = 16.4ml
One pint = 0.568 litre
One gallon = 4.55 litres
Wide use is made of decilitres (dl) and centilitres (cl): a half-litre carafe may be described as 5dl or 50cl, for example.

Rough and ready
A litre is a pint and three-quarters
Five litres is one-tenth more than a gallon

Weight

Exact conversions
One gramme (g) = 0.035 ounces
One kilogramme (kg) = 2.2 pounds
One ounce = 28.3g
One pound = 0.454kg

Rough and ready
100g is a tenth short of a quarter-pound
500g is a tenth more than a pound

Motorail

Services There are car-carrying sleeper train services from various points in northern France to the main holiday regions. The main routes of interest to cross-Channel travellers are:

Amiens to St-Gervais (844km)
Boulogne to Avignon (1,014km), Biarritz (1,062km), Bordeaux (853km), Brive (771km), Fréjus/St-Raphaël (1,296km), Narbonne (1,135km), Nice (1,369km), Toulouse (968km)
Calais to Narbonne (1,254km), Nice (1,404km)
Dieppe to Avignon (953km), Fréjus/St-Raphaël (1,235km)
Lille/Seclin to Avignon (1,005km), Biarritz (1,053km), Bordeaux (844km), Brive (762km), Fréjus/St-Raphaël (1,287km), Mulhouse (618km), Narbonne (1,126km), Nice (1,363km), St-Gervais (915km)
Rouen to Avignon (883km), Fréjus/St-Raphaël (1,164km)

Information and booking French Railways, 179 Piccadilly, London, W1V 0BA ☎ 01-409 3518. Also through British Rail Travel Centres, at some main-line stations.

Motoring regulations

It's important to make sure that you're properly equipped to drive on the Continent, and that you know the rules. There is a separate section on *Speed limits* later in the *Factfile*.

Registration document The official advice is to take the document with you; we have always found a photocopy sufficient. If the document is not in your name, it's wise to carry a letter of authority showing you're allowed to use the car. If you don't have your registration documents for any reason, you can get a temporary one – form V379 (from main UK post offices) tells you how.

GB plate This is not just a means of demonstrating to the neighbours that you're going abroad – a nationality plate is required, close to the rear registration plate. It has to be of an approved design and size – so don't be tempted by off-beat signs covered in Union Jacks or whatever.

Insurance Your normal policy should permit driving in France, but it will almost certainly give only the most basic third-party cover, and you will probably want better insurance. The simplest option is to get your existing insurer to issue a 'Green Card' which signifies that your normal insurance has been extended.

Insurance companies, being the bureaucracies they are, like a lot of notice – allow anything up to a month and £10 to £20 to get it. Most companies can issue Green Cards much more quickly in an emergency.

Equipment You must convert your headlamps so that when dipped they are not pointing to the left. Some cars have headlamps which are adjustable in this respect. For most, you need a conversion kit from garages and car accessory shops – simply strips of black tape you stick over a part of the headlamp glass (make sure you get the right one for your make and model of car). Although all French cars are equipped with yellow headlights, visitors' headlights can remain white. You must carry a spare set of light bulbs. If your car does not have hazard warning lights you must carry a red warning triangle, for use in breakdowns. You don't have to have wing mirrors, but it's a great help with a right-hand drive car if you have mirrors on both sides, particularly the left.

Special rules The *Driving* chapter tells you all about the infamous business of *priorité à droite*. The other main rules you need to be aware of are:

• If safety belts are fitted to the rear seats, passengers in those seats must use them

• You have to be 18 to drive a car in France and you can't drive on a British provisional licence

• Under-tens must not travel in the front seats

• You must not stop on open roads unless you can drive the car right off the road

• You must not overtake on the brow of a hill

Fines There's a system of on-the-spot 'fines' for many motoring offences. To be accurate, it's not a fine but a deposit system, and the police collect the money only from people who can't show that they are resident in France. You have to pay in cash (rarely, the police may accept vouchers from people covered by AA/RAC/Europ Assistance insurance) and the amounts are steep: up to 1,300F for speeding, and 2,500F for drinking

and driving. Theoretically, you can always attend the subsequent Court hearing: if you're not found guilty of the offence, your deposit will be returned; otherwise you'll be fined, usually the same amount as the deposit already paid. In practice, it's not worth going to all this trouble except for serious charges – it's usually more sensible to treat the deposit as an actual fine.

Opening hours

Tourist offices Hours vary a lot: 9.00am to noon, and 2.00pm to 6.00pm Monday to Saturday is common; but in busy tourist areas they may be open longer hours and on Sunday mornings (particularly in summer).

Shops 9.00am (7.00am for food shops) to 6.30pm or even 7.30pm (as late as 10.00pm for hypermarkets). Some food shops (particularly bakers) are open on Sunday mornings; and many are closed all or half-day Monday. In small towns, shops are often closed for lunch from noon to 2.00pm

Post offices 8.00am to 7.00pm (noon on Saturdays); smaller offices close for lunch from noon to 2.00pm. There is a 24-hour office in Paris, at 52 rue du Louvre.

Banks 9.00am to noon, and 2.00pm to 4.00pm – Monday to Friday in large towns, Tuesday to Saturday in other areas. Banks may close at mid-day on the day before a national holiday.

Restaurants See *Eating* chapter.

Museums Most public museums are closed on Tuesday and usually on national holidays. Museums charge for entry – usually between 10F and 16F, but half-price on Sunday. In Paris, some museums are closed on Monday, and some are free or half-price on Sunday or Wednesday

Package holidays

Packages to France are offered by the ferry operators and by some tour operators dealing through high-street travel agents; but they are also sold direct by small operators who advertise in newspapers. Operators who do not sell through agents have no need to become members of the Association of

British Travel Agents. Such operators are not necessarily 'bonded' – if they go bust before you travel or while you're away, you may lose your money (unless you are travelling by air on a charter flight, in which case another protective scheme comes into play). So check before booking direct with any holiday company to see if they offer protection for your money. If not, paying by credit card is just as good; because of the provisions of the Consumer Credit Act, you can reclaim losses from the card company.

The French Tourist Office produces a full list of package holiday operators.

Packing

General requirements
Passport, money, cheques, credit cards, camera and film, dictionary and phrase book, sewing kit, electric adapter-plug, loo paper, torch, scissors, sun-hat, sun-glasses, sun-cream, toys/games

Motoring requirements
Car registration document, GB (or other nationality) plate, headlamp converters, insurance Green Card, driving licence, owner's handbook, list of dealers, maps, spares, warning triangle (if your car does not have hazard flashers)

Picnic requirements
Bottle-opener/corkscrew, knives, clear plastic 'glasses'

Self-catering requirements
Bed linen (probably), tea towels, plastic bags, coat hangers, favourite cereals, tea, marmalade, basic foodstuffs – salt, spices etc

Parking

Restrictions The rules are similar to those in Britain, except that instead of yellow lines on the road, you should look for yellow marks on the kerbs. Areas controlled by parking meters or automatic ticket machines are called *grey zones* – you have to pay to park between 9.00am and 7.00pm. There are also *blue zones* in most large towns – between 9.00am and 12.30pm, and 2.30pm and 7.00pm you have to display a time disc, which allows up to an hour's parking. You can buy discs from police stations; some shops and tourist offices will give you one free.

Risks Tourists' cars are obvious targets for thieves in any country, and are particularly at risk where there are great concentrations of them – in Paris and the Channel ports, for example. Don't leave valuables in your car when it's parked in the street. Don't leave suitcases on the roof-rack. Take particular care about where you leave your car overnight.

Passports
There are three types of passport valid in France: they vary in how easy they are to get, and how much use they are. For a stay of up to 60 hours (not going beyond France) you can use an Excursion Document at a cost of only £2 but valid for only a month. For longer stays you must have at least a Visitor's Passport costing £10 and valid for a year. Either of these can be obtained while-you-wait at a main Post Office (Monday to Friday), provided you take along an appropriate document as proof of identity – your birth certificate, adoption certificate, NHS card, DHSS retirement pension book, pension card BR464 or uncancelled Standard or Visitor's Passport. Take your spouse if he or she needs documentation too.

Anyone who is going to travel abroad repeatedly will find it worth getting a Standard Passport, which costs £15 and takes several weeks to obtain by post (or several hours if you prefer to go in person to the Passport Office) but lasts for 10 years.

Documents used to prove your identity must bear your present name, and you need a document for everyone being included on the passport. You also need two passport photographs, and the form and the photographs must be countersigned by somone who has known you for at least two years – and not just anyone. For an Excursion Document or Visitor's Passport you need a 'responsible British citizen', and for a Standard Passport someone who is a Justice of the Peace, minister, lawyer, police officer, doctor, MP, bank official, established civil servant 'or person of similar standing'.

Petrol

Octane ratings are not always shown on pumps: *Essence Normale* is 90 octane, a low 2-star; *Essence Super* is 98 octane, 4-star. Watch out for *Essence Super sans plomb* – unleaded petrol which very few British cars can run on.

Postal services

Postal addresses French addresses resemble British ones, except that the postcode comes before the name of the town or city. The postcode system is of course more elegant and logical than ours – the first two digits identify the *département*, just as they do on car registration plates and elsewhere; in Paris, the number of the *arrondissement* comes at the end of the postcode.
Stamps Stamps are available at Post Offices (PTT – ask for the *Pay Tay Tay*) and from tobacconists (*tabacs*). Postboxes are painted yellow, and are usually sited near *tabacs*. Postcards from France to Britain cost 1.80F; letters up to 20g cost 2.40F.

Public holidays

Most shops and practically all museums are closed on national holidays. Dates in 1987:
New Year's Day Thursday 1 January
Easter Sunday and Monday 19/20 April
Labour Day Friday 1 May
VE Day Friday 8 May
Ascension Day Thursday 28 May
Whit Sunday and Monday 8/9 June
Bastille Day Tuesday 14 July
Assumption Day Saturday 15 August
All Saints Day Sunday 1 November
Remembrance Day Wednesday 11 November
Christmas Day Friday 25 December
When a holiday falls on a Thursday or a Tuesday, the Friday or Monday are often taken as holidays as well, to form a long weekend. When a holiday falls on a Saturday or Sunday, the Friday or Monday is often taken in lieu.

Public transport

Railways

The system France has a good rail network covering the country. Two services of special interest are the overnight through-trains from Calais (year-round to the Côte d'Azur and during the summer to the Languedoc-Roussillon region) and the very fast *TGV* running from Paris to Avignon, Bescançon, Chambéry, Dijon, Grenoble, Lyon, Montpellier, Marseille, St-Etienne, Toulon, the Alps, and (the latest line) from Lille to Lyon.

Unless you've bought your ticket outside France, you have to act as your own ticket inspector: use the orange automatic date-stamping machine at the platform entrance to validate (*composter*) your ticket before you travel, and if you make a break in your journey of more than 24 hours. Otherwise, you can be fined a 20 per cent surcharge.
Fares There are fare reductions if you travel on off-peak services (marked in blue in timetables), and there are *suppléments* on many main-line expresses in peak periods (marked in red). *France Vacances* rover tickets (1st or 2nd class) give you unlimited travel on any 9 or 16 days within a month. A *Billet-séjour* gives fare reductions on return tickets for long journeys (you can go out and return on different routes); there are restrictions on the trains you can use. Young people under 26 and senior citizens can get half-fare reductions.

There are various schemes, both for the young and for others, of discount rail travel throughout Europe; ask at a main-line British Rail Travel Centre for details.
Information and booking French Railways, 179 Piccadilly, London W1V 0BA ☎ 01-409 1224. (You can get Rail Rover and young people's rail cards here, as well.) Also through British Rail Travel Centres, at some main-line stations.

Air travel

Paris The main Paris airport is Roissy Charles de Gaulle. It has two terminals: Air France flights use Roissy 2 (so do many of the internal flights, by Air Inter) and other carriers use Roissy 1. Some flights use the other Paris airport is at Orly (divided into Orly Sud and Orly Ouest). There are rail and coach links from central Paris to both airports, running every 15min during the day and taking about 40min. There are regular flights to Paris from a number of UK provincial airports (several flights a day from Manchester, one a day from Newcastle, for example) as well as frequent flights from both London Heathrow and Gatwick.

Other destinations Other airports you can fly to from Britain (and airlines serving them) include: Biarritz AF; Bordeaux AF BA; Caen BT; Clermont-Ferrand TA; Deauville LA; Dinard JE; Le Havre BT; Lille AF; Lourdes/Tarbes DA; Lyon AF, BA; Marseille AF, BA; Montpellier AF, DA; Morlaix BT; Nantes AF; Nice AF, BA; Perpignan DA; Quimper BT; Rennes BT; Strasbourg AF; Toulouse AF, DA.

(AF= Air France from Heathrow; BT= Brit Air from Gatwick; BA= British Airways from Heathrow; DA= Dan Air from Gatwick; JE=Jersey European Airways from Gatwick; LA= Lucas/Aigle Azur from Gatwick; TA= Touraine Air Transport from Gatwick)

Radio and TV

French services

France Inter (on Long Wave, 1829m/164kHz) broadcasts news and information in English after the French news at 9.00am and 4.00pm during July and August, every day except Sunday.
BBC abroad Depending on the atmospheric conditions, your position and the sensitivity of your receiver, you may be able to keep in touch by picking up Radio 4 on Long Wave (1500m/200kHz). The BBC World Service broadcasts can be picked up in France during the summer on Medium Wave; at certain times the broadcasts are in English. More information from BBC World Service Information Centre, Bush House, Strand, London WC2B 4PH.

Self-catering

Most *gîtes* available to British travellers are privately owned, but are controlled through the Government-run Gîtes de France system and are subject to a national charter. There's a London booking service covering over 1,600

gîtes; to book you need a copy of the handbook listing the properties, which costs £3 from *Gîtes de France* Ltd, 178 Piccadilly, London WIV 9DB ☎ 01-493 3480.

The biggest *gîte* operator selling through travel agents is *Brittany Ferries*, The Brittany Centre, Wharf Road, Portsmouth PO2 8RU ☎ 0705 751833. Gîtes de France has a second brochure, published in conjunction with *Townsend Thoresen*, which is also available through travel agents.

Other companies selling through travel agents include: *Blakes Au Soleil Holidays*, Wroxham, Norwich NR12 8DH ☎ 06053 3224; *French Leave*, 21 Fleet Street, London EC4Y 1AA ☎ 01-583 8383; *French Life*, Holiday House, Leeds LS12 6HR ☎ 0532 450246; *French Travel Service*, Francis House, Francis Street, London SW1P 1DE ☎ 01-828 8131; *Sunvista Holidays*, 5a George Street, Warminster, Wiltshire BA12 8QA ☎ 0985 217373.

Many companies offering *gîte* holidays choose to sell direct to the public through advertising in national newspapers, rather than using travel agents. Among the better-known firms are: *Bowhill Cottages*, Mayhill Farm,Swanmore, Southampton SO3 2RD ☎ 0489 877627; *Les Propriétaires de l'Ouest*, Malton House, 24 Hampshire Terrace, Southsea, Hampshire PO1 2QE ☎ 0705 755715; *Vacances en Campagne*, Bignor, nr Pulborough, West Sussex RH20 1QD ☎ 07987 344; *Vacances Franco-Britanniques*, 1 St Margaret's Terrace, Cheltenham, Glos GL50 4DT ☎ 0242 526338.

The Gîtes de France organisation has over 30,000 properties in its network. If you want a wider choice contact *Fédération Nationale des Gîtes Ruraux de France*, 34 rue Godot-de-Mauroy, 75009 Paris ☎ (1) 47 42 25 43, who can give you the addresses and numbers of their regional offices.

The 1987 *French Farm and Village Holiday Guide* (FHG Publications £4.75) lists 1,000 *gîtes* throughout France which you can book direct with the owner.

You can find all sorts of self-catering properties to let in the brochure produced by *Interhome*, 383 Richmond Road, Twickenham TW1 2EF ☎ 01-891 1294.

Speed limits

Highways Unless road signs say otherwise the following general limits apply: 90km/hr (56mph) on ordinary roads, 110km/hr (68mph) on dual carriageways and toll-free motorways and 130km/hr (80mph) on toll motorways. When it's wet, the limits are lowered to 110km/hr (68mph) on toll motorways and 80km/hr (50mph) on other roads. There is a *minimum* speed limit of 80km/hr (50mph) in the outside lane of motorways during daylight.
Towns The limit in built-up areas is 60km/hr (37mph); the place-name sign marks the beginning of a town for speed-limit purposes; the end is marked by the name crossed out with a thin red line.

Taxis

The system You can't hail a taxi in the streets, as you can in large British cities; you have to pick one up from a taxi rank (*station de taxi*). In Paris, there's a pick-up charge of 8F, then a distance charge of at least 2.24F/km; outside Paris, the pick-up charge may be slightly less, but the rate per km is rather more.

Telephones

Codes and numbers All French numbers have eight digits (the system has recently changed, so old literature may show six or seven-digit numbers, often with an area code in brackets first). Unlike Britain's complex system of STD area codes, the French system has only *two* areas – Paris and everywhere else. Paris numbers are quoted with a (1) at the front; you don't need this when dialling within Paris. When dialling from Paris to the provinces or vice versa, you always preface the number with 16.

Numbers are always written in groups of two, as they are printed throughout this book. And in speaking, the French often quote a number as though it was made up of four decimal amounts, rather than in separate digits – so 12 34 56 78 will come out 'twelve, thirty four, fifty six, seventy eight', rather than 'one two three

four five six seven eight'. If your French vocabulary stops short at ten, ask for numbers to be expressed *chiffre par chiffre* (digit by digit).

Phoning Britain from France Dial 19 to get the international exchange; *wait* for a new dialling tone; then dial 44 to get Britain; then your STD code *but omitting* the first 0; then the number itself. So to dial Bath 1212 (STD code 0225), you dial 19; wait for tone; and then dial 44 225 1212.

Phoning France from Britain Dial 010 33 to get France; then 1 if you want a Paris number (nothing extra for a non-Paris number); then the eight-figure number itself.

Public phone boxes Older call boxes (*taxiphones*) still use tokens (*jetons*) which you can buy from the bar or restaurant where the box is sited; these allow only local calls. But most French call boxes now take real cash, and many allow international calls. You put your money in after lifting the receiver and hearing the dialling tone (a continuous note). Most modern boxes take 1F coins which should be sufficient for a local call. (They'll also take 5F coins, but the box returns unused coins, so using 1F coins normally saves money.) International call boxes are painted metallic grey; the rate to Britain is about 3F a minute at peak time, less between 9.00pm and 8.00am.

Hotels and restaurants are allowed to charge extra for calls made from boxes in their premises. More importantly, they are allowed to charge a lot more than the standard rates for calls made from your bedroom phone; the more stars the hotel has, the bigger mark-up you can expect.

Using the PTT For long calls it's often more convenient to find a major post office where you don't have to shovel cash into a slot. Go up to the counter and you'll be allocated a numbered kiosk with an ordinary phone – you may be given a correspondingly numbered token. When you've made the call, go back to the counter and pay the bill.
General numbers Operator ☎ 13; Directory Enquiries ☎ 12; see also *Emergencies*.

Tipping

Tipping in hotels, restaurants and cafés is not normally necessary – service is built into prices, or in some cases added to your bill; but people often leave a token amount on the table. Porters in posher places will hope for a franc or two. Public loos often have attendants who sit at a table at the entrance with a plate where you are expected to deposit coins. Cinema usherettes expect tips, petrol-pump attendants generally don't.

Tourist offices

In Britain For general information about France and French holidays, contact the French Government Tourist Office, 178 Piccadilly, London W1V 0AL. There's a 24-hour recorded information service on 01-449 6911; for *urgent* enquiries, ring 01-491 7622. Don't expect them to be able to book accommodation or travel (though French Railways are at the same address).

In France A tourist information centre may be called a *Syndicat d'Initiative* or an *Office de Tourisme*; there's one in most large towns and in small towns and villages which attract a lot of tourists. Use them for general information on local events, for local bus timetables and so on. In Paris, ANIT (the National Agency for Tourist Information) 8 avenue de l'Opéra, 75001 ☎ (1) 42 60 37 38 can give help; it won't book travel or accommodation. It's open Monday to Saturday 9.30am to 6.30pm (on the phone, 10.30am to 7.30pm). Each of the regions and *départements* also has its own tourist office in Paris.

In large towns, at stations and airports, there are offices which *can* book accommodation for you in their area or in another major town or city – but only for personal callers, and only for up to eight days in advance. They go by the name *Accueil de France* (French Welcome). Head office is in Paris at Office de Tourisme, 127 avenue des Champs-Elysées; open daily 9.00am to 8.00pm (6.00pm Sunday and national holidays).

The radio station *France Inter* runs a phone information service (from Paris) in English, with details of campsites and roads: ☎ (1) 43 06 13 13.

Weather

The table shows two measures of the weather in a selection of French holiday areas for spring, summer and autumn, compared with London. The temperature figure is the average over the month of the maximum temperature reached each day. The rainfall figure is the total for the month. Both figures are of course averaged over many years.

Don't let high daytime temperatures fool you into thinking that you won't need woollies; temperatures can often plummet in spring and autumn evenings, and in mountain areas at any time of the year.

Daily maximum temperature, in °C, on average

	April	July	October
Biarritz	16	23	19
Cannes	17	27	20
Dinard	13	21	16
La Rochelle	15	23	17
Tours	16	25	16
London	13	22	14

Monthly rainfall, in millimetres, on average

	April	July	October
Biarritz	90	90	165
Cannes	78	18	118
Dinard	39	55	63
La Rochelle	42	48	74
Tours	48	49	60
London	37	57	57

Help wanted

This is the first edition of *France Without Tears*; we hope it won't be the last. We're keen to have readers' help in revising the book when the time comes for a second edition. In particular, we should like to know whether you agree with our judgements on hotels, restaurants, shops and sights – and whether you have nominations for new entries.

Please write to: Good City Guides, PO Box 67, Bath BA1 1WN. Use a separate piece of paper for each town, village or resort on which you have observations to make. On the next page we have set out the headings to use when sending us a report. (If you have access to a photocopier, you could copy the page.)

What's in it for you? *A free copy* of the next edition *if*, after further investigation, we accept any of your suggestions. If you do write, please let us know what you think of *France Without Tears*, too.

Reader's report

Your name

Your address

Town, village or resort:

HOTELS

RECOMMENDED

NOT RECOMMENDED

RESTAURANTS

RECOMMENDED

NOT RECOMMENDED

SIGHTS

RECOMMENDED

NOT RECOMMENDED

SHOPS (in Channel ports only)

RECOMMENDED

NOT RECOMMENDED

TELEGRAPH FRENCH REGIONAL MAP SERIES

This new collection of nineteen regional maps is an invaluable aid to both the motorist and the tourist journeying in France. High in quality, detail and clarity, these all purpose maps are the perfect travelling companion.

Scale 1: 250,000

FRM 1	Brittany
FRM 2	Normandy
FRM 3	Val-de-Loire
FRM 4	Charentes-Périgord
FRM 5	Sud-Ouest-Pyrénées
FRM 6	Nord
FRM 7	Paris Region
FRM 8	Centre-Berry
FRM 9	Auvergne
FRM 10	Languedoc-Roussillon
FRM 11	Est
FRM 12	Bourgogne-Franche-Comté
FRM 13	Rhône-Alpes
FRM 14	Provence-Alpes-Côte-D'Azur
FRM 15	Corsica

- extensive index of place names
- vital road information – tolls, services, bridge heights
- clearly marked autoroute exits
- indexed tourist attractions and amenities

Scale 1: 550,000

FRM 16	North-West
FRM 17	North-East
FRM 18	South-West
FRM 19	South-East

- extensive administrative information
- clearly identified touring centres
- easy-to-read style

These maps are available through leading bookshops, the Telegraph Bookshop at 130 Fleet Street, price £2.50 per map for numbers 1-15 and £2.95 per map for numbers 16-19; or use our mail order service by sending to: Dept FRMS, The Daily Telegraph, 135 Fleet Street, London EC4P 4BL (adding 55p for postage and packing). Please allow up to 28 days for delivery.

Telegraph
PUBLICATIONS

Before you go
CONSULT THE EXPERT

Frank Barrett is acknowledged as one of the country's leading
authorities on air fares and package holidays.
With his two new books for the Daily Telegraph's Family Money-Go-
Round series he provides you with a guiding hand through the price
jungle. The theme of both *A Consumer's Guide to Air Travel*
and *A Consumer's Guide to Holidays Abroad* is how to get
value for money. Both books present the facts clearly and without
jargon. Both pinpoint the most suitable options and generally provide
enough information to enable you to spot the best deal and to make
the choice which best suits your needs. In short,
they help you to help yourself.

Index

Only major references are given; Paris, for example, is mentioned dozens of times in the book, but has only two page references here. Place names beginning with Le, La, L' or Les are indexed under the following word.